"What an incredible piece of evangelism encouragement! Dr. Johnston has compiled a wonderful work to help us understand evangelism's history so that we can have an evangelistic future. Use this book to fan the flames of evangelism fervor in your own life."

—Joel Southerland,
Executive Director of Evangelism,
North American Mission Board

"A serious book on the subject of evangelism, [this volume is] written by respected scholars and passionate evangelistic leaders. Johnston's love for evangelism inspires us to a great commitment to evangelism in the future."

—Ronnie W. Floyd,
President and CEO,
The Southern Baptist Convention Executive Committee

D1290681

A HISTORY *of*
EVANGELISM
in NORTH AMERICA

Thomas P. Johnston

EDITOR

KREGEL
ACADEMIC

A History of Evangelism in North America

© 2021 by Thomas P. Johnston

Published by Kregel Academic, an imprint of Kregel Publications, 2450 Oak Industrial Dr. NE, Grand Rapids, MI 49505-6020.

ISBN 978-0-8254-4709-9

Printed in the United States of America

21 22 23 24 25 / 5 4 3 2 1

*I dedicate this book to my colleagues in the
Southern Baptist Professors of Evangelism Fellowship.
They have truly held up my hands in seeking to instill a
passion for evangelism in new generations of students.*

*I also dedicate this volume to generations to come.
For myself and my wife, our eight grandchildren.
They themselves will experience new epochs in need
of the same old gospel story. Being confident of God's
faithfulness throughout all generations, I pray that they
will plow new furrows in the Lord's harvest fields.*

CONTENTS

....
....

INTRODUCTION

Few volumes have covered the history of evangelism as a focal point since the mid-1940s. Hence this present volume promises to fill a seventy-year void in concerted consideration. Evangelism in early America is discussed in helpful detail. Edwards, Brainerd, Wesley, Whitefield, Stearns, and Asbury all left their mark in the formation of the United States. The second half of this book prepares the reader for evangelism in the twenty-first century. Evangelistic movers and shakers in North America are considered: Henrietta Mears, Dawson Trotman, S. M. Lockridge, Billy Graham, Bill Bright, D. James Kennedy, the Jesus Movement, Donald McGavran, and John Piper. The goal was to offer a breadth of concurrent evangelism methodologies, which in some cases includes considerable interactions between the subjects. The result portrays God's oversight of evangelism as North American Christians sought to obey Christ's Great Commission in their generation.

In wonderfully cooperative spirit, twenty-one professors have contributed to this volume on the history of evangelism in North America. The overarching goal was to provide a biographical approach to evangelism, along with a focus on varieties of evangelism methodologies. Hence, when possible, each author combined the human and biographical side of their topic while also considering practical approaches to evangelism methodology.

Editing this volume has been exhilarating. I would like to thank the contributors for their time and effort. It has been a great blessing to work with the editors at Kregel. Thanks be to God for his grace in this venture, and a very hearty thank-you to all Southern Baptists for your Cooperative Program gifts that support all of our teaching efforts!

CHAPTER 1

JONATHAN EDWARDS: PREACHING *for an* AWAKENING

William D. Henard

In a poem written by Phyllis McGinley, one finds a critical caricature of Jonathan Edwards. In it, she introduces Edwards as one who preached only of the fear of God, even to the point that children would fear standing before him. At the close of her limerick, she pens:

> Abraham's God, the Wrathful One,
> Intolerant of error—
> Not God the Father or the Son,
> But God the Holy Terror![1]

McGinley offers a typical response to the preaching of Jonathan Edwards. In many literary and theological circles, people closely associate Edwards with one sermon. While being recognized as a literary masterpiece and a giant among American sermons by some,[2] there

---

1 Quoted in Michael D. McMullen, "Introduction to the Preaching of Jonathan Edwards," in *The Glory and Honor of God*, vol. 2 of *The Previously Unpublished Sermons of Jonathan Edwards*, ed. Michael D. McMullen (Nashville: Broadman & Holman, 2004), 4.

2 The editors of *Sermons and Discourses 1739–1742* interject that "Sinners in the Hands of an Angry God," as a sermon, "surely stands as the most famous of all of Jonathan Edwards' writings, and possibly the most famous American sermon." Harry S. Stout, Nathan O. Hatch, and Kyle P. Farley, "Editors' Introduction: Sinners in the Hands of

remains much more to Edwards than just "Sinners in the Hands of an Angry God." His preaching possessed a higher motivation than simply wanting to cause people to fall into terror.[3] Seeing people saved provided the passion and the motivation for him, and even when he preached terror and fear, his thoughts focused on conversion.[4] In a sermon preached early in his ministry, Edwards asserted:

> However great your aversion is to Jesus Christ, yet hell—one would think—should be enough [to] overcome it. . . . The consideration of hell commonly is the first thing that rouses sleeping sinners. By this means their sins are set in order before them and their conscience stares them in the face, and they begin to see their need of a priest and sacrifice to satisfy for them. . . . Consider how earnestly Jesus Christ invites you to come to him and trust in him.[5]

---

an Angry God," in *Sermons and Discourses 1739–1742*, vol. 22 of *The Works of Jonathan Edwards*, eds. Harry S. Stout, Nathan O. Hatch, and Kyle P. Farley (New Haven, CT: Yale University Press, 2003), 400.

3   Edwards himself criticized preachers who used terror just for the sake of frightening people. He declared, "Another thing that some ministers have been greatly blamed for, and I think is unjustly, is speaking *terror* to them who are already under great terrors, instead of comforting them. Indeed, if ministers in such a case go about to terrify persons with that which is not true, or to affright them by representing their case worse than it is, or in any respect otherwise than it is, they are to be condemned." Jonathan Edwards, "Some Thoughts Concerning the Present Revival of Religion in New England, and the Way in Which It Ought to be Acknowledged and Promoted; Humbly Offered to the Public, in a Treatise on that Subject," in vol. 1 of *The Works of Jonathan Edwards*, ed. Edward Hickman (Peabody, MA: Hendrickson, 2003), 392.

4   The term "saved" was not foreign to Edwards. He used the word in the titles of several sermons. See Jonathan Edwards, "There Are Some Christians Who, Though They Are Saved, Yet It Is as It Were by Fire (1742)" (Beinecke Rare Book and Manuscript Library, Yale University, New Haven, CT).

5   Jonathan Edwards, "Christ's Sacrifice," in *Sermons and Discourses 1720–1723*, vol. 10 of *The Works of Jonathan Edwards*, ed. Wilson H. Kimnach (New Haven, CT: Yale University Press, 1992), 603. Edwards first preached the sermon in early 1723. Manuscript evidence, however, indicates that he preached it at later times: namely, the addition of a few numbered subheadings in a different ink and the crossing out of a ten-line passage. See Wilson H. Kimnach, "Editor's Introduction: Christ's Sacrifice," in *Sermons and Discourses 1720–1723*, vol. 10 of *The Works of Jonathan Edwards*, ed. Wilson H. Kimnach (New Haven, CT: Yale University Press, 1992), 593.

Edwards believed that preaching on eternal punishment served the purpose of awakening unregenerate persons to their lost condition. He proclaimed such truth out of a love for the lost, not a masochistic ire.

EDWARDS'S PERSPECTIVE ON PREACHING

John E. Smith writes:

> We must not allow our interest in Edwards as a theologian and philosopher to overshadow his importance as a preacher and interpreter of Scripture. . . . In addition to his major treatises, Edwards wrote and delivered a great many sermons through his career as pastor. . . . Some 1,200 sermon manuscripts have survived, and it is estimated that these amount to no more than four-fifths of Edwards's actual output."[6]

Conrad Cherry concurs, elucidating how preaching connected to Edwards's conversion theology:

> Those sermons of Edwards which elicited strong emotions from the members of the congregation and had them crying to God for deliverance were carefully reasoned, doctrinally exacting pieces of work. . . . The sermon, therefore, was to instruct the mind, and as instruction it could become a means of grace.[7]

For Edwards, the proclamation of the Bible became the primary means through which God brought people to a converting experience. Edwards taught that "God has ordained that his Word be opened,

---

6 John E. Smith, *Jonathan Edwards: Puritan, Preacher, Philosopher* (Notre Dame, IN: Notre Dame University Press, 1992), 138.
7 Conrad Cherry, *The Theology of Jonathan Edwards: A Reappraisal* (Indianapolis: Indiana University Press, 1966), 50–51.

applied and set home upon men, in *preaching*."[8] He determined that preaching allowed him the opportunity to reason with people's minds so that they might be awakened to their need for Christ. Drawing this perspective from his study of the New Testament, he wrote, "How often have we an account in the Acts of the Apostles, reasoning and disputing with men to bring them to believing, and of many being brought to believe through that means. How often did they use that argument, especially of the resurrection of Christ."[9] Edwards thus believed that preaching provided an effective way to speak to the hearts and minds of the unregenerate.

HIS PASSION FOR PREACHING

Richard Bailey related that an often-neglected understanding of Edwards was his passion for preaching. He wrote, "Although scholars portray Jonathan Edwards in a variety of ways—as a theologian, a philosopher, an exponent of revival, and America's greatest sensationalist—few focus on his passion. . . . Edwards expressed fervor in one place where it is most often judged absent—in his preaching."[10] Bailey pointed out three areas that demonstrate Edwards's passion for preaching. He explained:

> First, he understood the relationship between divine revela-
> tion and human reason differently than many proponents
> of the Enlightenment. Second, Edwards desired both to en-
> courage the onset of the millennium and to fulfill his divine
> commission. As a result, he not only used contemporary
> models to frame his preaching but also modified the pre-
> vailing preaching pattern. Third, prompted by his affective

8   Jonathan Edwards, *A Treatise Concerning Religious Affections*, in vol. 1 of *The Works of Jonathan Edwards*, ed. Edward Hickman (Peabody, MA: Hendrickson, 2003), 242, emphasis original.

9   Jonathan Edwards, *The Miscellanies 501–832*, vol. 18 of *The Works of Jonathan Edwards*, ed. Ava Chamberlain (New Haven, CT: Yale University Press, 2000), 163.

10 Richard A. Bailey, "Driven by Passion: Jonathan Edwards and the Art of Preaching," in *The Legacy of Jonathan Edwards*, eds. D. G. Hart, Sean Michael Lucas, and Stephen J. Nichols (Grand Rapids: Baker Academic, 2003), 64.

theology, Edwards passionately prepared and proclaimed his message in order to guide his flock to their eternal home.[11]

Two mistaken assumptions continue to circulate that call into question Edwards's passion for preaching. First, the idea exists that he always read his sermons word for word from a manuscript. Second, some scholars believe that he lacked any emotion in his delivery. For example, Edward M. Collins Jr. says of Edwards that "in middle life he appeared emaciated by intense study and hard labour; hence his voice was a little low for a large assembly, but much helped by proper emphasis . . . and great distinctness in pronunciation. He did not use gestures, and a heavy dependence on his manuscript prevented any rapport with his congregation."[12]

While it is true that he carried extensive notes into the pulpit, even ones that could be called a manuscript, his actual handwritten notes assuredly demonstrate that he progressed to be more extemporaneous in his preaching. Early in his ministry, he wrote manuscripts in a neat and orderly fashion. Wilson H. Kimnach substantiates this idea in his "Preface to the New York Period," footnoting:

> Given the preference of JE's father and grandfather Stoddard for *extempore* or *memoriter* preaching, one must assume the JE made an initial effort to preach without relying upon his manuscripts, at least for some months. There are in fact a number of formal or stylistic devices in these early sermons (discussed in the appropriate places) which might have functioned as mnemonic aids also. On the other hand, there is no record that JE ever preached without his manuscript.[13]

---

11   Bailey, "Driven by Passion," 64–65.
12   Edward M. Collins Jr. "The Rhetoric of Sensation Challenges the Rhetoric of the Intellect: An Eighteenth Century Controversy," in *Preaching in American History: Selected Issues in the American Pulpit, 1630–1967*, ed. Dewitt Holland (New York: Abingdon, 1969), 102.
13   Wilson H. Kimnach, "Preface to the New York Period," in *Sermons and Discourses 1720–1723*, vol. 10 of *The Works of Jonathan Edwards*, ed. Wilson H. Kimnach (New Haven, CT: Yale University Press, 1992), 282, emphasis original.

Upon assuming the Northampton pastorate, however, Edwards moved to an abbreviated form of outlining his sermons. This new preparation style allowed Edwards more freedom in his delivery.[14] Kenneth Minkema elucidates:

> Contrary to time-honored descriptions of Edwards as a statue-like, inflectionless speaker, his sermon manuscripts indicated that he varied his delivery, sought eye contact with his listeners, and extemporized on occasion. Having succeeded the master preacher Stoddard, who had condemned the common practice of reading sermons from the pulpit, Edwards experimented with ways to free himself from total reliance on his manuscripts. Increasingly he employed special marks or cues, which allowed him to look up from his notes and then easily locate where he had left off. . . . He even began to compose portions of his sermons in outline, undeveloped introductory statements, and fragmentary phrases for extemporaneous delivery. Switching from octavo-sized booklets to duodecimo leaves meant more frugal use of paper, but the smaller format may also have been Edwards' way of forcing himself to memorize his sermons since they were less easily read.[15]

Along with the influences of two excellent and passionate preachers in the likes of his father Timothy Edwards[16] and his grandfather Solomon Stoddard,[17] Malcolm McDow and Alvin Reid add that George Whitefield heavily influenced the preaching passion of

---

14   Kenneth P. Minkema, "Preface to the Period," in *Sermons and Discourses, 1723–1729*, vol. 9 of *The Works of Jonathan Edwards*, ed. Kenneth P. Minkema (New Haven, CT: Yale University Press, 1997), 12.

15   Minkema, "Preface to the Period," 12–13.

16   George Marsden, *Jonathan Edwards, A Life* (New Haven, CT: Yale University Press, 2003), 33–34.

17   Bailey, "Driven by Passion," 69.

Edwards.[18] Speaking of Edwards, they write, "Early in his ministry, sermon manuscripts were read; after Whitefield visited Northampton, Edwards began using outlines instead."[19]

HIS AIM IN PREACHING

While Edwards had many specific objectives in his preaching, his essential goals or aims can be divided into three categories. J. I. Packer elaborates, "Like his seventeenth-century predecessors, he preached with a threefold aim: to make men understand, feel, and respond to gospel truth."[20] Edwards expressed himself this way:

> God hath appointed a particular and lively application of his word, in the preaching of it, as a fit means to affect sinners with the importance of religion, their own misery, the necessity of a remedy, and the glory and sufficiency of a remedy provided: to stir up the pure minds of the saints, quicken their affections by often bringing the great things of religion to their remembrance, and setting them in their

---

18   In at least one sermon, Edwards made reference to Whitefield. Preached in a private meeting in December 1739, with no reference that it was ever used again, Edwards spoke of the revival occurring in England and how "God has raised up in England a number of young ministers. . . . I have heard of the news of several, particularly Mr. Wesley, and Mr. Whitefield, and Mr. Harris, a young minister that has preached in Wales." See Harry S. Stout, Nathan O. Hatch, and Kyle P. Farley, "Editors' Introduction: God's Grace Carried on in Other Places," in *Sermons and Discourses 1739–1742*, vol. 22 of *The Works of Jonathan Edwards*, eds. Harry S. Stout, Nathan O. Hatch, and Kyle P. Farley (New Haven, CT: Yale University Press, 2003), 104. See also Jonathan Edwards, "God's Grace Carried On in Other Places," in *Sermons and Discourses 1739–1742*, vol. 22 of *The Works of Jonathan Edwards*, eds. Harry S. Stout, Nathan O. Hatch, and Kyle P. Farley (New Haven, CT: Yale University Press, 2003), 108.

19   Malcolm McDow and Alvin L. Reid, *Firefall: How God Shaped History through Revivals* (Nashville: Broadman & Holman, 1997), 213. McDow and Reid offer an obvious disagreement with some of the other scholars as to when Edwards began using sermon outlines. Minkema and Ehrhard supply the most critical proof of the timetable of Edwards's move from manuscript to outline. McDow and Reid provide an important look at the influence of Whitefield, and thus their conclusion proves helpful.

20   J. I. Packer, "Jonathan Edwards and the Theology of Revival," in vol. 2 of *Puritan Papers* (Phillipsburg, NJ: Presbyterian & Reformed, 2001), 26.

proper colours, though they know them, and have been fully instructed in them already.[21]

Edwards conveyed a perspective that moved beyond just the communication of biblical truth. He desired to speak to people's hearts. Though distinctly Puritan in his approach,[22] Edwards offered a fresh means by which people could experience God through the preaching of the Bible.

Understanding the Supremacy of God

John Piper relates that Edwards's first goal in preaching was to bring people to an understanding of God's supremacy.[23] As he spoke of the coming judgment of God, Edwards declared:

> Now how congruous is it that God, in the winding up of things, when the present state of mankind shall come to a conclusion, should manifest in the most public and open manner his dominion over the inhabitants of the earth, by bringing of them all—both high and low, rich and poor, both kings and subjects—together before him to be judged with respect to all that they ever did in the world; that he should thus openly discover his dominion in this world, where his authority has been so much questioned, denied, and proudly opposed. . . . Yet at the conclusion of the world he should thus make his dominion visible to all, and with respect to all mankind: so that every eye shall see him, even they which have denied him, and shall find that *God is supreme Lord of them and of the whole world.*[24]

---

21 Jonathan Edwards, *The Treatise on Religious Affections* (New York: American Tract Society, n.d.), 30–31. This particular edition probably dates c. 1850.

22 Packer, "Jonathan Edwards and the Theology of Revival," 26.

23 John Piper, *God's Passion for His Glory: Living the Vision of Jonathan Edwards* (Wheaton, IL: Crossway, 1998), 31.

24 Jonathan Edwards, "The Day of Judgment," in *Sermons and Discourses 1723–1729*, vol. 14 in *The Works of Jonathan Edwards*, ed. Kenneth P. Minkema (New Haven, CT: Yale University Press, 1997), 515, emphasis added. This sermon dates 1729, with the

It became the goal of Edwards for people to see God's majesty. When confronted with God's supremacy, people discover that "the majesty of God is exceedingly great and awful, but according to his awfulness, so is his wrath; this is the meaning of the words; and therefore we must conclude that the wrath of God is indeed beyond all expression and signification terrible. How great and awful is his majesty."[25] In his preaching, Edwards focused his congregation's mind on God's supremacy in order to prove humanity's absolute need for Christ.

Touching People's Affections

Edwards desired not just to impact the mind of his hearers for understanding but also to touch their hearts through his preaching. In his treatise *Religious Affections*, Edwards spoke of this goal of reaching people's affections by instructing them in the Scriptures:

> Holy affections are not heat without light; but evermore arise from some information of the understanding, some spiritual instruction that the mind receives, some light or actual understanding. The child of God is graciously affected, because he sees and understands something more of divine things than he did before, more of God or Christ, and of the glorious things exhibited in the gospel. . . . Hence it also appears, that affections arising from texts of Scripture coming to the mind, are vain, when *no instruction* received in the understanding from those texts, or any thing taught in them, is the ground of the affection, but the *manner* of their coming to the mind. When Christ makes the Scripture a means of the

---

great possibility that it was re-preached at least once. See Harry S. Stout, Kenneth P. Minkema, and Caleb Maskell, eds., "A Chronological List of Jonathan Edwards's Sermons and Discourses," The Jonathan Edwards Center at Yale University, accessed December 3, 2005, http://www.edwards.yale.edu.

25 Jonathan Edwards, "The Portion of the Wicked," in vol. 2 of *The Works of Jonathan Edwards*, ed. Edward Hickman (Peabody, MA: Hendrickson, 2003), 884.

heart's pruning with gracious affection, it is *by opening the Scriptures to their understandings.*[26]

Piper concludes that Edwards believed that the aim of preaching was to bring about "high affections rooted in, and proportioned by, the truth."[27] Edwards himself wrote, "The main benefit obtained by preaching is by impression made upon the mind at the time."[28] In other words, "Preaching . . . must first of all touch the affections."[29]

Evangelizing the Lost

Finally, Edwards established as his goal in preaching the salvation of the lost. Preaching served as his primary method for reaching those who were unbelievers, with evangelism providing an essential theme in his pastoral preaching. In a sermon preached two months prior to his delivering "Sinners in the Hands of an Angry God" to his Northampton congregation in June of 1741, Edwards proposed that one can discover God's concern for lost sinners through the fact of his undertaking to subdue the impenitent. Speaking of the unregenerate and God's concern for them, Edwards reasoned:

> Now they are always doubting of the truth of the Scriptures, questioning whether they be the word of God, and whether the threatenings of Scripture be true, but God hath undertaken to convince them that those threatenings are true, and he will make them to know that they are true, so that they will never doubt any more for ever. . . . Now ministers often tell sinners of the great importance of an interest in Christ, and that that is the

---

26 Jonathan Edwards, "A Treatise Concerning Religious Affections," in vol. 1 of *The Works of Jonathan Edwards*, ed. Edward Hickman (Peabody, MA: Hendrickson, 2003), 281–82, emphasis original.

27 Piper, *God's Passion for His Glory*, 40.

28 Jonathan Edwards, "Thoughts on the Revival of Religion in New England," in vol. 1 of *The Works of Jonathan Edwards*, ed. Edward Hickman (Peabody, MA: Hendrickson, 2003), 394.

29 Marsden, *Jonathan Edwards*, 282.

one thing needful. They are also told the folly of delaying the care of their souls, and how much it concerns them to improve their opportunity. But the instructions of ministers do not convince them, therefore *God will undertake to convince them.*[30]

Even when Edwards preached a more doctrinal sermon or one directed at the church, he would often make application to those who were not believers. His sermon titled "The Excellency of Christ," preached in 1738, provides an illustration of this tactic. With Revelation 5:5–6 serving as his text, Edwards essentially presented the various reasons for the supremacy of Christ:

There do meet in Jesus Christ, infinite highness, and infinite condescension. Christ, he is God, is infinitely great and high above all. . . . And yet he is one of infinite condescension. None are so low, or inferior, but Christ's condescension is sufficient to take a gracious notice of them. . . . There meet in Jesus Christ, infinite justice, and infinite grace. As Christ is a divine person he is infinitely holy and just. . . . And yet he is one that is infinitely gracious and merciful. . . . In the person of Christ do meet together, infinite glory, and lowest humility. . . . In the person of Christ do meet together, infinite majesty, and transcendent meekness.[31]

In the same sermon, Edwards then applied the message to nonbelievers, proclaiming, "Let the consideration of this wonderful meeting of diverse excellencies in Christ induce you to accept of him, and close

---

30 Jonathan Edwards, "The Future Punishment of the Wicked Unavoidable and Intolerable," in *Seeking God: Jonathan Edwards' Evangelism Contrasted with Modern Methodologies*, ed. William C. Nichols (Ames, IA: International Outreach, Inc., 2001), 128, emphasis added.

31 Jonathan Edwards, "The Excellency of Christ," in *The Sermons of Jonathan Edwards: A Reader*, eds. Wilson H. Kimnach, Kenneth P. Minkema, and Douglas A. Sweeney (New Haven, CT: Yale University Press, 1999), 164–67.

with him as your Savior. As all manner of excellencies meet in him, so there are concurring in him all manner of arguments and motives, to move you to choose him for your Savior."[32]

One of the clearest evangelistic sermons of Edwards, which includes a call to accept Christ, was one preached in 1733 titled, "The End of the Wicked Contemplated by the Righteous: The Torments of the Wicked in Hell, No Occasion of Grief to the Saints in Heaven." In the message, Edwards offered a very clear understanding of a sinner's need for conversion, asserting:

> God the Father hath sent his Son, who hath made way for your salvation, and removed all difficulties, except those which are with your own heart. And he is waiting to be gracious to you; the door of mercy stands open to you; he hath set a fountain open for you to wash in from sin and uncleanness. Christ is calling, inviting, and wooing you; and the Holy Ghost is striving with you by his internal motions and influences.[33]

Edwards did not shy away from his belief in the sovereignty of God. God is absolutely sovereign in matters of salvation. In his sovereignty, he chooses to call people to seek him and he seeks the unregenerate. While "the saints will know, that it is the will of God the wicked should be miserable to all eternity,"[34] it is also true that "Christ is now seeking your salvation; such an opportunity have you now in your hands."[35] One thus sees the evangelistic thrust and theological foundation of Jonathan Edwards's preaching.

---

32 Edwards, "The Excellency of Christ," 184.
33 Jonathan Edwards, "The End of the Wicked Contemplated by the Righteous: The Torments of the Wicked in Hell, No Occasion of Grief to the Saints in Heaven," in vol. 2 of *The Works of Jonathan Edwards*, ed. Edward Hickman (Peabody, MA: Hendrickson, 2003), 212.
34 Edwards, "End of the Wicked," 210.
35 Edwards, "End of the Wicked," 212.

SELECTED EXAMPLES OF EDWARDS'S
EVANGELISTIC SERMONS

An excellent beginning point for analyzing Edwards' evangelistic preaching comes from the sermons that helped spark the Great Awakening. Five years after assuming the pastorate in Northampton, Edwards preached four sermons that led to the first wave of the Revival.[36] He published these sermons as *Five Discourses on Important Subjects, Nearly Concerning the Great Affair of the Soul's Eternal Salvation.*[37] The sermons offer an enlightening look into his soteriology and his specific connections between seeking God and conversion. Delivering these sermons during the years 1734 and 1735, they represent his philosophy about the importance of theology in bringing about the Revival. According to Edwards, the Revival began as he preached doctrinal answers for the rising problem of Arminianism.[38] Edwards explained:

> About this time began the great *noise*, in this part of the country, about *Arminianism*, which seemed to appear with a very *threatening* aspect upon the interest of religion here.

---

36 Edwards mentioned in his preface to these sermons that a fifth sermon titled "The Excellency of Christ" was actually "added on my own motion, thinking that a discourse on such an evangelical subject, would properly follow others that were chiefly legal and awakening, and that something of the excellency of the Savior, was proper to succeed those things that were to show the necessity of salvation." M. X. Lesser, "Editor's Introduction: The Excellency of Christ," in *Sermons and Discourses, 1734–1738*, vol. 17 of *The Works of Jonathan Edwards*, ed. M. X. Lesser (New Haven, CT: Yale University Press, 2001), 560.

37 Jonathan Edwards, "Preface to Five Discourses on Important Subjects, Nearly Concerning the Great Affair of the Soul's Eternal Salvation," in vol. 1 of *The Works of Jonathan Edwards*, ed. Edward Hickman (Peabody, MA: Hendrickson, 2003), 620.

38 Unfortunately, this same controversy over Arminianism led to a decline in the revival fever. In recording his recollections of the Revival in a letter to Benjamin Colman, Edwards requested prayer for Hampshire County and Northampton because "in its present melancholy circumstances into which it is brought by the Springfield quarrel, which doubtless above all things that have happened, has tended to put a stop to the glorious work here, and to prejudice this country against it, and hinder the propagation of it." Jonathan Edwards, *The Great Awakening*, vol. 4 of *The Works of Jonathan Edwards*, ed. C. C. Goen (New Haven, CT: Yale University Press, 1972), 211.

The friends of vital piety trembled for fear of the issue; but it seemed, contrary to their fear, strongly to be *overruled* for the promoting of religion. Many who looked on themselves as in a *Christless* condition, seemed to be awakened by it, with fear that God was about to withdraw from the land, and that we should be given up to *heterodoxy* and corrupt principles; and that then their *opportunity* for obtaining salvation would be past.[39]

Thus, as Edwards proclaimed messages which explained God's sovereignty and the means by which a person sought salvation, the initial stirrings of the Awakening began. While his intentions originated more out of correction and instruction than revival, the results of the sermons proved astounding.[40]

"Justification by Faith Alone"
Edwards used the text Romans 4:5, which states, "But to him that worketh not, but believeth on him that justifieth the ungodly, his faith is counted for righteousness."[41] He proposed through this sermon to show how, in regard to humanity, "We are justified only by faith in Christ, and not by any manner of virtue or goodness of our own."[42] Edwards set the standard declaring the means by which one

---

39 Jonathan Edwards, "A Narrative of Surprising Conversions," in *Jonathan Edwards on Revival* (Carlisle, PA: The Banner of Truth Trust, 1984), 11, emphasis original.

40 Edwards recounted, "This dispensation has also appeared very extraordinary in the *numbers* of those on whom we have reason to hope it has had a saving effect. We have about *six hundred and twenty communicants*, which include almost all our adult persons. The church was very *large* before; but persons never *thronged* into it as they did in the late extraordinary time. Our *sacraments* are eight weeks asunder, and I received into our communion about a *hundred* before one sacrament, *fourscore* of them at one time, whose appearance, when they presented themselves together to make an open explicit *profession* of Christianity, was very affecting to the congregation. I took in near *sixty* before the next sacrament day." Edwards, "A Narrative of Surprising Conversions," 19, emphasis original.

41 All Scripture quotations in this chapter are from the 1611 Authorized Version, unless otherwise noted.

42 Jonathan Edwards, "Justification by Faith Alone," in *Sermons and Discourses, 1734–1738*, vol. 19 of *The Works of Jonathan Edwards*, ed. M. X. Lesser (New Haven, CT: Yale University Press, 2001), 149.

was converted. Salvation came as an act of God, not as the result of the individual's goodness. This concept espousing God's sovereignty in the provision of eternal life serves as a foundational premise within Edwards's conversion theology.

From this sermon, Edwards offered some initial understanding into his steps to conversion. In Edwards's mind, one might ask, "How does a person become a Christian?" Edwards provided an answer, explaining:

> Here, if I may humbly express what seems evident to me, though faith be indeed the condition of justification so as nothing else is . . . in one sense, Christ alone performs the condition of our justification and salvation; in another sense, faith is the condition of justification; in another sense, other qualifications and acts are conditions of salvation and justification too.[43]

One final important aspect of the sermon arises out of Edwards's use of the terms "coming to Christ" and "receiving Christ." In relating these terms to justification and faith, he explained:

> I don't now pretend to define justifying faith, or to determine precisely how much is contained in it, but only to determine thus much concerning it, viz. That it is that by which the soul, that before was separate, and alienated from Christ, unites itself to him, or ceases to be any longer in that state of alienation, and comes into that forementioned union or relation to him, or to use the Scripture phrase, that 'tis that by which the soul COMES to Christ, and RECEIVES him: and this is evident by the Scriptures using these very expressions to signify faith.[44]

43　Edwards, "Justification by Faith Alone," 152.
44　Edwards, "Justification by Faith Alone," 157, emphasis original.

"Pressing into the Kingdom of God"

One of the most distinct sermons Edwards preached that reflects his understanding of the doctrine of seeking is this sermon, the second in his series on *Five Discourses on Various Important Subjects*. Lesser notes that Edwards preached this sermon in February 1735, "Some ten weeks after the November lecture on justification and within five weeks of the onset of 'the present season of the pouring out of the Spirit of God on this town' and the many 'instances of sudden conversions.'"[45]

Luke 16:16 provided the text, which reads, "The law and the prophets were until John: since that time the kingdom of God is preached, and every man presseth into it." In introducing this topic, Edwards proclaimed, "In discoursing on this subject, I would, first, show what is that way of seeking salvation that seems to be pointed forth, in the expressing of 'pressing into the kingdom of God'; second, give the reasons why it concerns everyone that would obtain the kingdom of God, to seek it in this way; and then make application."[46]

An important part of the sermon comes from the application section where Edwards offered possible objections from people concerning the act of seeking, and then provided an answer to that objection. Edwards recognized that there existed a proper way in which a person should seek salvation, admonishing, "There are many that in time past have sought salvation, but not in this manner, and so they have never obtained. . . . Be exhorted therefore not to seek salvation as they did."[47] He then concluded with this exhortation, "Therefore as you regard the interest of your soul, don't run yourself into a like difficulty, by unsteadiness, intermission, and backsliding; but press right forward, from henceforth, and make but one work of seeking converting and pardoning grace, however great, and difficult, and long a work that may be."[48]

---

45   M. X. Lesser, "Editor's Introduction: Pressing into the Kingdom of God," in *Sermons and Discourses, 1734–1738*, vol. 19 of *The Works of Jonathan Edwards*, ed. M. X. Lesser (New Haven, CT: Yale University Press, 2001), 272.

46   Jonathan Edwards, "Pressing into the Kingdom of God," in *Sermons and Discourses, 1734–1738*, vol. 19 of *The Works of Jonathan Edwards*, ed. M. X. Lesser (New Haven, CT: Yale University Press, 2001), 276.

47   Edwards, "Pressing into the Kingdom of God," 282–83.

48   Edwards, "Pressing into the Kingdom of God," 304.

"Ruth's Resolution"

This sermon not only typifies Edwards's conversion preaching, but it also represents his love for typology in his messages. Edwards saw Ruth as "a type of the Gentile church, and also of every sincere convert. . . . Ruth forsook all her natural relations, and her own country, the land of her nativity, and all her former possessions there, for the sake of the God of Israel; as every true Christian forsakes all for Christ."[49]

His intention appears to be to emphasize the importance of watching what other Christians do with the purpose of imitating their resolve to follow Christ. Edwards preached, "Unless you follow them, in their turning to God, their conversion will be a foundation of an eternal separation between you and them."[50] Conversion, therefore, finds a portion of its motivation in relationships. People should desire heaven because family and friends who are converted will be there. Edwards concluded his message by asking a question and offering a challenge. He offered this appeal, "Shall everyone take heaven, while you remain, with no other portion but his world? Now take up that resolution, that if it be possible you will cleave to them that have fled for refuge to lay hold of the hope set before them."[51]

"The Justice of God in the Damnation of Sinners"

The title for this sermon provides a foundational understanding in Edwards's mind concerning God's sovereignty in all areas of salvation. The sermon also points to humanity's depravity and consequences associated with sin. In the message, Edwards continued his theological understanding of "the free grace of God, in the salvation of men by Jesus Christ; especially as it appears in the doctrine of justification by faith alone."[52]

---

49 Jonathan Edwards, "Ruth's Resolution," in *Sermons and Discourses, 1734–1738*, vol. 19 of *The Works of Jonathan Edwards*, ed. M. X. Lesser (New Haven, CT: Yale University Press, 2001), 307.

50 Edwards, "Ruth's Resolution," 316.

51 Edwards, "Ruth's Resolution," 320.

52 Jonathan Edwards, "The Justice of God in the Damnation of Sinners," in *Sermons and Discourses, 1734–1738*, vol. 19 of *The Works of Jonathan Edwards*, ed. M. X. Lesser (New Haven, CT: Yale University Press, 2001), 339.

Edwards's imprecations served the purpose of alarming his listeners with the dreadfulness of eternal damnation. He warned, "This is what you are in danger of: you that are a Christless sinner; are a poor condemned creature: God's wrath still abides upon you; and the sentence of condemnation lies upon you: you are in God's hands, and 'tis uncertain what he will do with you."[53] Coupled with this alarm came a call to respond to Christ. If individuals recognized their own lostness, then those persons needed to demonstrate a willingness to receive Christ. In a very important statement in which Edwards connected conversion, God seeking humanity, and people receiving Christ, he asserted:

> There is certainly a great deal of difference between a forced compliance, and a free willingness. Force and freedom can't consist together. Now that willingness that you tell of, whereby you think you are willing to have Christ for a Savior, is merely a forced thing. Your heart does not go out after Christ of itself; but you are forced and driven to seek an interest in him. Christ has no share at all in your heart; there is no manner of closing of the heart with him. This forced compliance is not what Christ seeks of you; he seeks a free and willing acceptance, Ps. 110:3, "Thy people shall be willing in the day of thy power." He seeks not that you should receive him against your will, but with a free will: he seeks entertainment in your heart and choice. And,
>
> If you refuse thus to receive Christ, how just is it that Christ should refuse to receive you! How reasonable are Christ's terms, who offers to save all those that willingly, or with good will, accept of him for their Savior![54]

---

53   Edwards, "Justice of God," 348.
54   Edwards, "Justice of God," 361. The context of this quote stemmed from Edwards's belief that some people had a willingness to receive Christ, but on their own terms. He considered selfish motives to equal a forced compliance rather than a free willingness. Edwards stated that these motives for this forced compliance came from the fact that "you are willing not to be miserable. . . . And surely it would be very dishonorable for Christ to offer himself upon lower terms." Edwards, "Justice of God," 361–62. In other words, individuals must receive Christ in the manner demanded by Jesus. Though

Edwards concluded the sermon with a plea for persons, in spite of their sinfulness, to seek God. He implored:

> He will show mercy only on Christ's account, and that according to his sovereign pleasure, on whom he pleases, when he pleases, and in what manner he pleases: you can't bring him under obligation by your works, do what you will, he will not look on himself obliged. But if it be his pleasure, he can honorably show mercy through Christ, to any sinner of you all, not one in this congregation excepted. Therefore, here is encouragement for you still to seek and wait, notwithstanding all your wickedness.[55]

CONCLUSION

Jonathan Edwards represents the best in a theological evangelist. He understood the distinguishing marks of human nature. Sinners were bound for an eternal hell without Christ. He also stood unwavering on God's sovereignty. God chooses, draws, and convicts people about their need for salvation. God then does the converting.

Yet in the midst of Edwards's theology came an overwhelming burden for the salvation of people. The means God used to awaken sinners was the preaching of the gospel. When an individual experienced awakening, it was then that seeking could begin. And preach Edwards did. Throughout his ministry he preached hundreds of sermons and stood in the pulpit many days a week exhorting, evangelizing, and counseling his congregation. Edwards opened God's Word to people who would listen.

In his sermons, Edwards taught people about God's sovereignty, humanity's depravity, and the need for people to seek salvation. Even when he came under the greatest attacks from his own church members, he did not give up. God would do all in his power to change

---

they may desire salvation, anything outside of Christ's demands deemed nothing but a forced compliance through selfish motivation. Thus, the person decided to comply in order to avoid hell, not in order to trust in Christ.

55 Edwards, "Justice of God," 375.

the fallen individual. A person, therefore, needed to do all within that individual's ability to be saved, namely, seek God.

When one examines Jonathan Edwards's theology, especially as seen through his Northampton sermons and treatises, an awareness quickly emerges concerning this man's passion for those who are not believers. Edwards preached God's Word. Gerstner comments:

> He preached every doctrine he found in the Bible. His texts range over both Testaments and all the books of each. He preached about sovereignty and he preached about responsibility; he preached about hell and about heaven; he preached about grace and about law; he preached about individual piety and about social obligations; he preached about principles and about persons; he preached about terror and he preached about comfort."[56]

Edwards, though unashamedly Calvinistic, provided a provocative yet balanced perspective in his theology. He believed in God's absolute sovereignty, but he also taught of humanity's responsibility. His ability to harmonize the two doctrines allows for a greater understanding in reference to how one can attest to God's sovereignty and maintain a passionate interest in evangelism. The two ideas appear to be at odds with one another. Edwards demonstrated how one can hold intensely to both ideals without conflict.

Edwards, additionally, did not profess an easy religion. His call for spiritual evidence in salvation gives proof of his belief in perseverance and persistence. His desire, though, always remained to see individuals converted to Christ.

---

56   John Gerstner, *Jonathan Edwards, Evangelist* (Morgan, PA: Soli Deo Gloria, 1995), 190.

CHAPTER 2

DAVID BRAINERD: EVANGELISM *of the* NATIVE AMERICAN INDIANS

J. D. Payne

On Tuesday, Oct. 6, [1747] he lay for a considerable time as if he were dying; at which time he was heard to utter, in broken whispers, such expression as these: 'He will come, he will not tarry. I shall soon be in glory. I shall soon glorify God with the angels.'[1]

After writing this commentary describing the last days of David Brainerd, Jonathan Edwards notes Brainerd revived a little from his sickness, but such progress was short-lived. Years of tuberculosis' effect had taken its toll, and Brainerd's life was coming to an end. For the past few months the Edwards family had taken Brainerd into their home and care. Three days later, at twenty-nine years of age, the apostle to the Indians would enter into his heavenly rest.[2]

After editing Brainerd's journal, written for his mission society, and his personal diary, Edwards published *An Account of the Life of the*

---

1 Jonathan Edwards, *The Life of David Brainerd* (Grand Rapids, MI: Baker Book House, 1978), 343.

2 It is likely, based on descriptions of his health, Brainerd had the disease for seven years. If such was the case, then tuberculosis was with him during his college days and ministry to the Native Americans.

Reverend Mr. David Brainerd in 1749.[3] This lengthy work, filled with
daily entries and thoughts from Brainerd and interrupted at times
with Edwards's reflections, highlights significant events in the man's
life, giving most attention to his last five years. It was Edwards's publication that brought the story of Brainerd to the masses.[4] Throughout
the eighteenth and ninteenth centuries, Brainerd became a household
name among American Christians and his writings would become a
powerful catalyst for the development and growth of the Protestant
Missionary Movement. Hearing of his devotion to God, sacrificial
lifestyle, and simple gospel message, early Moravians, William Carey,
and John Wesley were just a few who looked to Brainerd as an example
and source of motivation for their global efforts. The young man—
expelled from Yale and who had suffered greatly in the wilderness to
take the gospel to the Native Americans of Pennsylvania, New Jersey,
and New York—became a model for the Christian life.

In this chapter, I provide a brief introduction to the life and
ministry of Brainerd. Who was this American legend who had such
influence on his and subsequent generations? What were his methods
of evangelizing the Native Americans of the Northeast?

CHILDHOOD AND COLLEGE

Little is known about the early years of David Brainerd. He was born
April 20, 1718 in Haddam, Connecticut to Hezekiah and Dorothy
Hobart Brainerd. The couple had nine children, four daughters and
five sons. Hezekiah was a man of means. John A. Grigg writes, "The

---

3   Jonathan Edwards, *An Account of the Life of the Reverend Mr. David Brainerd* (Boston:
    D. Henchman, 1749).

4   By the end of the nineteenth century, at least thirty editions of Edwards's book had
    been published. David C. Calhoun notes that it was Edwards's most reprinted work
    and was the first biography in America to achieve widespread attention throughout
    the world. David C. Calhoun, "David Brainerd: 'A Constant Stream'," *Presbyterion*
    13, no. 1 (Spring 1987): 49. Joseph Conforti makes the claim that this publication
    served as "the archetype" for the literary category of "missionary memoir." See Jo-
    seph Conforti, "David Brainerd and the Nineteenth Century Missionary Movement,"
    Journal of the Early Republic 5, no. 3 (Autumn 1985): 322.

Brainerds were a prosperous family that enjoyed the growing availability of consumer goods, and they were increasingly connected to
wider colonial and possibly even Atlantic society."[5] However, life for
Brainerd came with great difficulty. Hezekiah died when he was nine
years old, and Dorothy followed suit five years later. Brainerd was
about fourteen when he buried his mother.

Such tragedies possibly contributed to psychological problems for
Brainerd. A simple reading of his writings revealed a man deeply de-
pressed and possibly suffering with other mental illness. He described
himself as "inclined to melancholy" from his youth.[6] While there is
no doubt he recognized and struggled with the weight of his sin,
extreme mood swings are noted with extensive regularity in his diary.
These would be described as ranging from the depths of despair to
the heights of delight, generally lasting for a few days but sometimes
occurring within hours of one another.

Brainerd's account of his conversion can be traced to when he was
seven or eight years old and experienced conviction for his sin and fear
of death. He was raised in a Christian home and regularly participated
in religious activities. At twenty years of age, he noted that he read
his Bible "more than twice through in less than a year, spent much
time every day in prayer and other secret duties, gave great attention
to the word preached, and endeavored to my utmost to retain it."[7]
Though he was proficient in Christianity, Brainerd admitted he was
not converted at the time, but "had a secret hope of *recommending
myself to God by my religious duties.*"[8] After nearly a year of religious
actions, struggles with conviction, worrying about hell and the loss of

---

5   John A. Grigg, *The Lives of David Brainerd: The Making of an American Evangelical
    Icon* (Oxford: Oxford University Press, 2009), 27. Grigg has written an outstanding
    scholarly biography on Brainerd.
6   Edwards, *Account of the Life,* 10. The word "melancholy" frequently occurs in his
    writings to describe his feelings. David L. Weddle labels Brainerd as "the melancholy
    saint." See David L. Weddle, "The Melancholy Saint: Jonathan Edwards's Interpre-
    tation of David Brainerd as a Model of Evangelical Spirituality," *Harvard Theological
    Review* 81 #3 (1988): 297–318.
7   Edwards, *Account of the Life,* 11–12.
8   Edwards, *Account of the Life,* 13.

God's Spirit, praying and fasting, Brainerd described his conversion as the recognition of an inward breakthrough that brought joy, peace, and a new perspective of God:

> As I was walking in a dark thick grove, *unspeakable glory* seemed to open to the view and apprehension of my soul. I do not mean any *external* brightness, for I saw no such thing; nor do I intend any imagination of a body of light, somewhere in the third heavens, or any thing of that nature; but it was a new inward apprehension or view that I had of God, which as I never had before, nor any thing which had the least resemblance of it. I stood, wondered, and admired! . . . Thus, God, I trust, brought me to a hearty disposition to *exalt him*, and set him on the throne, and principally and ultimately to aim at his honor and glory, as King of the universe.[9]

Two months later, Brainerd entered Yale College. He eventually was caught up in the religious fervor of the revivals and awakening sweeping the colonies. His newfound zeal would cause vexation among college officials and result in expulsion from the school.

Brainerd's removal from Yale would have likely been seen as a tragic blow to his future ministry plans. The novel religious climate was pressing against ministers (and Christians) who lacked some of the pietistic enthusiasm scattered throughout the colonies. In the fall of 1740, the college passed a rule that no student was allowed to question the conversion or lifestyles of the rector, trustees, or tutors. Generally, the details of Brainerd's expulsion are attributed to transgressing this policy. However, Grigg notes that Brainerd trended in the direction of the new expressions, had visited a religious meeting that was to be off limits to students, and joined others in preaching to separate meetings.[10]

---

9   Edwards, *Account of the Life*, 24–25.
10 For details on the "Yale Radical," see Grigg, *The Lives of David Brainerd*, 8–25. Brainerd writes of his religious shift in January 1741: "I grew more cold and dull in religion by means of my old temptation, ambition in my studies. But through divine

A freshman overheard someone referring to tutor Chauncey Whittelsey as a man who "has no more grace than this chair." The freshman then told a woman what he heard. She reported it to Rector Thomas Clap who then followed up with the freshman to obtain the names of the malicious talkers. When confronted, Brainerd confessed to the infraction made in private. His punishment was to make a public confession before the college. Brainerd refused and was expelled in November 1741.[11]

LICENSE TO PREACH

Without his degree, it appeared his future ministry prospects had come to an end. However, several ministers of a nearby association accepted Brainerd into their fellowship and put him on a pathway to be licensed to preach. From April to July of 1742, Brainerd prepared for his licensing examination. On July 29, he described his experience with the Fairfield East Association:

> [I] Was examined by the Association met at Danbury, as to my *learning,* and also my *experiences* in religion, and received a licence from them to preach the Gospel of Christ. Afterward felt much devoted to God; joined in prayer with one of the ministers, my peculiar friend, in a convenient place; went to bed resolving to live devoted to God all my days.[12]

COMMISSION TO NATIVE AMERICANS AT KAUNAUMEEK

Brainerd's expulsion resulted in an invitation to engage in apostolic work among some of the Native American tribes in the Northeast.

---

goodness, a great and general *awakening* spread itself over the college, about the end of February in which I was much quickened, and more abundantly engaged in religion" (Edwards, *Account of the Life,* 30).

11 John Grigg, "A Principle of Spiritual Life: David Brainerd's Surviving Sermon," *The New England Quarterly* 77 #2 (Jun 2004): 274–275.

12 Edwards, *Account of the Life,* 44. Brainerd would be ordained on June 11, 1744 in Newark (94).

Several ministers of New York and its vicinity—including Ebenezer Pemberton, Aaron Burr, and Jonathan Dickinson—contacted the Society in Scotland for Propagating Christian Knowledge (SSPCK) for assistance in reaching "the deplorable and perishing state of the Indians in the provinces of New York, New Jersey, and Pennsylvania." The Society agreed to provide funding for two missionaries. Azariah Horton was sent to Long Island in 1741. November 19, 1742, Pemberton and others met with Brainerd and challenged him to consider serving as the other missionary. Six days later, Brainerd was examined and approved to go to the Native Americans.[13] He was sent to Kaunaumeek (about twenty miles from Albany, NY) April 1, 1743 and served there for one year.

Shortly after his arrival, he began his evangelistic work through a native interpreter.[14] His entry for April 10, 1743 is representative of much of his actions at Kaunaumeek:

> Rose early in the morning and walked out and spent a considerable time in the woods, in prayer and meditation. Preached to the Indians, both forenoon and afternoon. They behaved soberly in general: two or three in particular appeared to be under some religious concern; with whom I discoursed privately; and one told me "that her heart had cried ever since she first heard me preach."[15]

After a month of service, Brainerd noted he had little success to bring him comfort. He experienced great loneliness and had poor lodging and food. In addition to these matters, the Dutch community threatened to drive the Indians off the land. Brainerd claimed they hated him because he came to evangelize the native peoples.[16] Edwards notes

---

13 Sereno Dwight, ed., *Memoirs of the Rev. David Brainerd: Missionary to the Indians* (New Haven, CT: S. Converse, 1822), 3, 4, 5.

14 John Wauwaumpequunnaunt served as his translator. John had lived in Stockbridge, Massachusetts, and, under the ministry of John Sergeant, had been instructed in Christianity (Edwards, *Account of the Life*, 64).

15 Edwards, *Account of the Life*, 62.

16 Edwards, *Account of the Life*.

that Brainerd traveled to New Jersey on May 30, 1743, to discuss with the commissioners of the SSPCK his need for funding to start an English school for the Indians. The commissioners agreed to his proposal and provided the resources for his interpreter to serve as the schoolmaster.[17]

The commissioners wanted him to learn the native language. John Sergeant of Stockbridge, Massachusetts, had experienced some effectiveness with the Indians and was selected as Brainerd's tutor. He began language study on November 29, 1743. There was a significant problem, however, with this educational experience. Winter was approaching and Stockbridge was a difficult ride of twenty miles from Kaunaumeek. Brainerd never became fluent and credited this geographical distance as one of the reasons for his shortcoming.[18] March 11, 1744 was his last day of preaching to the community.[19] Though the school had been in place less than a year, Brainerd encouraged the few Native Americans to move to Stockbridge to be under the ministry of Sergeant. They agreed to this suggestion and relocated twenty miles away. The commissioners of the SSPCK relocated Brainerd to the Delaware Indians.[20]

Brainerd experienced few conversions, if any, at Kaunaumeek. He wrote to one of the commissioners, providing an update on his work. His greatest encouragement was that "God's word seemed, at times, to be attended with some *power* upon the hearts and consciences of the Indians. . . . Several of them came, of their own accord to discourse with me about their soul's concerns; and some, with tears, inquired what they should do to be saved?"[21] Brainerd does not offer any elaboration on what occurred after they raised the Philippian jailer's question other than "I cannot say that I have satisfactory evidences

---

17 Edwards, *Account of the Life,* 65.
18 Two months after beginning his studies, he writes, "Those weeks that I am obliged now to be from home, in order to learn the Indian tongue, are most spent in perplexity and barrenness, without much sweet relish of divine things; and I feel myself a stranger at the throne of grace for want of more frequent and continued retirement" (80).
19 Edwards, *Account of the Life,* 86.
20 Dwight, *Memoirs of the Rev. David Brainerd,* 142.
21 Edwards, *Account of the Life,* 88–89.

of their being 'renewed in the spirit of their mind,' and savingly converted to God."[22]

FORKS OF DELAWARE AND SUSQUEHANNA

On May 1, 1744, with most of the Native Americans now at Stockbridge, Brainerd traveled 112 miles to a remote location "above New Jersey" to a settlement "within the Forks of the Delaware."[23] While there, he regularly preached to the Native community as well as to any white settlers in the area.

An entry in his diary revealed social tensions between the natives and the European settlers. Such points of conflict interfered with Brainerd's evangelism, requiring him to adjust to the context: "Preached twice to the poor Indians; and enjoyed some freedom in speaking, while I attempted to remove their prejudices against Christianity." Realizing the cultural struggle, he recognized his limitations: "My soul longed continually for assistance from above; for I saw I had no strength sufficient for that work." In his report to the commissioner, he noted that the ungodly actions of so-called "Christians" had biased the Native Americans against the faith. Some of the people shared with him that they refused to become Christians because they feared they would become wicked like the white people.[24]

The work at the Forks of the Delaware proved to be difficult. Brainerd "longed for the presence of God" in his work that "the poor heathen might be converted."[25] On June 27, 1744, he attempted to obtain a plot of land whereby the Delaware could relocate and have a better opportunity for instruction in the faith. During this trip to obtain the necessary resources, he noted the challenge facing his evangelistic labors:

---

22   Dwight, *Memoirs of the Rev. David Brainerd*, 173.
23   It is worth noting that along this journey he did stop to speak of the Christian faith with some Indians at a place called Miunissinks (Edwards, *Account of the Life*, 92).
24   Edwards, *Account of the Life*, 108.
25   Edwards, *Account of the Life*, 96.

> While I was riding, had a deep sense of the greatness and
> difficulty of my work; and my soul seemed to rely wholly
> upon God for success, in the diligent and faithful use of
> means. Saw, with the greatest certainty, that *the arm of the
> Lord* must be *revealed*, for the help of these poor Heathen,
> if ever they were delivered from the bondage of the powers
> of darkness.[26]

While preparing to preach the next day, he confessed to God that
though he was burdened for their conversion, the work was not his
and he did not wish to receive any glory for it. If the people were to
come to faith, God would have to move them to Himself. Brainerd
seemed to have received some peace at this moment, recognizing it
was not his responsibility to convert them.

During this period of Brainerd's ministry, he traveled to the
Susquehanna River to evangelize a settlement called Opeholhau-
pung, where he found twelve native houses.[27] Here he approached
the "king" of the community, and requested the opportunity to teach
Christianity to the people. He was granted permission to preach. Once
again, Brainerd was impressed by the difficulty of the use of human
means to reach the Native Americans. After his initial sermon at the
Susquehanna, he wrote, "I was exceeding sensible of the impossibility
of doing any thing for the poor Heathen without special assistance
from above; and my soul seemed to rest on God, and leave it to him
to do as he pleased in that which I saw was his own cause."[28] After a
few days, Brainerd returned to the Forks of the Delaware.

While at the Forks, Brainerd observed the conversion of his interpreter (Moses Finda Fautaury) and his wife. These were the first Native

---

26 Dwight, *Memoirs of the Rev. David Brainerd*, 151.
27 Brainerd's brother, Byram, his interpreter, and two "chief Indians from the Forks of
    Delaware," went on this trip. This was an extremely difficult trip. One of the challeng-
    es included Brainerd's horse falling. Though he was not injured in the fall, the horse's
    leg was broken and had to be killed in the wilderness "thirty miles" from any house
    (Edwards, *Account of the Life*, 110).
28 Edwards, *Account of the Life*, 111.

Americans he baptized. Soon after, he baptized Moses's children.[29] Later, he was told these public baptisms served as a powerful witness to the gospel, as the watching natives became more troubled than ever "about their souls' concerns."[30] Brainerd decided since he did not have "any considerable appearance of special success" in the Forks or the Susquehanna, he would venture eighty miles to the community in Crossweeksung, New Jersey, "and see what might be done toward Christianizing them."[31] It would be at this location that Brainerd would experience an unprecedented work of the Spirit among the Native Americans.

CROSSWEEKSUNG AND CRANBERRY

He arrived in Crossweeksung in August 1745. He wrote on August 2, "In the evening I retired, and my soul was drawn out in prayer to God; especially for my poor people, to whom I had sent word that they might gather together, that I might preach to them the next day."[32] Both young and old came to hear him share the gospel over the next several days. On one occasion, approximately fifty people gathered. During this month, Brainerd noticed many people quickly falling under conviction for their sins. He wrote, "as fast as they came from remote places round about, the Spirit of God seemed to seize them with concern for their souls."[33]

After preaching on August 8, to approximately sixty-five people, Brainerd remained to talk with those who desired more instruction. It was in this moment that there was "much visible concern" among the people and "the power of God seemed to descend upon the assembly *like a mighty rushing wind,*' and with an astonishing energy bore down all before it." People were frightened and cried out for God's mercy.

29   Dwight, *Memoirs of the Rev. David Brainerd,* 214.

30   Dwight, *Memoirs of the Rev. David Brainerd,* 215.

31   Edwards, *Account of the Life,* 133.

32   Dwight, *Memoirs of the Rev. David Brainerd,* 215.; Edwards records this entry as August 3 (Edwards, 144).

33   Edwards, *Account of the Life,* 148. He also observed that some had been burdened for their salvation since June when he spent a brief time in the area before moving in August.

Brainerd noted, "I must say I never saw *any day like it*, in all respects: it was a day wherein I am persuaded the Lord did much to destroy the kingdom of darkness among this people."[34] Seventeen days later, Brainerd baptized twenty-five persons and began immediate discipleship training. The size of the community engaging with Brainerd's preaching swelled to ninety-five.[35] He summarized his observations:

> Their hearts were engaged and cheerful in duty; and they rejoiced that they had, in a public and solemn manner, dedicated themselves to God. Love seemed to reign among them! They took each other by the hand with tenderness and affection, as if their hearts were knit together, while I was discoursing to them. . . . Numbers of the other Indians, on seeing and hearing these things, were much affected, and wept bitterly; longing to be partakers of the same joy and comfort.[36]

From Crossweeksung, Brainerd made trips to settlements where he had preached in the past. His preaching at Crossweeksung continued, and he baptized additional converts before the end of the year. In early November, he traveled throughout New Jersey attempting to raise funds needed for an English school and schoolmaster for the native community.[37]

By March 1746, 130 Native Americans were gathering at Crossweeksung. Brainerd was delighted that the Lord had planted His church among this people. Social transformation took place in

---

34 Edwards, *Account of the Life*, 148–150.

35 Dwight, *Memoirs of the Rev. David Brainerd*, 227–229. Without explanation, Edwards' edition of *The Life of David Brainerd* replaces Brainerd's language of baptism with the language of public profession of faith. Though Brainerd also notes the baptisms of many children and includes them in his numbers, Edwards removes all such references.

36 Dwight, *Memoirs of the Rev. David Brainerd*, 228.

37 Dwight, *Memoirs of the Rev. David Brainerd*, 254. The schoolmaster would arrive January 31, 1746 to a school of "about thirty children and young persons" in the day school and "about fifteen married people" in the evening school (Edwards, *Account of the Life*, 217).

the lives of individuals and families, as marriages were restored and drunkenness avoided. The people turned away from their old religious practices. A Christian ethic began to permeate the community. Believers began to share their faith with other indigenous peoples. The ordinances were incorporated into the worshipping community. Brainerd included the following reflections, noting how quickly the church was birthed among the people:

> I know of no assembly of Christians where there seems to be so much of the presence of God, where brotherly love so much prevails, and where I should take so much delight in the public worship of God in general, as in *my own congregation*; although not more than nine months ago, they were worshipping *devils* and *dumb idols* under the power of Pagan darkness and superstition. Amazing change this! [sic.] effected by nothing less than divine power and grace. This is the doing of the Lord, and it is justly marvelous in our eyes.[38]

Brainerd believed their uncivilized lifestyle was not conducive to the public worship of God, proper education of children, and comforts of life. Therefore, in March, he began discussing with the new believers the need to resettle in another community where they could have the aforementioned advantages. By May, Cranberry, some fifteen miles away, became their new home where they could overcome being "slothful in business" as they had known, live together, and enjoy "the means of grace and instruction."[39]

By late fall, Brainerd's poor health took its toll on his body and forced him to leave the ministry in Cranberry. John Brainerd, David's brother, oversaw the church.[40]

---

38 Edwards, *Account of the Life*, 223.
39 Edwards, *Account of the Life*, 234–235.
40 Edwards, *Account of the Life*, 301, 308.

BRAINERD'S METHODS

Prayer

Brainerd's writings reveal a man deeply surrendered to God and regularly engaged in extensive prayer for himself and others. His diary is filled with entries related to his praying and fasting. For example: "My soul was ardent in prayer, was enabled to wrestle ardently for myself, for Christian friends, and for the church of God; and felt more desire to see the power of God in the conversion of souls, than I have done for a long season."[41] As his ministry developed, he confessed that he became more burdened for the conversion of Native Americans and directed his prayers accordingly.

Christocentric Preaching

Brainerd conducted personal evangelism in homes and evangelistic sermons in public places. Regardless of the message, he made "Christ as the *substance* of every subject" on which he preached. His preaching offered an exclusivist message of salvation. Christ was described as the *only* way to the Father. The invitation was open for all, "to come *empty* and *naked, weary* and *heavy laden*" and cast themselves upon him. Christ was the One who supplied "the wants" and answers to "the utmost desire of immortal souls."[42]

In his initial report to the SSPCK, he commented on his approach to preaching:

> I studied what was most *plain* and *easy,* and best suited to their capacities; and endeavoured to set before them from time to time, as they were able to receive them, the most *important* and *necessary* truths of Christianity; such as most immediately concerned their speedy conversion to God, and such as I judged had the greatest tendency, as means, to effect that glorious change in them.[43]

---

41 Edwards, *Account of the Life,* 77.
42 Dwight, *Memoirs of the Rev. David Brainerd,* 321–23.
43 Dwight, *Memoirs of the Rev. David Brainerd,* 171.

Brainerd credited his emphasis on the "doctrines of grace" as what God used to make "such a powerful influence upon the minds of these people." The doctrines were wed to his preaching method and "blessed of God for the awakening," and "the saving conversion of numbers of souls." Brainerd did not criticize the people's external works or challenge them to be morally upright before God. Rather, he drew attention to "the fallen creature," "the misery of his *natural* state," God's "sovereign mercy," and "the great Redeemer." These were given to the Native Americans for acceptance.[44] Moral and social transformation would come, but only if the heart was supernaturally transformed.

Public Baptisms
During his first eleven months at Crossweeksung, he baptized seventy-seven people (38 adults, 39 children). While Brainerd made no comments regarding the children, he writes that he only baptized adults who "appears to have a work of special grace wrought in their hearts." If his private examination revealed that any candidate remained under the conviction of sin without "*comfortable evidence*" of change, then he did not baptize them.[45] These baptisms were a powerful witness to the other Native Americans who observed from a distance.

Catechetical Meetings
Following his preaching, Brainerd gathered the people for growth in knowledge. After they received some of the truths of the faith, Brainerd would use the Old Testament to explain the historical account of God's mission in and through the Jewish people leading up to the Incarnation, crucifixion, resurrection, and the Holy Spirit. He then held evening gatherings in his home to exposit biblical books.[46]

He described these meetings as "lectures," though the people were allowed to dialogue with him regarding such biblical instruction.

---

44 Dwight, *Memoirs of the Rev. David Brainerd,* 324–27.
45 Dwight, *Memoirs of the Rev. David Brainerd,* 227–28.
46 Dwight, *Memoirs of the Rev. David Brainerd,* 172.

Brainerd initially had reservations with the substance of his catechet-ical method that occurred on Wednesdays and Saturdays.[47] He feared his teaching would fail to connect with the Native Americans on an emotional level given his attention toward doctrine. His concerns were short-lived: "When I first entered upon it, I was exercised with fears, lest my discourses would unavoidably be so doctrinal that they would tend only to enlighten the head, but not to affect the heart. But the event proved quite otherwise; for these exercises have hitherto been remarkably blessed in the latter, as well as the former respects."[48]

He took two approaches to teaching doctrine, disciplines, and biblical history. The first method was a systematic use of questions and answers "agreeably to the Assembly's *Shorter Catechism*." The second approach was topical, based on an "important subject" he deemed "difficult to them" at the moment of their need.[49]

Cultural Study

Brainerd was not ignorant to the numerous expressions of the Na-tive American ways of life. He described in his writings, individuals' actions, tribal beliefs, and religious events. Though he was never concerned with what moderns have come to describe as an ethnog-raphy, his study, sometimes as a participant-observer, influenced his approach to ministry. Brainerd learned from the people and made some adjustments to his methods while on the field.

Brainerd was a product of colonialism. British culture was viewed as far superior to what he observed in the wilderness. One of the highlights in his reflections on the work at Crossweeksung is that the Native Americans, "now appear like rational creatures, fit for human society, free of that savage roughness and brutish stupidity which

---

47   Edwards, *Account of the Life,* 274.
48   Edwards, *Account of the Life,* 213.
49   Dwight, *Memoirs of the Rev. David Brainerd,* 338–42. It is important to note that though he did not learn the language of the people, he attempted to innovate his cat-echetical method to the limited native vocabulary. For example, Brainerd was unable to explain *acquitted* in relation to justification, so he called it "God's looking upon us as good creatures" (340).

rendered them very disagreeable in their Pagan state."[50] The hunting practices of the tribes interfered with his methods of instruction. Native Americans needed to become more tied to farming practices which would remove their perennial hunting excursions and keep them in the community for learning.

The evolution of the English language over centuries had accommodated to Hebrew and Greek words and concepts. Native tongues had not. The abstract theological language he had heard throughout his life did not exist among the people. Brainerd fell short in language learning and acknowledged that in a lengthy, and somewhat frustrated, report to the SSPCK.[51] He was limited to working with interpreters and described his frustrations with them. Euro-American influence was the way of the future. Many Native Americans recognized this and desired to learn English. Therefore, the long-term health of the native church and her ability to grow in favor with God and (white) man was dependent on the believers learning the truths of the faith in another's heart language.

Establishment of English Schools and Settlements

Following the example of his predecessors, particularly Sergeant at Stockbridge, Brainerd established schools and communities for the Native Americans. These included a schoolmaster who would oversee the daily education of both children and adults. English was taught as the community learned to read the Bible.[52] The development of such structure and the relocation of new believers to a new settlement required Brainerd to become a businessman and oversee the Native American affairs.

---

50 Edwards, *Account of the Life*, 273.
51 Dwight, *Memoirs of the Rev. David Brainerd*, 335–37. Brainerd worked with an interpreter to do some translation work, in the end found the task not worthy of the time involved when the Native Americans could be taught English. He writes, "Although I have not made that proficieny which I could wish to have made, in learning the Indian languages; yet I have use all endeavours to instruct them in the English tongue; which perhaps will be more advantageous to the Christian interest among them, than if I should preach in their own language" (337).
52 Edwards, *Account of the Life*, 273.

Preference toward Receptive Peoples

While Brainerd received assignments from the SSPCK, he made lengthy trips via horseback to other remote settlements. This itinerant ministry continued even after placing his home in communities such as Kaunaumeek, Forks of the Delaware, and Crossweeksung. Regardless of location, Brainerd never revealed how he discerned it was time to leave to a new location other than passing comments about the small size of the indigenous numbers or their disinterest. He would sometimes revisit these areas, months later, and make another attempt to preach the gospel.

Church Planting from the Harvest

Brainerd had at least two opportunities to serve established congregations, but did not accept their invitations. He chose a more apostolic way of ministry. His focus was upon the wilderness area. His desire was to evangelize and plant churches in territories where the gospel was unknown. Brainerd was often frustrated at the poor examples of the Christian faith set by white people. Such matters biased the native populations against the gospel. Commenting on some Native Americans who had recently arrived in his area and "who had frequently lived among Quakers; and, being more civilized and conformed to English matters than the generality of the Indians," he noted the challenge of ministering to them. These people "had imbibed some of the Quaker's errors." Unhealthy exposure to the faith caused such Native Americans to be "much worse to deal with than those who are wholly under Pagan darkness; who make no pretences to knowledge in Christianity at all, nor have any self-righteous foundation to stand upon."[53] Brainerd wanted to plant churches where the gospel foundation was nonexistent.

CONCLUSION

Few Protestant missionaries preceded Brainerd to the Native Americans. Models and methods were limited. Forerunners such as Thomas

---

53 Dwight, *Memoirs of the Rev. David Brainerd*, 260–61.

Mayhew and John Eliot developed personal evangelism and public preaching methods. Praying towns and English schools had been used elsewhere. Brainerd took the evangelistic methods of his day and adjusted them to his contexts. He emphasized God's love in his preaching, more typical of the Moravians than many New England Puritans. While he believed in civilizing native tribes, social transformation came *after* evangelization. English learning and cultural change *followed* conversion.[54] Brainerd's ministry lasted only a few years, but his influence continues to this day.

---

54   For an excellent discussion of matters mentioned in this conclusion see R. Pierce Beaver, "Methods in American Missions to the Indians in the Seventeenth and Eighteenth Centuries: Calvinist Models for Protestant Foreign Missions," *Journal of Presbyterian History (1962–1985)* 47, no. 2 (June 1969): 124–48.

CHAPTER 3

JOHN WESLEY: ITINERANT PREACHING *and* PREACHERS' CONFERENCES

Jeff Brown

John Wesley (1703–1791) will forever be connected to passionately and meticulously preaching the gospel. His passion for the Word of God and for those who were lost without the hope of its glorious message has been studied, written about, discussed, taught, and analyzed for more than two hundred years. Indeed, very few preachers from the eighteenth century on have held equal influence to Wesley. His ministry has been quite difficult to duplicate; and his contribution to the church at large is so wide-reaching that it too is difficult to equal. He stands tall—and also stands alone—in his efforts to proclaim the good news to those without its hope.

His approach to evangelism, mainly through the avenues of itinerant preaching and preachers' conferences, was quite unique to his context. Indeed, one cannot approach the topic of the history of evangelism without giving serious consideration to Wesley's work. His approach to soul-winning continues to have a great deal to speak into the current evangelical church.

THE LIFE OF JOHN WESLEY

Family

Without a doubt, Wesley's upbringing helped to shape the evangelist that he became. He was born on June 17, 1703, at Epworth Rectory, Lincolnshire, England, to Samuel and Susannah Wesley. He was the fifteenth of the nineteen children. His father was a godly, gifted Anglican priest, and his mother was the daughter of a "non-conformist preacher" and a descendent of a medieval baron. She greatly influenced John's life through her strict regimen of reading and study that she required of all her children at a very young age. One of his siblings was Charles Wesley, who would make a name for himself as a hymn writer. The brothers worked together in ministry throughout their lives. Though they were very poor, both became very educated, and Christian piety remained important staples of daily life for the Wesley family.

Education and Early Ministry

A strict regimen of learning in-home, as well as a formal education that began at age ten, prepared him for the academic rigors of Oxford University, where he received a B.A. and M.A., and was eventually chosen as a fellow of Lincoln College. He attempted to work with his father at his parish, but soon returned to Oxford at the age of twenty-six to join his brother Charles, along with Robert Kirkham and William Morgan, as "Methodists." The term "Methodist" was given due to the meticulous way in which they practiced the faith. They consistently, painstakingly approached Christianity daily in a very serious and disciplined manner. Eventually John took leadership of the Methodists and it expanded into a larger movement. This group was also called the Holy Club due to its focus on strict piety. The group was uncommon in many other ways as well, including the practice of social ministry—a conviction that followed Wesley throughout his life and ministry.

In his early thirties he went as a missionary to the state of Georgia in the United States; it did not go well at all on several levels. Wesley struggled greatly and felt a failure. He wrote in his *Journal,* January 24, 1738, "I went to America to convert Indians; but Oh! Who shall convert me? . . . I have a fair summer religion. I can talk well; nay, and believe myself, while no danger is near; but let death look me in the face, and my spirit is troubled."[1] He then concluded, "Nor can I say, 'To die is gain!'"[2] These years were very difficult for Wesley. Having left in 1735, he returned home in 1737 with more questions than answers and more frustrations than clarity.

Much of his conviction on spirituality and evangelism came from the influence of the Moravian Brethren that sprang from the German Lutheran Pietist movement. These groups impacted him much more than he was shaped by his own upbringing. Books that were influential included Thomas à Kempis's *The Imitation of Christ,* Jeremy Taylor's *Holy Living* and *Holy Dying,* as well as William Law's *Christian Perfection* and *Serious Call.* It was clear that he was interested in a more spiritually focused approach to Christianity beyond what the current Anglican church of his childhood was providing. This focus proved to have a strong impact on his evangelism work, both in method of reaching out and in expectation of the saved.

THE ALDERSGATE EXPERIENCE: WESLEY'S OWN CONVERSION

A beginning point for Wesley's new life began with a simple conversation while he was on mission in Georgia with a Mr. Spangenberg, who was a German pastor working as a missionary there at the same time as Wesley. His conversion/new birth experience finally happened a couple of years later on May 4, 1738, at the age of thirty-five on Aldersgate Street. He describes this notable event with some detail and states, "I felt my heart strangely warmed. I felt I did trust in Christ, Christ alone for salvation, and an assurance was given me

---

1   Albert Henry Newman, *A Manual of Church History* (Philadelphia: The American Baptist Publication Society, 1957), 642.
2   Newman, *Manual of Church History,* 642–43.

that he had taken away my sins, even mine, and saved me from the law of sin and death."[3]

This experience radically impacted everything that he did from that point on, especially his passion for reaching the lost. He began to focus on soteriology, specifically the conversion of lost souls through the proclamation of the gospel.[4] He clearly demonstrated these changes in a sermon at his alma mater of Oxford. He soundly rebuked unsaved churchmen, faculty, city, and the nation of England! He challenged them to bear the Spirit's fruit in their lives.[5] Consequently, he was never invited back.

WESLEY THE EVANGELIST

Due to these influences, experiences, and commitment to kingdom service, Wesley stands out as perhaps the greatest English-speaking evangelist of all time. This is true for several reasons. First and foremost, he was gifted in many areas of ministry and therefore emphasized a holistic approach to fulfilling the Great Commission. Evangelism was always at the core of what he was aiming to accomplish, as his overarching goal was the conversion of lost souls. He saw a very clear connection between theology and practice, between head and heart, and between the call to holiness and compassion on humankind. He was not just reaching the lost; he was working to make disciples.

Second, he insisted on taking the gospel outside of the walls of the church. It was no longer a "come and see" approach but rather a more biblical "go and tell" method of outreach. Early on, he had adopted this conviction personally and was committed to training

---

3   Frederick A. Dreyer, *The Genesis of Methodism* (Bethlehem, PA: Lehigh University Press, 1999). 27.

4   Jim R. Coleman, "Text and Performance in John Wesley's Final Oxford Sermon: Antithesis and Appeal in Scriptural Christianity," http://mds.marshall.edu/cgi/viewcontent.cgi?article=1016&context=sermon_conference. Also see William Cannon, "John Wesley's Years in Georgia," 5, http://archives.gcah.org/bitstream/handle/10516/1330/MH-1963-07-Cannon.pdf?sequence=1&is%20Allowed=y. He makes a direct correlation between his evangelistic failures and the absence of his Aldersgate experience.

5   Coleman, "Text and Performance."

others to practice it as well. He was devoted to confronting the lost and unsaved in their context, which is demonstrated in his declaration, "The world is my parish."

Third, he was self-disciplined and meticulous in his work. He was defined a great deal by this very thorough, focused, and calculated approach to the Christian life, church ministry, and outreach to the lost world. He was spiritual in his thinking but was also able to uniquely balance the spiritual and the practical. In evangelism, he both worked as hard as he possibly could, and also waited patiently for the Spirit to move. This approach caught on and many, many others joined the ranks of these orderly and disciplined followers of Christ.

Finally, and perhaps most notably, Wesley stands out because he was very human. Wesley was unique in many ways, and this also included his failure and self-doubt. He was a great man, but even so, there is a side to his story that is often overlooked and is so crucial to understanding how God used him. Looking at Wesley from this angle might actually do more to humanize him, explain more about why he seemed so suspicious of his own ability, and at the same time make him a much more attainable model for evangelism and disciple-making. As mentioned, Wesley's mission in the United States was a disaster. Albert Newman explains that Wesley's personal immaturity and stringent approach pushed people away.[6] Newman also adds, "By such proceedings he made himself so obnoxious to the community that he found it best to return from Georgia to England in 1738."[7] Wesley admitted his failure in his journal.[8] These failures caused great religious doubt within himself.[9] However, this very sad, failed evangelistic mission to the Native Americans became a catalyst for a greater harvest. It was in these moments of truth, struggle, awakening, and resoluteness that one sees the full picture of this great Christian leader who was far from

---

6   Newman, *A Manual of Church History*, 643–44.
7   Newman, *A Manual of Church History*.
8   Percy Livingstone Parker, ed. Wesley, *The Journal of John Wesley* (Chicago: Moody Press, 1951), 22–26.
9   Clyde Fant and William Pinson, *A Treasury of Great Preaching*, Vol. 3: Wesley to Finney (Dallas: Word Publishing, 1995), 5.

perfect but offered such a strong standard of impassioned commitment while also breaking new ground for the Savior.

WESLEY'S UNIQUE APPROACH TO EVANGELISM

Spurred on by his adult conversion, Wesley immediately began a breakneck pace of travelling the countryside to proclaim the good news. It is estimated that he traveled around four thousand miles annually and that the crowds he preached to were quite large. While he had a small band of enlisted ministers to help with this solemn and urgent task, he soon realized that they had more people to reach, teach, and train than they could handle among themselves.

As a result of need and conviction, Wesley began to take notice of the unique gifts of the faithful servants around him. He "soon discovered that some of his helpers had gifts for exhortation and preaching, and he put them to work."[10] His answer was found in enlarging his team with both ordained clergy and lay ministers in order to reach more and more people through their ministry.

This new development moved things forward quite quickly by simultaneously distributing labor among more people, while at the same time reaching more listeners through a multiplied army of preachers. Above all else, Wesley continued to insist on piety and purposeful, focused service. He was careful to choose the most committed and able preachers that he could find. As they were available, he recruited, trained, and released them, and even followed up with frequent evaluations of their performance.

A second key point about his use of lay preachers was his conviction that they be local lay leaders. He did this for many purposes. Among the central reasons were that they had an understanding of the community, a personal love for the people, credibility among the locals, and more accessibility to the congregation. This logical approach was successful on many fronts, and it often ensured both intentional evangelism and committed discipline.

---

10   Fant and Pinson, *Treasury of Great Preaching.*

Next, Wesley was committed to utilizing women preachers. He was committed to seeing them preach if they felt called. Wesley did qualify them officially, which was quite unique and controversial within his context. With regard to expectation of these women, he was fair in requirements, evaluation of quality, and in holding them accountable— being committed to holding them to the same standards as the men that he had allowed to preach under the umbrella of the Methodists.[11]

The requirements were both biblical and practical. Key among them was the expectation of genuine love. Lay preachers were to be truly alive to God, evidenced by true love of God and neighbor. Second, they were required to have competent knowledge of the Word of God. Third, they had to have evidence of a true calling that was demonstrated, "by converting sinners from the error of their ways." While informal, the qualifications and expectations were both real and lofty. Even so, one critic labeled these lay preachers as "intruders" who would be "swallowed by a pit." Wesley replied, "Such an intruder are you, if you convert no sinners to God. Take heed lest a deeper pit swallow you!"[12] His high expectations of one hoping to preach the gospel are clear. They must be called, qualified, and effective. This was logical, practical, biblical, and—in Wesley's view—God-honoring.[13]

HIS USE OF PREACHING CONFERENCES

Once the numbers of lay preachers grew, organization among them became a must. As a result, in 1744, a mere six years following his

---

11 See Jennifer M. Lloyd, *Women and the Shape of British Methodism: Persistent Preaching 1807–1907* (Oxford: Manchester University Press, 2009).

12 John Wesley, *The Works of the Rev. John Wesley*, 490. Reverend Mr. Fleury was the critic referred to here. He was especially critical about the use of lay preachers. Fleury attacked the Methodists, saying that they "used the most ignorant and illiterate of them, provided they have the inward call of the Spirit."

13 One historian notes that Wesley was impressive and very unique in church history regarding how he was able to keep such a large group of preachers so focused over his long life. The qualities he expected included being diligent, honest, punctual, pure, biblical, and an impartial servant to all. See Robert Southey, *The Life of Wesley: And the Rise and Progress of Methodism, Volumes 1–2* (New York: Evert Duyckinck, 1820), 90–93.

conversion, Wesley began a series of annual conferences with his preachers at which questions of doctrine, discipline and strategy were discussed. Through this work, he discovered what he believed would be the most effective plan for spreading the gospel outward; they would go "a little and a little further from London, Bristol, St. Ives, Newcastle, or any other Society. So, a little leaven would spread with more effect and less noise and help always be at hand."[14]

Along with the annual conferences, Wesley found and utilized ways to evaluate and recruit preachers during the gaps between conferences. One notable model was that of "tickets." Quarterly, Wesley would issue tickets to preachers as evaluations. If they were given a handwritten ticket by Wesley, they were able to continue their preaching on behalf of the kingdom under the Methodists. If not, they were dismissed and replaced. One instance shows Wesley writing one preacher, warning him that songs were to be limited to two, one before and one after the sermon. If he would not comply, he would be replaced. The note was cordial, encouraging, but clear. Wesley continued to be committed to order (often being accused of legalism) even as his preachers were spread across the countryside.[15]

Wesley, in giving advice to Methodist preachers gave some very practical and helpful points that range from punctuality to honesty and from premarital advice to believing the best about people. He shared his wisdom in a proposed motto, "Holiness to the Lord" and encouraged a seriousness toward ministry and relationships. He stressed a holy life, meaningful and sacrificed unto the Lord; "Be ashamed of nothing but sin . . ."[16] he encouraged, as he prodded his students toward a holy, fruitful, and meaningful life.

---

14   Howard A. Snyder, *The Radical Wesley & Patterns for Church Renewal* (Downers Grove, IL: InterVarsity Press, 1980), 35.
15   F. M. Parkinson, "Proceedings of the Wesley Historical Society," *The Wesleyan Historical Society*, 1898, 143–44.
16   Southey, *The Life of Wesley*, 93.

HIS UNWAVERING CONVICTION

Among the profound yet basic and practical advice that he often shared, John Wesley made a statement that defines the foundation of his work as an evangelist of the gospel.

> You have nothing to do but to save souls. Therefore, spend and be spent in this work. And go always, not only to those that want you, but to those that want you most. Observe: it is not your business to preach so many times, and to take care of this or that society; but to save as many souls as you can; to bring as many sinners as you possibly can to repentance, and with all your power to build them up in that holiness without which they cannot see the Lord . . . you will need all the sense you have, and to have all your wits about you![17]

He, like Nehemiah, "inspected the gates" to strategize his gospel work. In his journal dating December 2, 1737, he made the following entry, "During this time I had frequent opportunities of making many observations and inquiries concerning the real state of the province, the English settlements therein, and the Indians that have intercourse with them. These I minuted down from time to time a small extract of which I have subjoined." He follows this statement with twenty-eight observations about the land, the people, and his experiences.[18] He was observant, thorough, meticulously detailed, and constantly focused on the work that was before him.

His decisions about using the gifted and willing, and then making sure they were prepared was quite impressive and laid the groundwork for the future Methodist Annual Conference. Wesley then organized

---

17 "Minutes of Several Conversations Between the Rev. Mr. Wesley and Others; From the Year 1744 to the Year 1789," in John Emory, *The Works of the Rev. John Wesley Volume V* (New York: Emory and B. Waugh for the Methodist Episcopal Church, at the Conference, 1831). 219.

18 *Journal of John Wesley,* December 2, 1737, 45–50.

his followers into a "connection," and a number of societies into a "circuit" under the leadership of a "superintendent." Periodic meetings of Methodist clergy and lay preachers eventually evolved into the "annual conference," where those who were to serve each circuit were appointed, usually for three-year terms.[19]

The final numbers at Wesley's death are significant. An indication of his organizational genius, we know exactly how many followers Wesley had when he died: 294 preachers, 71,668 British members, nineteen missionaries (five in mission stations), and 43,265 American members with 198 preachers. Today Methodists number about 30 million worldwide.[20]

For Wesley, each sermon was evangelistic, and preaching was the key to evangelism. He insisted on "offering Christ" to the congregation. As well, he was always intentional about making the connection between conversion and discipleship—always.[21] Proclamation was Wesley's most powerful and most utilized evangelistic tool. It was portable, so he could take it with him as Christ and the disciples did to any place they felt led to go. For him, the church had been stagnant and stationary for too long. He knew that many people would never come to the church to hear the gospel, so he logically concluded that the gospel should be brought to them by capable people who were well trained.

The use of lay preachers in the open air were two calculated risks taken at once. He spoke of his conviction about this choice and it does well to define why he insisted on lay preaching and the proclamation of God's Word outside of the church and away from the pulpit: "It is no marvel that the devil does not love field preaching! Neither do I; I love a commodious room, a soft cushion, a handsome pulpit. But where is my zeal if I do not trample all these underfoot

---

19   *Christianity Today*, "John Wesley: Methodical Pietist," https://www.christianitytoday.com/history/people/denominationalfounders/john-wesley.html.

20   *Christianity Today*, "John Wesley."

21   Francis Gerald Ensley, *John Wesley, Evangelist* (Nashville: Methodist Evangelistic Materials, 1908), 42.

in order to save one more soul?"[22] It was clear that his passion for the lost is what drove him from town to town and mandated that he find quality help wherever he could. The hand and heart of the heavenly Father reaching out to the lost was the vision that kept him riding across the countryside looking for lost souls to share hope with. He concluded, "The best thing of all is God is with us." This message of Immanuel was what fueled his fire, sparked his creativity, challenged his behavior and defined his person.

HIS THEOLOGY: GOD'S GREAT GRACE

While most famous as a founder of methodism and a charismatic preacher, he was first and foremost an evangelist. The foundation of his ministry, the conversion of sinners from their lostness and hopelessness was founded in God's desire to save, not man's goodness. Wesley was plainly asked, "Is there any clear scripture promise of this; that God will save us from *all* sin?" He replied, "There is. . . . No promise can be more clear"[23] than God's assurance to save the repentant sinner. When asked if it was explicitly stated in the New Testament, he responded that it was and "that (it was) laid down in the plainest terms."[24]

To additional questions about the broad witness of the New Testament to this hope of salvation for humankind he answered, "Undoubtedly it does, both in those prayers and commands which are equal to the strongest assertions."[25]

While his line of questioning then leads to his well-known doctrine of perfectionism, it is clear that his foundation for conversion was based in both Testaments of Scripture, offered by a holy and kind God who always intended to save lost people.

---

22 *Journal of John Wesley*, chapter 11, "I Do Indeed Live by Preaching"; "Wesley's Advice to Travelers Wesley and the French Prisoners," Saturday, [June] 23 [1759] entry, https://onlinechristianlibrary.com/book/the-journal-of-john-wesley, 148.
23 Wesley, *Works of Wesley*, 209.
24 Wesley, *Works of Wesley*, 209.
25 Wesley, *Works of Wesley*, 209–10.

HIS INTENDED AUDIENCE: THE LEAST OF THESE

Years after returning home, his heart for the desperate was recorded multiple times, as he reflected on the native Americans he met on his Georgia mission. In his journal, Wesley speaks often of his ministry to the different tribes of the Choctaw, Cherokee, and Chickasaws. He described them as "inured to hardships of all kinds, and surprisingly patient of pain"—having no letters, no religion, no laws, no civil government, nor kings or princes, living in a way that "every one doeth what is right in his own eyes."[26] Even as a defeated man and on his way out of Georgia, the gospel was of paramount concern.

Upon his return to England, it was the miners whom he sought out particularly. "At five in the morning, as they went down into the pits, he was there to deliver the glad tidings, and when, after incredible hours, they came up from the bowels of the earth, he was there to meet them. As they heard the word of redemption, tears guttered down their blackened cheeks." For them, the new birth meant a rough time; to make a clean break was neither easy nor a simple process. At least they were no longer forgotten and now possessed home for the future.

One writer puts it quite well in an historical perspective.

> Then came John Wesley and his "helpers." They were the first preachers since the days of the Franciscan Friars in the Middle Ages who ever reached the working classes. In England, as in France, Germany, and everywhere else, the Reformation was essentially a middle-class movement. Unfortunately, it never captured either the upper classes or the working classes.[27]

Another historian notes that what was clearly a gospel endeavor to the poor and disadvantaged eventually evolved as a social work. As

---

26   *Journal of John Wesley*, 26.
27   Hugh Price Hughes, introduction to *The Journal of John Wesley* (Chicago: Moody Press, 1951), 3.

converts, they became sober, industrious and gained wealth. "By converting the poor, Wesley brought the British proletariat within the orbit of the Gospel."[28] The gospel made them productive, and eventually influential, as they abandoned many of the habits that had held them back and they chose instead to cling to their new lives in Christ. The gospel had a powerful effect on not only the person but the community, the economic situation, and the nation.

He was so well-known for God's power in his ministry that the highly respected George Whitefield called for him to join what was being experienced in Bristol, which was nothing short of a revival![29] Wesley was drawn to Bristol's poor; and great success for the gospel was found in both prisons and churches. Unfortunately, "He preached so enthusiastically during this time that he was barred from a number of churches."[30] Again, as was the case in nearly every circumstance, Wesley made a difference among the lost, and in those most in need of it. It was not always an easy endeavor at first, but an enormous difference was made.

Wesley, on horseback, set out for the hamlets and mines. The mobs regarded a field preacher as fair game. When the crowds assembled, the town crier would bellow, horns would blow, a cow or a bull would be driven into the crowd. . . . At the end of his long career when he returned to places where once he had been mobbed, the crowds now hailed him as if he had been King George.[31]

Under attack by a mob, Wesley noted the sudden change of one group as God moved in their hearts: "My heart was filled with love, my eyes with tears and my mouth with arguments. They were abased, they were ashamed, they were melted down, they devoured every word. What a turn was this!"[32]

---

28 Roland H. Bainton, *Christendom, A Short History on Christianity and Its Impact on Western Civilization* (New York: Harper and Row, 1966), 125.

29 Snyder, *The Radical Wesley*, 32.

30 Jason E. Vickers, *Wesley: A Guide for the Perplexed*, 2009, 14. See also Bainton, *Christendom*, 121.

31 Bainton, *Christendom*, 122–23.

32 *Journal of John Wesley*, October 18, 1749.

THE "FINISHED PRODUCT"

The fifth and final emphasis of Wesley's approach to evangelism was on what he considered to be the end result of the Great Commission: his emphasis on small groups and discipleship.

Both Wesley and Whitefield were aware that they held differing views of theology. Both were asked about the other and the mutual respect was clear. Once asked of Whitefield if he thought that he'd see Wesley in heaven, he said, "no." He qualified this answer by noting that he believed that he would be at a far distance, while Wesley would be much closer to the throne than him.

When he spoke of fulfilling the Great Commission, he was not simply speaking of witnessing or converting sinners, he was committed to the full expectation of Christ's task of disciple-making. He was as passionate about holy Christians as he was about converting the lost from the snares of sin. He was convinced that nominal Christianity was not to be tolerated because Christ's call was for self-denying followers. He organized the process of discipleship in a manner that would make the process most efficient and most effective. Borrowing from the Pietists and Moravians, Wesley organized believers into small groups. The purpose was for a more open forum, a more clear and honest confession of sin, and clarity with regard to doctrine and action. They could not stop their spiritual growth at conversion. Maturity in Christ was a must.

Wesley was quite joyful when the biblical description of the church in Acts began to form out of these small cell groups of six or so people, separated by gender.[33] "Many now happily experienced that Christian fellowship of which they had not so much as an idea before. They began to 'bear one another's burdens,' and naturally to 'care for each other.'"[34]

The unity and fellowship of the smaller group had shown the same type of fruit as it had for Spener's *Collegia Pietatus* as well as the Moravian small groups. These seemingly small convictions of

---

33 Snyder, *The Radical Wesley*, 37.
34 Snyder, *The Radical Wesley*.

Wesley continued to build the church and make a difference in the lives of those who were growing in their new faith and being actually conformed to Christ.

HIS LEGACY OF SOUL-WINNING

Wesley indeed had a unique, varied approach to evangelism. He once stated, "We must build with one hand and fight with the other, and this is a great work, not only to bring souls to believe in Christ, but to build them up in our most holy faith."[35] For him, very uniquely to the time, evangelism was clearly intentional, aimed outside of the walls of the church through traveling to the people (as Jesus did). It began with a direct and intentional sharing of the gospel and ended with disciplined loyalty to Christ through both thought and behavior as the Great Commission demanded. His approach was uncommon, but never unbiblical. He saw the dire need for the gospel to be proclaimed among a lost yet willing audience, and was willing to do whatever he could to reach them. The results were indisputable and widely accepted.[36]

- He preached forty thousand sermons in his lifetime, wrote more than thirty volumes, averaging eight hundred sermons per year or fifteen per week.
- He traveled more than 4,500 miles annually on horseback until the age of sixty.
- He organized 550 itinerant preachers, and perhaps more than 1,500 local preachers as well.
- When Wesley died, there were seventy thousand Methodists in England alone with perhaps another seventy thousand having passed during his lifetime.
- In the United States, Methodists consisted of 1,160 parishioners in 1773, reached nearly 15,000 by 1784, and 57,631 by 1790.

---

35 Ensley, *John Wesley, Evangelist*, 40.
36 Ensley, *John Wesley, Evangelist*, 6–7.

- He died with a few coins. He had given away all of his wealth throughout his life.[37]

"The crowds he drew were the greatest in the Kingdom's long religious history and continue to hold the record. He was probably heard by more men in his lifetime than any other human being until the advent of the radio."[38] It is truly difficult to put into perspective the amount of importance that he continues to have even in the postmodern era.

Wesley is known for many things: his successful work in England, his failure in America, his unique approaches in a time when the gospel struggled to have effect within the church. What made Wesley stand out then is what continues to bring him to the front of all serious conversations about evangelism, preaching, and theology: he truly meant what he said, and he was sure to say exactly what he intended in the clearest of terms. One such statement that was from both his heart and mind was this: "I want the whole Christ for my Savior, the whole Bible for my book, the whole Church for my fellowship and the whole world for my mission field." He truly felt the burden of the lost world on his shoulders and a continual "fire in his bones" to preach the gospel those without Christ's hope. He understood that a strong view of Scripture, the correct understanding of the role of the church, and the commitment of the individual were all key to fulfilling the intention of the Great Commission.

Wesley's exhortation stands, "You have one business on this earth—to save souls." With all that he did for the kingdom, evangelism was at the heart. He was determined to win the world for Christ and had little patience with those who thought that the point of Christianity was something else. Regardless of the place, the message remained the same. The Wesley who struggled to find his footing among the Native Americans and made many mistakes early on in his

---

37   Stanley T. Ling, "What Did Wesley Practice and Preach about Money?" West Ohio Conference Center, 2019, https://www.westohioumc.org/conference/news/what-did-wesley-practice-and-preach-about-money. Wesley believed that if he died with even ten pounds, he would be a thief.
38   Ensley, *John Wesley, Evangelist*, 8, 53.

life offers the church a fuller and clearer picture of one who endured. He endured both the attacks of the enemy and his own personal deficiencies. On his way out of America, with shoulders slumped, he witnessed. Whether people responded or not, he shared the gospel. He was quite imperfect, while still being very effective for the work of the kingdom. The history of evangelism within the church is filled with such individuals.

CHAPTER 4

GEORGE WHITEFIELD: METHODS *for* EFFECTIVE EVANGELIZING

Jake Roudkovski

George Whitefield played a seminal role in the movement of God commonly known as the First Great Awakening. Between 1738 and 1770, Whitefield undertook seven evangelistic tours of the American colonies. Some estimate that 80 percent of the American population residing in the colonies heard him preach in person, making him seen by more American settlers than George Washington. His name was recognized more widely by American colonialists than any living person except those of British royalty.[1] Arnold Dallimore asserted that "God has had His great and good men in all ages, but there can be little doubt that Whitefield deserves the primacy often accorded to him: 'The greatest evangelist since Paul.'"[2] Albert Belden emphasized the prominence of Whitefield in evangelism by stating, "No man secured such a hearing for the gospel amongst

---

1   Steven Lawson, *The Evangelistic Zeal of George Whitefield* (Sanford, FL: Reformation Trust Publishing, 2013), 7.
2   Arnold Dallimore, *George Whitefield* (Carlisle, PA: The Banner of Truth Trust, 1980), 2:536.

the common people in all the history of Protestant Christianity."[3] In his lifetime, he preached at least 18,000 times, addressing perhaps ten million hearers.[4] In this chapter, the author will analyze the life and ministry of George Whitefield by providing a brief biographical background with major ministerial milestones, followed by salient factors that contributed to his evangelistic effectiveness.

George Whitefield was born to Thomas and Elizabeth Whitefield on December 16, 1714, in Gloucester, England. His father died when Whitefield was only two years old. Elizabeth was left to care for seven children and the family's inn. When Whitefield turned ten, his mother remarried, but the marriage ended in a bitter divorce. At the age of twelve, young George was enrolled in the Saint Mary de Crypt grammar school where he developed an interest in drama and public speaking. Young Whitefield was fond of reading various plays, studying them intently, and then preparing to act the parts. He even trained his voice and gestures to generate best effects. As a result of his hard work, he was the recognized orator of the school frequently chosen to represent his school in oratorical contests, which at that time played a prominent role in school life.[5]

The decline of his mother's business at the inn led Whitefield to withdraw from school so that he could help his mother by serve guests and clean the inn. A guest at the inn, a servitor from Pembroke College at Oxford, informed his mother that Whitefield could attend Oxford if he worked his way through college as he was doing. Both son and mother agreed that George should finish grammar school and then attend Oxford. Whitefield's decided to attend Oxford in 1732, when he was about eighteen years old. With a loan of nearly fifteen dollars from one of his friends and a recommendation of several others, he entered Pembroke College and was granted a "servitor's" spot. The servitors' responsibilities included cleaning rooms, polishing shoes,

---

3   Albert Belden, "What America Owes to George Whitefield," *Religion in Life* 20, no. 3 (Summer 1951): 446.

4   Kevin A. Miller, "Did You Know?" *Christian History* 38, no. 2 (1993): 7.

5   Edwin Hardy, *George Whitefield: The Matchless Soul Winner* (New York: American Tract Society, 1938), 30.

washing clothes, and running errands for the students from higher socioeconomic backgrounds in exchange for free tuition.[6]

Even though the spiritual atmosphere at Oxford at that time was not stimulating for spiritual growth and health, Whitefield pursued a right standing with God by praying three times per day and fasting frequently. In spite of his ardent spiritual efforts, he found no peace for his troubled soul. So stringent was Whitefield in his efforts to earn salvation through his works that his severe discipline caused him to suffer a lifelong physical illness.[7] Near the end of his first year at Oxford, Charles Wesley, the future hymn writer, introduced him to a small group of students commonly knowns as the "Oxford Holy Club." Charles's brother, John Wesley, and ten others met to pursue pure and moral lives. Urgently searching for acceptance by God, Charles Wesley gave Whitefield a book in the spring of 1735 titled *The Life of God in the Soul of Man* written by Henry Scougal. George learned that the way of salvation was not accomplished by his religious works but by God's grace. Under conviction of the Holy Spirit, he confessed, "I must be born or be damned!"[8]

At the age of twenty-one, as Whitefield came to repentance and faith in Christ, he testified: "God was pleased at length to remove the heavy load, to enable me to lay hold on His dear Son by a living faith, and, by giving me the Spirit of adoption, to seal me, as I humbly hope, even to the day of everlasting redemption."[9] Upon his conversion, Whitefield began reading the Bible on his knees, often accompanied by Matthew Henry's *Exposition of the Old and New Testament*. When the Wesley brothers departed for the mission field in the American colony of Georgia, Whitefield became the leader of the Holy Club. With a passion for Christ, he evangelized his fellow students and enlisted new believers into small-group Bible studies.

---

6   Dallimore, *George Whitefield,* 1:61.

7   Lawson, *The Evangelistic Zeal,* 7.

8   Arnold Dallimore, *George Whitefield: God's Anointed Servant in the Great Revival of the Eighteenth Century* (Wheaton, IL: Crossway, 1990), 17.

9   George Whitefield, *George Whitefield's Journals* (1738–1741, reprinted; Edinburgh: Banner of Truth, 1998), 58.

The strict discipline in Bible study earned the members of the Holy Club the derisive term "Methodists."

Upon graduating from Oxford in 1736, Whitefield returned to Gloucester, where he was ordained a deacon in the Church of England. "I can call heaven and earth to witness," Whitefield stated, "that when the bishop laid his hands upon me, I gave myself up to be a martyr for Him who hung upon the cross for me."[10] Almost immediately, Whitefield sensed the call of God to preach. One week later, he delivered his first sermon in Saint Mary de Crypt Church, Gloucester, where he had been baptized. When he returned to Oxford to further his studies, the compulsion to proclaim God's Word intensified. As he was given opportunities to fill pulpits in London, he was instantly recognized as a "young preaching phenomenon."[11] In 1737 six of his sermons were published after thousands came to hear him preach in towns around England.

Without prior notice, correspondence arrived from John and Charles Wesley in Georgia, inviting the young preacher to assist in their new missionary work in the American colonies. On May 7, 1738, Whitefield arrived in Georgia where he toured the colony and met its leaders. He preached at every opportunity and visited in homes to share Christ. During his first trip to America, Whitefield decided to build an orphanage in Georgia. To raise funds for the endeavor, he returned to England in 1739. While in England on January 11, 1739, Whitefield was ordained as a priest in the Church of England. After this momentous occasion, he set out to preach throughout England and seek contributions for his orphanage. After several refusals to preach in churches, the young evangelist preached his first open-air message to a group of miners in Kingswood, in a field on the outskirts of Bristol. This first open-air preaching experiment proved to be the turning point not only for Whitefield's evangelistic ministry but for evangelicalism in general. As Whitefield continued to preach throughout the English countryside, it was common for crowds of

---

10   George Whitefield, *George Whitefield's Letters* (1771, reprinted; Edinburgh: Banner of Truth, 1976), 16.
11   Lawson, *The Evangelistic Zeal*, 9.

ten to twenty thousand individuals to gather in the fields to hear him proclaim the gospel.[12]

The crowds in England did not deter Whitefield from focusing on his ministry in America. On August 14, 1739, he embarked on the second voyage to the American colonies. As the First Great Awakening began to spread in the colonies, the preaching of Whitefield played a major role. The evangelist preached in cities and towns from New York to Savannah. In Philadelphia, more than ten thousand gathered to hear Whitefield.[13] In Boston, fifteen thousand listened eagerly to one of his sermons.[14] It was uncommon for Whitefield to have less than one thousand people in the audience at any given time. Wherever Whitefield traveled, shops closed, commerce ceased, farmers suspended their work, and even judges delayed their hearings. This preaching tour would set the American landscape ablaze with the truths of the gospel and need for saving faith in Christ alone. In the near future, a fledgling nation would arise out of the flames.

In addition to preaching, Whitefield formed relationships with leaders of the First Great Awakening such as Jonathan Edwards, Gilbert Tennent, and William Tennent. Several of those spiritual leaders continued to follow up on Whitefield's evangelistic efforts even upon his departure from the colonies. Benjamin Franklin, who became a good friend of Whitefield during this time, set out to make the itinerant evangelist famous in the colonies. He printed ten editions of Whitefield's bestselling *Journals* securing the services of eleven printers in the process. During 1739–1741, more than half of the books published by Franklin were by or about Whitefield.[15] During the second trip to America, Whitefield commenced construction of the Orphan House in Georgia which was one of the primary reasons, after all, for traveling to America.[16]

---

12 Joseph Belcher, *George Whitefield: A Biography* (New York: American Tract Society, 1857), 468.
13 George Whitefield, *George Whitefield's Journals*, 359.
14 Whitefield, *George Whitefield's Journals*, 460.
15 Walter Isaacson, *Benjamin Franklin: an American Life* (New York: Simon and Schuster, 2003), 111.
16 Timothy McKnight, "George Whitefield's Theology and Methodology of Evangelism" (PhD diss., The Southern Baptist Theological Seminary, 2003), 6.

In March of 1741, Whitefield returned to England. He encountered a hostile reception by various groups who had been partially incited by John Wesley's published sermons against Calvinism. In response to Wesley's sermon "Free Grace," Whitefield published a letter that dealt with each point of Wesley's argument. Despite some opposition to his ministry in England, Whitefield stayed three years in his native land. Toward the end of this visit, the evangelist married Elizabeth James. A tragedy struck the newly formed family when their four-month-old son, John, died unexpectedly in the very home in which George himself had been born.

Less than eight months after the loss of their son, the Whitefields left together for America, Elizabeth's only trip to the colonies. During this third trip (1745–1748), the evangelist faced opposition similar to what he had encountered in England. Critics derided Whitefield for exploiting people's passions, emphasizing the new birth, dividing the clergy, and preaching in towns without the approval of the local clergy. The evangelist wrote responses to his critics and continued to preach to large audiences. As his health deteriorated, Whitefield was encouraged by his doctor to convalesce, which he did in Bermuda in 1748.

Whitefield undertook the fourth trip to America in 1751. The trip was cut short in 1752 due to a dire financial situation at the orphanage. He felt that he needed to return to England to secure contributions for the survival of the orphanage. During a time of great financial need, the great evangelist providentially came into contact with a wealthy aristocrat, Selina Hastings, Countess of Huntington. As he became her personal chaplain, Lady Huntington became a faithful supporter of Whitefield's ministry and lessened his financial duress. Furthermore, this relationship afforded Whitefield the opportunity to preach to many British aristocrats at her numerous estates.[17]

During the fifth trip to America (1754–1755), Whitefield generally preached twice a day. He would wake up usually at 4 a.m. before beginning to preach at 5 a.m. or 6 a.m. A visit from Whitefield remained a major event in the colonies drawing large crowds. Near

---

17   Lawson, *The Evangelistic Zeal*, 22.

Philadelphia, the newly formed College of New Jersey, which later became Princeton College, confirmed upon him an honorary Master of Arts degree. After only a year in the colonies, Whitefield was forced to return to England in 1755 to recover physically. He would minister in England for the next eight years due to the French and Indian War, which prevented a trip back to America.[18]

During the sixth voyage to America (1763–1765), the evangelist's health deteriorated substantially. He suffered from asthma and angina. Rather than preaching twice a day, he would be confined by sickness to preach twice a week. Dallimore describes the way many reacted to Whitefield's illness: "The people, however, had heard earlier of his invalided condition, and it is evident that now, seeing him so changed and so weak, they looked upon him as indeed a dying man, and more than ever they held him in affection. Realizing they might have but few further opportunities, they came in still greater earnestness to hear him preach."[19]

Shortly before Whitefield's seventh and final voyage to America, his wife Elizabeth died of fever. Whitefield lamented her loss, "I feel the loss of my right hand daily; but right hands and right eyes must be parted with for Him, who ordereth all things well."[20] Whitefield didn't allow his personal loss to impede his passage to America. In November 1769, the aging evangelist arrived in Charleston where he preached to large congregations. Whitefield then traveled to Savannah to attend a dedication ceremony for an addition to the Orphan House. In the last few months of his life, Whitefield preached in Philadelphia and various towns in New England. On the night of September 29, 1770, in Exeter, Massachusetts, George Whitefield preached his last sermon. The great evangelist died the next day.[21]

Upon brief examination and analysis of the life and ministry of the great preacher, the author of this chapter identified several salient factors which contributed to Whitefield's evangelistic effectiveness. The

---

18   Lawson, *The Evangelistic Zeal*, 24.
19   Dallimore, *George Whitefield*, 2:426.
20   Whitefield, *George Whitefield's Letters*, 382.
21   McKnight, "Whitefield's Theology and Methodology," 8.

first notable factor is Whitefield's evangelistic fervor which stemmed from his immersion in the Scriptures. Once he became converted, Whitefield intentionally saturated himself with the Word of God, internalizing biblical truths into his daily life and ministry. Reflecting on his study of the Bible as a new believer, Whitefield comments, "I began to read the Holy Scriptures upon my knees. . . . This proved meat indeed and drink indeed to my soul. I daily received fresh light and power from above."[22] After reading the text, young Whitefield prayed over "'every line and every word' in both the English and Greek, feasting his mind and his heart upon it till its essential meaning became a part of his very person."[23] One can almost envision the young evangelist on his knees glancing back and forth from the English Bible to the Greek to Matthew Henry's commentary, "seeking to discern and digest Scripture's divine truths."[24]

Whitefield continued to immerse himself in the Word of God throughout his life and ministry. Whitefield's evangelistic preaching vocabulary reflected his internalization of the Scriptures. He employed biblical metaphors, drew biblical analogies, and illustrated biblical truth with other biblical passages. He commented on how the Word of God became primary in his life and ministry, "I got more true knowledge from reading the Book of God in one month, than I could ever have acquired from the writings of men."[25] The more Whitefield immersed himself in the Word of God, the deeper his soul was set ablaze to love Christ and share the gospel. Whitefield confessed how his daily devotion to the Scripture became like "fire upon the altar" of his soul, fueling his love for Jesus and evangelism.[26]

The second prominent factor was Whitefield's prayer life. Through time spent on his knees, his passion for God and souls was further deepened. According to one prominent biographer, Whitefield's prayer life was a main source for his evangelistic effectiveness: "The

22 Whitefield, *George Whitefield's Journals*, 60.
23 Dallimore, *George Whitefield*, 1:22.
24 Lawson, *The Evangelistic Zeal*, 32.
25 Whitefield, *George Whitefield's Journals*, 60.
26 Whitefield, *George Whitefield's Journals*, 48.

grand secret of Whitefield's power was, as we have seen and felt, his devotional spirit. Had he been less prayerful, he would have been less powerful."[27] Whitefield saw time alone with God as the avenue that brings God and man together, "It raises man up to God, and brings God down to man."[28] He viewed prayer not just as a spiritual discipline but as utter delight. Recalling one particular season of prayer, he mentioned: "Oh, what sweet communion had I daily vouchsafed with God in prayer. . . . How often have I been carried out beyond myself when sweetly meditating in the fields! How assuredly have I felt that Christ dwelt in me and I in Him."[29] The great preacher viewed prayer as "a fountain of refreshing water for his parched soul."[30] Whitefield's evangelistic effectiveness didn't stem from his oratory skills or Oxford education but primarily from prayer spent alone with God. As he poured his heart to God in prayer, he was used effectively by God to reach more people for Christ.

The third noteworthy factor was Whitefield's pursuit of holiness. Holiness was the goal of his spiritual disciplines. In the midst of his demanding ministry, Whitefield pleaded with others to intercede for his pursuit of holiness. For his holiness to deepen, he believed that he needed to be turning away from sin continuously in repentance before God. Whitefield proclaimed, "Abhor thy old sinful course of life, and serve God in holiness. . . . If you lament and bewail past sins, and do not forsake them, your repentance is in vain, you are mocking of God, and deceiving your own soul; you must put off the old man with his deeds, before you can put on the new man, Christ Jesus."[31] In his Christian walk, Whitefield recognized holiness as a progressive transformation from one degree of glory to another (2 Cor 3:18). His sanctification was a continual process realized though spiritual disciplines. From his conversion until his last breath, Whitefield pursued

---

27   Robert Philip, *The Life and Times of George Whitefield* (1837, reprinted; Edinburgh: Banner of Truth, 2007), 565.
28   George Whitefield, *The Works of the Reverend George Whitefield*, vol. V (London: Edward and Charles Dilly, 1772), 28.
29   Whitefield, *George Whitefield's Journals*, 61.
30   Lawson, *The Evangelistic Zeal*, 37.
31   Whitefield, *The Works of the Reverend George Whitefield*, vol. VI, 6–7.

personal holiness. Ryle asserted that among preachers of the eighteenth century, Whitefield was "one of its most saintly characters, if not the saintliest of all."[32] God honored his pursuit of holiness by countless lives that came to know Christ and the fact that a legitimate scandal never surrounded his life.

The fourth substantial factor of Whitefield's evangelistic effectiveness included his Christocentric approach to life and ministry. The intense focus on Christ was the dominant focus of his life: "His one true life was always the person of Jesus. The risen Christ was the fixed star of his life's voyage, the sole object of his affections. It was for Jesus that he lived, Jesus whom he sought to please, and Jesus in whom he hoped to find his rest."[33] Whitefield urged people to look for Christ in the Scriptures always, "He is the treasure hid in the field, both of the Old and New Testaments. In the Old you will find Him under prophecies, types, sacrifices, and shadows; in the New, manifested in the flesh, to become a propitiation for our sins as a priest, and as a prophet to reveal the whole will of his heavenly Father."[34] Every stone in the Bible, he believed, must be overturned in search of Christ. Whitefield pleaded with his listeners to keep Christ in view when studying the Scriptures and to use each verse to bring them closer to Jesus.[35] He was convinced that the written Word should always lead to a deeper knowledge of the living Word, Jesus Christ.[36]

Whitefield's Christocentric approach to life and ministry was anchored to the cross of Christ. Whitefield was convinced that any presentation of the gospel must begin by exposing sin in the life of the listener and his or her urgent need for salvation. He next proceeded to the saving death of Jesus as he proclaimed the perfect atonement accomplished by the death of the Son of God. Moving from man's

---

32   J. C. Ryle, "George Whitefield and His Ministry" in *Select Sermons of George Whitefield* (Edinburgh: Banner of Truth, 1958), 5.

33   Stephen Mansfield, *Forgotten Founding Father: The Heroic Legacy of George Whitefield* (Nashville: Cumberland House, 2001), 214.

34   George Whitefield, *Sermons of George Whitefield* (Peabody, MA: Hendrickson, 2009), 199–200.

35   Whitefield, *Sermons of George Whitefield,* 199–200.

36   Lawson, *The Evangelistic Zeal,* 39.

ruin in sin to Christ substitutionary death on the cross, Whitefield proclaimed Christ crucified as the only means of salvation: "Look on His hands, bored with pins of iron; look on His side, pierced with a cruel spear, to let loose the sluices of His blood, and open a fountain for sin, and for all uncleanness . . . only believe in Him, and then, though you have crucified Him afresh, He will abundantly pardon you."[37] Throughout his sermons, journal entries, correspondence, and personal conversations, Whitefield gloried in the cross of Christ as the supreme and singular hope for the world. It was the Christocentric approach to life and ministry firmly anchored to the cross that drove Whitefield relentlessly in evangelistic passion, pursuit, and practice.

The fifth salient contributing factor to Whitefield's evangelistic effectiveness consisted of his continuous emphasis on the necessity of the new birth. Dallimore asserted, "The one great truth which had been the foundation of Whitefield's ministry from the first was that of the new birth."[38] Whitefield's sermon "The Nature and Necessity of the New Birth" was his most widely circulated material. The famed evangelist made the new birth a dominant theme in his preaching, "The doctrine of our regeneration or new birth in Christ Jesus . . . is one of the most fundamental doctrines of our holy religion . . . the very hinge on which the salvation of each of us turns."[39] Where regeneration was not a central focus of the preachers in those days, Whitefield made it a prevailing emphasis in his life and ministry.

The sixth striking factor that contributed to Whitefield's evangelistic effectiveness incorporated a universal appeal for people to come to repentance and faith in Christ. While he unapologetically identified himself as a Calvinist, he was committed more to Christ and to the Scriptures than any theological system. He disagreed with Hyper-Calvinists like John Hussey who argued against general appeals for salvation and contended that persons who believe in particular redemption "cannot preach consistent with general offers

---

37   Whitefield, *The Works of the Reverend George Whitefield*, vol. VI, 62.

38   Dallimore, *George Whitefield*, vol. 1, 345.

39   Whitefield, *The Works of the Reverend George Whitefield*, vol. VI, 257.

of grace."[40] Whitefield believed strongly that ministers should "offer salvation freely to all by the blood of Jesus."[41] He urged ministers to stay faithful to the Great Commission in proclaiming the gospel to "every creature" (Mark 16:15). The great evangelist contended, "The grand topics Christ's ministers are to preach, are, 'repentance toward God, and faith in our Lord Jesus Christ.'"[42] He maintained that all men, elect or not, have responsibility to repent and believe in Christ. Whitefield did not observe a contradiction in extending a universal appeal for people to respond to Christ while, at the same time, upholding a belief in unconditional election. He believed that God intended the preaching of the gospel to all of humanity and offering of such invitations as a means of drawing the elect to Him through the effectual call of the Holy Spirit.[43] The English evangelist believed and practiced extending universal appeals for all to come to Christ.

Personal evangelism constituted another significant factor of Whitefield's evangelistic effectiveness. He intentionally shared the gospel verbally with individuals he encountered during his travels and daily life. He famously stated, "God forbid that I should travel with anybody a quarter of an hour without speaking of Christ to them."[44] This habit of personal evangelism began shortly after Whitefield's conversion. He shared his newfound faith with a woman and several young people who subsequently came to faith in Christ.[45] The great evangelist was not content in proclaiming the gospel publicly as he sought ways to share the gospel privately. He shared Christ with fellow travelers who sailed with his numerous journeys across the Atlantic Ocean. Whitefield witnessed to sick family members, leading one fever-stricken boy to Christ.[46] Once, he witnessed to the captain and

---

40   John Hussey, *God's Operations of Grace but No Offers of Grace* (Elon, NC: Primitive Publications, 1973), 72.
41   Whitefield, *George Whitefield's Letters*, 156.
42   George Whitefield, *Sermons on Important Subjects by the Rev. George Whitefield* (London: B. Fisher, 1841), 653.
43   McKnight, "Whitefield's Theology and Methodology," 160.
44   Miller, "Did You Know?" 1.
45   Whitefield, *George Whitefield's Journals*, 60.
46   Whitefield, *George Whitefield's Journals*, 143.

sailors of the ship as well as the British Army troops on board. The itinerant evangelist would walk the decks late at night to gain a hearing from the sailors.[47] At times, he would witness to individuals for hours at a time, answering any of their questions regarding the gospel. In fact, his goal was to speak to each person on the ship regarding his or her spiritual condition.[48]

In addition to speaking with individuals privately regarding the gospel, Whitefield employed written correspondence to communicate the gospel. He wrote letters to his family members such as his mother and his brother James as well as people he just met urging all to trust Christ. Whitefield wrote letters to the poor and common as well as individuals of nobility and fame such as Benjamin Franklin.[49] Just as prayer provided fuel for Whitefield's spiritual power, personal evangelism provided passion for his evangelistic ministry.

The final major feature to be rendered in this analysis of Whitefield's methodologies was his willingness to take the gospel outside the walls of a church building. In describing this biblical initiative, J. C. Ryle commented about Whitefield:

> He was the first to see that Christ's ministers must do the work of fishermen. They must not wait for souls to come to them, but must go after souls, and "compel them to come in." He did not sit tamely by his fireside. . . . He dived into holes and corners after sinners. He hunted out ignorance and vice wherever they could be found. In short, he set on foot a system of action which, up to his time, had been comparatively unknown.[50]

Like Jesus and his disciples, Whitefield became a fisher of men not being constrained by church buildings. He proclaimed the gospel in

---

47 Whitefield, *George Whitefield's Journals*, 110–111.
48 Whitefield, *George Whitefield's Journals*, 139.
49 McKnight, "Whitefield's Theology and Methodology," 215–217.
50 J. C. Ryle, *The Christian Leaders of the Last Century* (1868, reprinted; Moscow, ID: Charles Nolan, 2002), 44.

the fields and mines, city squares and ships, houses and carriages. "The whole world is now my parish," he proclaimed. "Whosesoever my Master calls me I am ready to go and preach the everlasting Gospel."[51]

After a brief examination and analysis of the major biographical milestones, the author of this chapter identified several foremost factors that contributed to Whitefield's evangelistic effectiveness. Whitefield possessed an unusual evangelistic fervor that stemmed from his immersion in and saturation with the Scriptures. Whitefield's prayer life fueled his passion for God and souls. His pursuit of holiness precluded Whitefield from any legitimate scandal and further provided an impeccable credibility to his life and evangelistic ministry. Whitefield's Christocentric focus anchored in the cross drove the great evangelist to pursue souls relentlessly across the continents. The great evangelist's emphasis on the new birth became a prevailing theme for his proclamation ministry. Whitefield's universal appeal for people to come to repentance and faith in Christ was the soteriological necessity in the theology of the great evangelist. Personal evangelism evident in Whitefield's verbal conversations and written correspondence provided passion and greater intensity to his proclamation ministry. Whitefield's marketplace evangelism of taking the gospel outside of the walls of the church was the major methodological avenue that enabled the gospel to be heard across the continents. God give us more Whitefields for this century!

---

51 Whitefield, *George Whitefield's Letters*, 110.

CHAPTER 5

SHUBAL STEARNS *and the* SANDY CREEK ASSOCIATION

···
···

Larry Steven McDonald

I f a Hall of Fame was established in the United States for its
religious leaders, Shubal Stearns would surely be among its
inductees. Undoubtedly Stearns ranks as one of America's greatest, although largely unheralded, religious leaders and innovators.[1]
Few other American Baptists prior to the twentieth century wielded
as great of an influence in his homeland. His personal charisma and
magnetic power over audiences rivaled that of George Whitefield,[2]
and his extensive labor, both directly and indirectly, left a legacy that
endures into the twenty-first century.[3]

---

1 Thomas S. Kidd, *The Great Awakening: The Roots of Evangelical Christianity in Colo-
    nial America* (New Haven, CT: Yale University Press, 2007), 187. An earlier version of
    the paper was published as "Frontier Thunder: Principles of Evangelism and Church
    Growth from the Life of Shubal Stearns," *The Journal of the Academy for Evangelism in
    Theological Education*, 15 (1999–2000): 57–69.
2 Kidd, *The Great Awakening*, 260–261.
3 For information on Stearns see George W. Paschal, "Shubal Stearns," *The Review and
    Expositor* 36:1 (January 1939): 43–57; and Charles E. Taylor, "Elder Shubal Stearns,"
    North Carolina Historical Papers 2:2 (January 1898): 99–105. Also see William L.
    Lumpkin, *Baptist Foundations in the South: Tracing through the Separates the Influ-
    ence of the Great Awakening, 1754–1787* (Nashville: Broadman Press, 1961); H. Leon
    McBeth, *The Baptist Heritage* (Nashville: Broadman Press, 1987); A. H. Newman, *A
    History of the Baptist Churches in the United States*, 4th Edition (New York: Charles
    Scribner's Sons, 1902); and John Sparks, *The Roots of Appalachian Christianity: The*

Stearns was the key leader of one early Baptist group settling into Virginia and North Carolina,[4] later extending its influence into South Carolina and Tennessee, commonly understood to be the southernmost area of the Appalachian region. Indeed, so extensive was their influence that a present-day study of the Appalachian region is incomplete unless one considers the pervasive voice and experience of religion upon the people. One of the prominent historical influencers of Appalachian Christianity was Stearns. John Sparks has even labeled him as the founding father of Appalachian Christianity.[5] This group of early Baptist settlers, the Separates, became the most important of the area's Baptist assemblies. In fact, Sandy Creek Baptist Church, founded by Stearns, has been designated the mother of Separate Baptists churches and of Southern Baptist churches.[6] Thus, Stearns's influence reaches beyond historical Appalachian Christianity and extends to modern-day churches.

Separate Baptist progress between 1760 and 1770 is unparalleled in modern Baptist history. As historians Thomas Kidd and Barry Hankins stated, "the church at Sandy Creek grew like wild fire."[7] Sandy Creek Baptist Church's influence was pervasive and almost irresistible. Baptist churches of the South owe much of their evangelistic fervor and zeal for church planting to Stearns and the Separate Baptists. This intensely evangelistic preaching consumed the Separate Baptists as they preached anywhere, they were able to gain the attention of people. They are largely responsible for planting Baptist faith and polity so deeply in Southern soil.

Indeed, the South's best-known Baptists, the Southern Baptists, owe much of their success to Stearns and Sandy Creek's legacy. Charles

---

Life and Legacy of Elder Shubal Stearns (Lexington: The University Press of Kentucky, 2001).

4   See Thomas S. Kidd and Barry Hankins, *Baptist in America: A History* (New York: Oxford Press, 2015), 35–38.

5   Sparks, *The Roots of Appalachian Christianity*, 1.

6   Morgan Edwards, *Materials Towards A History of the Baptists in the Providence of North-Carolina*, vol. 4 (n.c.: n.p., 1772), 19. Also see Newman, *A History of Baptist Churches*, 292; and Walter B. Shurden, "The Southern Baptist Synthesis: Is It Cracking?" *Baptist History and Heritage* 16:2 (April 1981): 2–11.

7   Kidd and Hankins, *Baptist in America*, 36.

Taylor noted, "that the number and prosperity of the Baptists within the limits of the Southern Baptist Convention is largely due, under God's blessing, to the work begun by Elder Stearns."[8] Likewise, Leon McBeth acknowledged the impact of Separate Baptists upon the Southern Baptist Convention as he wrote, "Understanding the later development of the Southern Baptist Convention apart from the contributions of Separate Baptists would be impossible."[9]

Walter B. Shurden identified four traditions within the Southern Baptist Convention, one of which is the Sandy Creek tradition. He characterized the Sandy Creek tradition as primarily one of ardor and revivalism.[10] This ardor and revivalism has been described as an intensely evangelistic preaching which consumed the Separate Baptists with a sense of urgency and enthusiasm, almost like Pentecost.[11] The Separate Baptists "preached anywhere; in homes, in farm buildings, in open fields, in public markets, in houses of worship, or anywhere they were able to gain the attention of people."[12] The zeal of Shubal Stearns and Separate Baptists had a profound impact upon the Southern Baptist Convention.

Stearns's impact in evangelism and church planting stemmed from principles which could be emulated by those desiring to have the same effect. In fact, Stearns appears to be a precursor to many of the teachings of modern-day evangelistic practices. He relied upon the Holy Spirit, made demographic observations, and understood the ministry issues of leadership, training, delegation, and multiplication. Stearns mobilized believers and churches to unite by casting the vision of reaching non-Christians. These principles rely on Stearns's understanding both of God's intrinsic holiness and

---

8   Taylor, "Elder Shubal Stearns," 101.
9   McBeth, *The Baptist Heritage*, 227.
10   Shurden, "The Southern Baptist Synthesis." Also see John F. Loftis, "Factors in Southern Baptist Identity as Reflected by Ministerial Role Models, 1750–1925" (PhD dissertation, The Southern Baptist Theological Seminary, Louisville, KY, 1978).
11   Noel Ray Lykins, "North Carolina Separate Baptists: A Study in Frontier Baptist Expansion in the Eighteenth Century" (ThM thesis, Southeastern Baptist Theological Seminary, Wake Forest, NC, 1961), 98.
12   Lykins, "North Carolina Separate Baptists."

his own personal piety. A brief biographical sketch of Stearns will help contextualize his unique understanding of evangelism in the eighteenth century.

STEARNS'S EARLY YEARS

Shubal Stearns was born on January 28, 1706 to Shubal and Rebecca Larriford Stearns in Boston, Massachusetts.[13] Reared in Connecticut, he joined a Congregationalist Church in Tolland. George Whitefield greatly influenced Stearns by his preaching during the Great Awakening in 1745. Through Whitefield's influence, Stearns attended a "New Light" or "Separate" church where Stearns ministered for six years.[14] This "New Light" congregation believed in emotional preaching, personal piety and evangelism, as opposed to the so-called "old lights" who repudiated raw emotionalism and defended the existing state church order. Additionally, the new lights became known as "separates" because they separated from the state churches and required a profession of regeneration prior to membership.[15]

In addition, these New Light churches experienced a controversy over infant baptism. Wait Palmer, the New Light pastor of the Baptist church in North Stonington, Connecticut, may have been the first to challenge Stearns on the issue of infant baptism versus believer's baptism. After a thorough study of the Bible, Stearns declared himself a Baptist and received baptism from Palmer on May 20, 1751 in Tolland. Ordained by Palmer and Joshua Morse, Stearns became the pastor of a new Baptist church in Tolland where he served for approximately three years.[16]

---

13   Letter from Edward C. Stearns of the New York State Association of the Stearns Family along with a Genealogy of the Stearns Family from Bonds Genealogies and History of Watertown of the Boston Genealogical Society. Obtained from the North Carolina Baptist History Archives at Wake Forest University, Winston-Salem, NC.

14   Robert B. Semple, *A History of the Rise and Progress of the Baptists in Virginia*, revised and extended by G. W. Beale (Richmond, VA: Pitt & Dickinson Publishers, 1894), 12.

15   James D. Mosteller, "The Separate Baptists in the South," *The Chronicle* 17:3 (July 1954): 143.

16   Lumpkin, *Baptist Foundations in the South*, 21.

The challenge to spread the gospel on the western frontier captured Stearns's heart. Requesting volunteers from his church to accompany him and his wife, Stearns set out to answer what he believed to be God's call. Five couples responded. And in 1754 the group departed for Virginia where they met Daniel Marshall, Stearns's brother-in-law.[17] Marshall had ministered to the Mohawk Indians before moving to Virginia. Under the guidance of Rev. John Garrard, they established a Baptist church on Cacapon Creek in Hampshire County, Virginia.[18]

Ministering to Virginians was difficult. The area was sparsely populated. Regular Baptists, already established in the area, did not look favorably upon their new neighbors, the Separate Baptists. On June 13, 1755, Stearns received a letter from friends in the Piedmont area of North Carolina. While that letter no longer exists, Stearns reiterated its contents in a letter to Noah Alden, who had followed him as pastor of the church in Tolland, Connecticut. He said the people in North Carolina reported "that the work of God was great in preaching to an ignorant people, who had little or no preaching for a hundred miles, and no established meeting. But now the people were so eager to hear, that they would come forty miles each way, when they could have opportunity to hear a sermon."[19]

Stearns and fifteen others left Virginia in the summer of 1755 traveling to the Sandy Creek area in Guilford County (now Randolph County), in central North Carolina. Joining Stearns and his wife were "Peter Stearns and wife, Ebenezer Stearns and wife, Shubal Stearns jur. and wife, Daniel Marshall and wife, Joseph Breed and wife, Enis Stinson and wife, Jonathan Polk and wife." Soon after

---

17   For more information on Daniel Marshall see Gregory L. Hunt, "Daniel Marshall: Energetic Evangelist for the Separate Baptist Cause," *Baptist History and Heritage*, 21:2 (April 1986): 5–18 and Larry Steven McDonald, "Daniel Marshall," *Encyclopedia of Christianity in the United States*, George Kurian and Mark A. Lamport, editors (Lanham, MD: Rowman & Littlefield Publishers, 2015), 3:1421–1422.

18   David Benedict, *A General History of the Baptist Denomination in American and Other Parts of the World*, 4th Edition (New York: Lewis and Colby, 1848), 683.

19   Isaac Backus, *A History of New England with Particular Reference to the Denomination of Christians Called Baptists*, vol. 2, 2nd Edition, with notes by David Weston (Newton, MA: Backus Historical Society, 1871), 530.

their arrival, they organized the Sandy Creek Baptist Church on
November 22, 1755.[20]

Stearns became the church's pastor and quickly established himself
as a dynamic preacher and leader. Benedict indicates Stearns "was a
man of small stature, but good natural parts and sound judgement.
His voice was musical and strong, and many stories are told respecting
the wonderful and enchanting influence which was exerted on his
hearers by his vocal powers, and the glances of his eyes."[21] Charles
Taylor glowingly writes, "He was undoubtedly one of the greatest
ministers that ever presented Jesus to perishing multitudes. Had he
been a Romish priest, he would long since have been canonized and
declared the patron saint of Carolina. Fervent supplications would
have ascended, and stately churches would have been dedicated to the
holy and blessed saint Shubael Stearns, the apostle of North Carolina
and the adjacent states."[22]

Daniel Marshall and Joseph Breed became his assistant ministers
even though they were not ordained. Under Stearns's leadership, Sandy
Creek's initial membership roll of sixteen ballooned to 606 people
as the church began aggressive outreach within the community.[23]
Rapid growth mandated the planting of new churches. In 1758, six
congregations organized themselves into the Sandy Creek Baptist
Association.[24] This new association eventually included churches in
Virginia and South Carolina.[25] Thus, a handful of transplanted New
Englanders electrified North Carolina. The question is "What made
Stearns and his cohorts so successful?" A thorough examination of
his ministry at the Sandy Creek Baptist Church suggests that Shubal
Stearns followed five distinct principles that enabled him to evangelize
America's early frontier.

20   Edwards, *North Carolina*, 18.
21   Benedict, *General History of the Baptist Denomination*, 386.
22   Charles E. Taylor, "Elder Shubael Stearns," *North Carolina Baptist Historical Papers*,
     II:2 (January 1898): 105.
23   Taylor, "Elder Shubael Stearns."
24   Lumpkin, *Baptist Foundations in the South*, 46.
25   George W. Purefoy, *A History of the Sandy Creek Baptist Association, from Its Organization in A.D. 1758, to A.D. 1858* (New York: Sheldon & Co., 1859), 62.

DEPENDENCE UPON THE HOLY SPIRIT

For Stearns, evangelism and church planting began with his own personal piety. Stearns believed that the Holy Spirit of God established personal purity within believers and empowered them for ministry. Contemporaries noted that purity of life, godly simplicity, pious ardor, invincible boldness, and perseverance characterized Stearns, Marshall, and Harris.[26] Later, historians would testify that Stearns's "character was indisputably good as a man," and that Stearns "evidenced complete dependence upon the Holy Spirit."[27]

Stearns's desire to maintain a pious lifestyle before God and others, as well as his personal piety became hallmarks both of the Sandy Creek Baptist Church and Association and the Separate Baptist movement. One historian stated that the "most [noteworthy] characteristic of the Separates was their dependence on the Holy Spirit and their sense of his presence in their meetings."[28] The strict discipline practiced by the Separates resulted in high moral and ethical standards, earning them high praise as simple, sincere Christians of remarkably sound judgment. The associational meetings were characterized by a pervasive sense that God's power rested upon the preachers.[29] On October 16, 1765, Stearns wrote a letter to friends in Connecticut discussing revival meetings in which he had participated. Stearns concluded the letter by stating, "The power of God was wonderful."[30]

Stearns endeavored to live his life in submission to the Holy Spirit's leadership. He believed that personal holiness and the ability to minister effectively were inseparable. That is, submission to the Holy Spirit's leadership produced a purity of life that was readily apparent to others. Subsequently, he believed this purity resulted in the power of the Holy Spirit upon his ministry. Thus, church growth in Stearns's

---

26   Benedict, *A General History of the Baptist Denomination*, 684.
27   Edwards, *North Carolina*, 21; and Lumpkin, *Baptist Foundations in the South*, 40.
28   Paschal, "Shubal Stearns," 51.
29   See Mosteller, "The Separate Baptists in the South," 148; and Purefoy, *A History of the Sandy Creek Baptist Association*, 64.
30   Isaac Backus, *An Abridgment of the Church History of New-England, from 1602–1804*, (Boston: n.p., 1804), 251.

mind began with discipleship among church leadership, especially among pastors. As spiritual leaders, Stearns believed pastors needed to mind their own spiritual health before they could care for others.

PRIORITIZING EVANGELISM

Beyond personal holiness, Shubal Stearns believed that ministers and their congregations should practice intentional evangelism. Evangelism rarely happens by accident, and Stearns was described as having rousing missionary zeal.[31]

This priority Stearns placed on evangelism quickly became a distinguishing feature of the Separates at the Sandy Creek Church. By contrast, the Particular Baptists in the Jersey Settlement, an area near Sandy Creek, began one year prior to the Sandy Creek church.[32] While having two of the most able pastors and preachers of the Philadelphia Association, Rev. Benjamin Miller and Rev. John Gano, the Particular Baptists had little impact beyond their own membership and neighborhood. New church planting never became a part of the Jersey Church ministry. In the years to come, however, the Separates influenced Gano, and he became an evangelist.[33]

The history of the Sandy Creek Church clearly portrays commitment to evangelism. As noted earlier, the church began with sixteen members and multiplied to 606 within a short time. Not only did the Sandy Creek Church grow, but it started other churches in the process. From 1755 to 1772, a seventeen-year period, forty-two churches traced their lineage to the Sandy Creek Church.[34] Contemporaries claimed that Stearns and his friends were aggressive

---

31 Lumpkin, *Baptist Foundation in the South*, 28.
32 Separate Baptists were primarily known for their revivalist/evangelistic emphasis where the Particular Baptist were primarily known for their theological focus. For further study see Anthony L. Chute, Nathan A. Finn, and Michael A.G. Haykin, *The Baptist Story: English Sect to Global Movement* (Nashville: Broadman, 2015) and Thomas S. Kidd and Barry Hankins, *Baptists in America: A History* (New York: Oxford University, 2015).
33 Paschal, "Shubal Stearns," 53.
34 Edwards, *North Carolina*, 18–20.

and possessed an invincible boldness which spread throughout that church body.[35]

The impiety and generally poor religious state of the Southern colonies in the eighteenth century are well documented.[36] Stearns preached the basic message of new birth, conviction and conversion, with a definite time and place of conversion being a key element in one's personal salvation.[37] Stearns's innovations may have led to the earliest record of a public invitation in American church history.[38]

Shubal Stearns and the Separate Baptists had an urgent commitment to make a clear and simple gospel presentation to as many lives as possible. This message centered on Jesus Christ coming in the flesh, living a sinless life, dying on the cross for the world's sin, and his resurrection following three days in the grave. Stearns believed that responding to this message by exercising personal faith in Christ produced a conversion experience. William L. Lumpkin observed, "With relentless intensity a twofold conviction was borne in upon the hearts of the Separates . . . the urgency of the missionary task and the readiness of men to accept the truth if only they could hear it . . . a frantic urgency filled the missionary enterprise."[39] Stearns had both a passion for evangelism and the ability to excite that same passion in others.

MOBILIZATION OF LAITY FOR MINISTRY

If Stearns relied on the Holy Spirit's empowerment and believed strongly in personal evangelism, he also understood the value of

---

35   See Newman, *A History of Baptist Churches*, 293–294; Benedict, *A General History of the Baptist Denomination*, 684; and Lumpkin, *Baptist Foundations in the South*, 38.

36   See Rhys Isaac, *The Transformation of Virginia, 1740–1790* (Chapel Hill: The University of North Carolina Press, 1982).

37   Benedict, *A General History of the Baptist Denomination*, 683. Also see Roger Finke and Rodney Stark, *The Churching of America, 1776–1990: Winners and Losers in Our Religious Economy* (New Brunswick, NJ: Rutgers University Press, 1992).

38   Steve O'Kelley, "The Influence of Separate Baptists on Revivalistic Evangelism and Worship" (PhD dissertation, Southwestern Baptist Theological Seminary, Fort Worth, TX, 1978), 130.

39   Lumpkin, *Baptist Foundations in the South*, 24.

mobilizing his churches' laity for evangelizing the unconverted. Lay participation in ministerial acts distinguished the Sandy Creek Baptist Church from its beginnings. Members at Sandy Creek were always encouraged to exercise their gifts of ministry.[40]

Four factors stimulated and reinforced lay participation in Separate Baptists.[41] First, the pastors encouraged the development of leadership from within their own congregations. Second, the Separates used a style of discipleship in which pastors used lay assistants in ministry. Whether within a local church, or in newly planted branch churches, or as traveling companions, the laity received practical, hands-on ministry training. Third, the Separates' style of worship included a public confession of faith by a new convert, thereby encouraging even the newest lay person to share his or her faith. Fourth, the Separates emphasized a devotion to family and accountability to the local church that encouraged lay involvement.

Daniel Marshall and Joseph Breed, neither of whom were ordained, assisted Stearns at Sandy Creek even though the church initially had only sixteen members.[42] Certainly, such a small congregation had no compelling need for these two additional ministers. Yet Stearns had an eye on the future. These assistant pastors received "on the job training" for future ministries that would reach beyond the scope of Sandy Creek Church and even beyond Stearns himself.

Elnathan Davis stands as another example of Stearns's ability to mentor his disciples and inspire dedicated service to the church. Davis heard that Stearns, being small in stature, was to baptize John Steward, a very large man. Convinced that drowning would be the inevitable outcome, Davis took several of his friends to observe the baptism. However, Stearns's preaching so captivated Davis that it frightened him away. It was not long until Davis returned and converted to Christianity.[43] In recounting this story, Morgan Edwards

40   Loftis, "Factors in Southern Baptist Identity," 83.
41   Loftis, "Factors in Southern Baptist Identity," 139–148.
42   Benedict, *A General History of the Baptist Denomination*, 683.
43   Edwards, *North Carolina*, 26–27.

states, "Immediately he [Davis] began to preach conversion work, raw as he was, and scanty as his knowledge must have been."[44]

Although Stearns enjoyed a certain celebrity status within the Sandy Creek Church and Association, he was undergirded by a multitude of others committed to strengthening the church and evangelizing the unconverted. When the laity of a church is trained and organized for ministry, a strong foundation exists.

STRATEGIC CHURCH PLANTING

Stearns's vision went beyond the Sandy Creek Baptist Church of which he was pastor. Having a vision to plant other churches, he instilled this concept in those near him. Daniel Marshall, his assistant and brother-in-law, founded Abbott's Creek Church located approximately thirty miles from Sandy Creek.[45] In 1760, another church was organized at Little River, North Carolina. Church membership of Little River grew from five to five hundred within three years.[46]

Stearns applied careful, strategic planning in choosing the physical locations for these new church plants. This is best illustrated with the Sandy Creek Church, where Stearns observed road patterns and population makeup before choosing the church site. The designated spot he chose promised to become a strategic center from which he could minister to a growing and spiritually needy population.[47]

The population makeup of the area where Stearns started the Sandy Creek Baptist Church was English-speaking newcomers moving from north of the Carolinas, most of whom were not Christians. This English-speaking element became more predominant than all the foreign-speaking groups combined.[48]

Three trails converged at Sandy Creek, which made it one of the busiest crossroads of the southern frontier. The first trail, the Settlers

---

44 Edwards, *North Carolina*, 27.
45 Benedict, *A General History of the Baptist Denomination*, 684.
46 Benedict, *A General History of the Baptist Denomination*, 685.
47 Lumpkin, *Baptist Foundations in the South*, 30.
48 Lumpkin, *Baptist Foundations in the South*, 37–38.

Road, ran from north to south from Pennsylvania to South Carolina. The second, Boones Trail, went from Wilmington westward to the Yadkin settlements. The third trail, the Trading Path, ran from southeastern Virginia (Norfolk) to the Waxhaw country.[49] William W. Barnes claims that when Stearns reached the Sandy Creek area, he heard a voice within that said, "Here I Stand."[50] The wisdom of this choice was soon evident.[51]

Stearns's planning paid high dividends. According to one source, "By 1776 the Baptists had become a power in the [NC] colony, having established at least one church in every county."[52] David Benedict identified an even greater area of influence as he stated, "the Separates in a few years became truly a great people, and their churches were scattered over a country whose whole extent from north to south was about 500 miles; and Sandy Creek Church, the mother of them all, was not far from the centre [sic] of the two extremes."[53] Edwards gives a more comprehensive statement of the breadth of this church planting vision as he stated, "From this Zion went forth the word, and great was the company of them who published it: it, in 17 years, has spread branches westward as far as the great river Mississippi; southward as far as Georgia; eastward to the sea and Chesopeck [sic] bay; and northward to the waters of Potowmack [sic]: it, in 17 years become mother, grand-mother, and great Grandmother to 42 churches, from which sprang 125 ministers, many of which are ordained."[54]

Stearns's far-reaching impact stemmed from his vision to plant new churches, his ability to instill that vision in others, and his insightful choices of church locations. He enjoyed remarkable influence for the kingdom of God through the multiplying of churches.

---

49   Lumpkin, *Baptist Foundations in the South.*
50   W. W. Barnes, "Sandy Creek—The Holy Land of Baptists," *The Chronicle* 19:2 (April 1956): 70.
51   Lumpkin, *Baptist Foundations in the South,* 30.
52   R. D. W. Connor, *The Colonial and Revolutionary Periods, 1584–1783, History of North Carolina,* vol. 1 (Chicago: Lewis Publishing, 1919), 196.
53   Benedict, *A General History of The Baptist Denomination,* 684.
54   Edwards, *North Carolina,* 19–20.

ORGANIZED ASSOCIATION OF CHURCHES

The final element in Stearns's master strategy was to organize churches into associations in order to promote corporate strength. In 1758, Stearns established the Sandy Creek Baptist Association. This association was the first in North Carolina, the second in the South, and the third in America.[55] Stearns believed the association would help to "establish stability, regularity, and uniformity among the Separate churches."[56]

Although no minutes of the Sandy Creek Association exist from 1758 to 1805, there are some accounts of the associational meetings. Benedict indicates the meetings were primarily preaching, exhortation, singing, and conversation about ministry. These assemblies provided ministers with a time of mutual encouragement and spiritual refreshment. Often people came long distances to observe the meetings simply out of curiosity. As a result of visiting these associational meetings, these guests would frequently petition the association to send preachers to their areas.[57] James Reed attended the first meeting of the association and described it by saying, "At our first Association we continued together three or four days . . . the great power of God was among us. The preaching every day seemed to be attended with God's blessing. We carried on our Association with sweet decorum and fellowship to the end. Then we took leave of one another, with many solemn charges from our reverend old father, Shubal Stearns, to stand fast unto the end."[58]

Unanimity in all decisions characterized the early Sandy Creek Baptist Association. But by 1770, the associational proceedings were blocked due to disunity. Lack of agreement existed on the issue of associational authority, especially in disciplining churches and ordaining pastors. Stearns also may have held too strong of control.[59] The second

---

55   See Purefoy, *A History of the Sandy Creek Baptist Association*, 104–107; and McBeth, *The Baptist Heritage*, 232.

56   Robert A. Baker, *The Southern Baptist Convention and Its People, 1607–1972* (Nashville: Broadman Press, 1974), 50.

57   Benedict, *A General History of the Baptist Denomination*, 685.

58   Benedict, *A General History of the Baptist Denomination*, 685.

59   Lumpkin, *Baptist Foundations in the South*, 57–59.

day of meetings and most of the third day were devoted to fasting and prayer. A proposal was then brought to divide the association into three groups, each one organized by its individual state. The churches in North Carolina kept the name Sandy Creek, while the churches in South Carolina took the name Congaree, and the churches in Virginia adopted the name Rapid-ann (Rapid-ann soon changed its name to the General Association of Separate Baptists). Yet even following this division, the churches continued to grow and multiply. Whereas in 1771, the Virginian churches had 1,355 members, by 1773, they had increased their enrollment to 3,195 members.[60]

The Sandy Creek Association of North Carolina faced more difficulties as families left the state. Edwards indicates that in 1771, fifteen hundred families left the area following the controversy with the Regulators and the battle of Alamance.[61] But as the families left, they carried with them the evangelistic and missionary zeal of their home churches and association. G. W. Purefoy describes this as he states, "This emigration into East Tennessee soon resulted in the formation of five Baptist churches, which for several years belonged to the Sandy Creek Association, but were afterward organized into the Holston Association, which is the mother of the Tennessee Association, and no doubt of others in the state."[62] The great influence of the Sandy Creek Baptist Association was evident even given the division of the association and the changing population of the area. Their example of wise and prayerful handling of their disagreements and difficulties only increased the spread of the Separate Baptist movement and the gospel message.

CONCLUSION

Shubal Stearns died on November 20, 1771, at the age of sixty-five. He served the Sandy Creek Baptist Church as pastor for sixteen years. As

---

60 Newman, *A History of the Baptist Churches*, 297–298.
61 Edwards, *North Carolina*, 18–19.
62 Purefoy, *A History of the Sandy Creek Baptist Association*, 72.

cited earlier Stearns and his church influenced many lives as it became "mother, grand-mother, and great Grandmother to 42 churches, from which sprang 125 ministers, many of which are ordained and support the sacred character as well as any sett [sic] of clergy in America."[63]

Roger Finke and Rodney Starke have suggested that American churches have grown in proportion to their aggressiveness and their otherworldliness.[64] Stearns's life and methodology lend credence to their argument. The Separate Baptists succeeded largely because of these defining characteristics,[65] with Shubal Stearns being the chief exemplar. From Stearns's life it is clear that he depended upon the Holy Spirit, had a clear priority of evangelism, was committed to mobilizing the laity, and had a vision to establish and organize together new churches. Stearns's primary goal remained the furtherance of God's kingdom. Lumpkin summarized the influence of Separate Baptists by stating,

> The Separate Baptist movement in the South was undoubtedly one of the most formative influences ever brought to bear upon American religious life. . . . [T]he Separate Baptist movement contributed notably to the spiritual life and vitality of American Christianity. It infused such life into the Baptist denomination in America as to raise it from obscurity to prominence within a quarter of a century. By reason of this brief history it made Baptists the principal beneficiaries in America of the Great Awakening.[66]

Lumpkin then stated that Stearns "was the chief light and the guiding genius behind the Separate Baptist movement . . . rarely has a religious leader seen such rapid and magnificent results from a few years of labor. Surely the Lord was in it."[67] Stearns's life emulated principles

---

63   Edwards, *North Carolina*, 20.
64   See Finke and Stark, *The Churching of America, 1776–1990*.
65   Mosteller, "The Separate Baptists in the South," 146.
66   Lumpkin, *Baptist Foundations in the South*, 147, 162.
67   Lumpkin, *Baptist Foundations in the South*, 59.

of evangelism and church planting which can still be followed today for the strengthening and expansion of churches.

Sparks indicated that although the name Shubal Stearns has been forgotten by many, he has never really left us. He believes Stearns's followers brought his spirit with them to Tennessee, Virginia, Kentucky, South Carolina, and Georgia.[68] Sparks stated, "Indeed Shubal Stearns is yet alive in the hearts and minds of Appalachian Christians and will always remain so as long as a distinctive Appalachian Christianity exits."[69] In today's postmodern era, perhaps more than ever, America needs a taste of God's power rumbling through its vast cities and plains. Through God's people, America and even the entire world needs to experience again the compelling effect of God's message which echoes through the hills of Appalachia.

---

68   Sparks, *The Roots of Appalachian Christianity*, 290.
69   Sparks, *The Roots of Appalachian Christianity*, 290.

CHAPTER 6

FRANCIS ASBURY
and the CIRCUIT RIDERS

....
....

Timothy K. Beougher

T he early Methodist leaders in America asked four questions about every candidate offering himself for the work of the ministry: 1) "Is this man truly converted?"; 2) "Does he know and keep our rules?"; 3) "Can he preach acceptably?"; 4) "Has he a horse?"[1] Readers today certainly can understand the first three of these questions, but why the fourth question? Why ask if the candidate has a horse? This chapter seeks to summarize the ministry of Francis Asbury and the circuit-riding Methodist preachers.[2]

FRANCIS ASBURY (1745–1816)

Francis Asbury was born into a working-class family near Birmingham, England. His Anglican parents had been among the early converts of John Wesley, the founder of Methodism. Francis dropped

---

1 William George Taylor, *Pathfinders of the Great South Land* (London: The Epworth Press, 1924), 52.

2 An excellent starting point in studying the topic is the issue of *Christian History* magazine devoted to Camp Meetings & Circuit Riders (Issue 45, Vol. XIV, No. 1). I wrote the opening article, "Did You Know? Little-known and Remarkable Facts about Camp Meetings and Circuit Riders," on pages 2–3.

out of school before the age of twelve to apprentice in a trade.[3] He was converted at the age of thirteen or fourteen and began to have preaching opportunities at age sixteen. By the age of twenty-one he was appointed a full-time Methodist preacher.[4]

His future life work was set in motion by his answer to a question John Wesley asked at a 1771 gathering of Methodist ministers in England: "Our brethren in America call aloud for help. Who are willing to go over and help them?" Asbury answered the call, and departed for America in the Fall of 1771, never again to return to England. On board the ship he wrote in his journal his reason for embarking on this journey: "I am going to live to God, and to bring others so to do."[5]

The first winter in America took a toll on his health, and for the remainder of his life he battled numerous health problems including colds, coughs, fevers, headaches, ulcers, and rheumatism, which at times prevented him from riding his horse. When Asbury could not mount his steed, he travelled by carriage.

During the Revolutionary War, he remained politically neutral, refusing to take sides in the conflict. But the Methodists, with their roots in the Anglican Church of England, continually had their loyalty questioned. To make matters worse, John Wesley had denounced the colonial uprising and made clear his support of the British side. Asbury learned in 1778 he must take an oath of loyalty to Maryland to continue to work in that colony, an oath which Asbury was not ready to take.

Asbury went into hiding for several months in Delaware, where no oath was required. Unable to preach regularly, he turned his unwanted

---

3   Historians debate the exact trade for which he was apprenticing. Options presented include blacksmith, button maker, buckle maker, leatherworker, and saddle maker.

4   The Methodist movement provided preaching and ministry opportunities for men like Asbury, who lacked the university training to become clergymen in the Church of England. But even though Wesley encouraged lay preachers, he did not want them to be ignorant. He constantly pressured them to read and to study, and Wesley's prolific pen provided them an abundance of reading material. Though Asbury's formal schooling was cut short, he applied himself to a lifetime of personal reading and study.

5   "September 12, 1771," in *Journals and Letters of Francis Asbury*, II:417, cited in L. C. Rudolph, *Francis Asbury* (Nashville: Abingdon Press, 1966), 14.

"sabbatical" into a time of deep study, reading dozens of books, but supremely the Bible, over and over and over again. Following the war, it took several years for Methodists in America to overcome the stigma of disloyalty, but overcome it they did.

After the war, John Wesley ordained Englishman Thomas Coke as superintendent for the Methodist Church in America. The famous Christmas Conference in Baltimore in 1784 marked the official beginning of The Methodist Episcopal Church in America. When Coke arrived in America, he ordained Asbury as a fellow superintendent, and then, six months later, returned to England. Against Wesley's wishes, Asbury assumed the title of bishop (instead of superintendent) and became the clear leader of American Methodism.

Asbury had become a full-fledged American, and he knew that unlike England, where John Wesley could dictate everything to the church, Asbury would need to involve pastors in some of the decision-making. Rudolph explained, "Asbury's way was to get the program he wanted through the actions of the American preachers. He was too wise to try and impose a program upon freedom-intoxicated circuit riders directly."[6] Yet Asbury never believed that the bishop and the preachers were equal. Bishops are ordained to rule, and Asbury intended to fulfill that role. Rudolph articulates Asbury's strategy: "Of course he would do the bidding of the conference, but as bishop he expected that in most cases he himself would shape what the bidding of the conference would be."[7]

Asbury was an organizational genius and drew up maps of circuits for men he would recruit as circuit riders. He realized the Methodist practice of utilizing traveling preachers would be even more strategic

---

6   Rudolph, *Francis Asbury*, 50.
7   Rudolph, *Francis Asbury*, 57. Rudolph adds on page 58, "Whether or not a thing was democratic, it had to look democratic." Nathan Hatch astutely observes, "It is one of the odd twists of American history that the Methodist Episcopal church, in the firm grip of Bishop Francis Asbury, outstripped the explicitly democratic Christian movement. The very church that most adamantly refused to share ecclesiastical authority with the laity actually came to have the greatest influence among them." Nathan O. Hatch, *The Democratization of American Christianity* (New Haven, CT: Yale University Press, 1989), 81–82.

in America than in England. Smith notes, "He was more concerned about the circuit in the wilderness than the cathedral in the city."[8] Crisscrossing the country many times, Francis Asbury became one of the best-known men in America. A letter addressed "Bishop Asbury, North America," was promptly delivered.[9]

Despite his numerous ministerial strengths, Asbury was not a particularly good preacher. Once while feeling ill he asked his travelling companion, Jesse Lee, to preach first and he would "exhort" briefly following the sermon. The parishioners assumed Lee was the bishop and testified that the bishop preached well, but they did not like what the old man who spoke after him had to say.[10] Asbury wrote about another preaching experience, remembering, "I attempted to preach . . . on 'the lame and the blind;' the discourse was very *lame*; and it may be, I left my hearers as I found them—*blind*."[11]

On another occasion he reflected on his vain attempt to imitate George Whitefield's preaching voice. Whitefield's powerful preaching voice was legendary, prompting Shakespearian actor David Garrick to declare he would give a hundred guineas if he could say "Oh!" like Whitefield. One day while riding a circuit, Asbury, in reflecting on Garrick's statement, tried to say "Oh!" as he imagined Whitefield must have said it. The only result was that his horse became so frightened he jumped the river![12]

Asbury labored tirelessly to communicate the gospel whenever he could. Smith maintains, "It was his custom, whenever he stopped, to have prayer, whether in taverns or private homes, among saints

8   George G. Smith, *Life and Labors of Francis Asbury* (Nashville: M. E. Church, South, 1898), 308.

9   Rudolph, *Francis Asbury*, 71. See also Charles Ludwig, *Francis Asbury: God's Circuit Rider* (Fenton, MI: Mott Media, 1984), 175, 182.

10 Circuit rider Jesse Lee, who travelled with Francis Asbury for three years, was elected chaplain of the U. S. House of Representatives (1809), and of the Senate (1814), and published the first *History of Methodism in the United States* (1810). See R. G. Tuttle, "Lee, Jesse (1758–1816)," in *Dictionary of Christianity in America*, edited by Daniel G. Reid (Downers Grove, IL: InterVarsity Press, 1990), 640.

11 Rudolph, *Francis Asbury*, 94, citing from "August 17, 1788," in *The Journal and Letters of Francis Asbury*, I:578 (emphasis original).

12 Ludwig, *Francis Asbury*, 49, 69.

or sinners, friends or strangers, and to speak to everyone about his soul."[13] Despite constant battles with illness, he continued to visit the various circuits until his death, even when he had to be tied to the saddle to remain upright. He had a simple method to determine whether he was well enough to travel: "If he could walk twice across the sickroom he declared himself fit for the road."[14] When he died, all his earthly possessions were in the two saddlebags on his horse.

Asbury was viewed as an autocratic leader by many of his associates, but he never asked his circuit riders to endure any hardship he was unwilling to endure. When one of his critics compared him to the pope, Asbury replied:

> For myself, I pity those who cannot distinguish between a pope of Rome, and an old, worn man of about sixty years, who has the *power given him* of riding five thousand miles a year, at a salary of eighty dollars, through summer's heat and winter's cold, traveling in all weather, preaching in all places; his best covering from rain often but a blanket; the surest sharpener of his wit, hunger—from fasts, voluntary and involuntary; his best fare, for six months of the twelve, coarse kindness; and his reward, suspicion, envy, and murmurings all the year round.[15]

During his forty-five-year ministry, Asbury rode more than a quarter million miles on horseback, crossing the Allegheny Mountains some sixty times.[16] He visited nearly every state in the young Union at least once a year. George Smith eulogizes Asbury's life by saying, "He was

---

13   Smith, *Life and Labors of Francis Asbury*, 241.
14   Rudolph, *Francis Asbury*, 215. See also Herbert Asbury, *A Methodist Saint: The Life of Francis Asbury* (New York: Alfred A. Knopf, 1927), 131–132, cited in Ludwig, *Francis Asbury*, 135.
15   "December 15, 1803," in *Journals and Letters of Francis Asbury*, II:417, cited in Rudolph, *Francis Asbury*, 79 (emphasis original).
16   Noll argues Asbury traveled over more of America than "probably any other person of his generation." See Mark Noll, *A History of Christianity in the United States and Canada* (Grand Rapids: William B. Eerdmans, 1992), 170.

remarkable in that he had but one aim and but one way to advance it. His aim was simply to save men from sin, and his way to advance that was by the simple preaching of the gospel."[17]

When Francis Asbury came to the colonies in 1771, there were only six hundred American Methodists. When he died forty-five years later, there were 214,235 American Methodists. The number had grown from 1 in 5,000 to 1 in 40 of the total population of the country, largely through the means of camp meetings[18] and circuit riders.[19] Wigger portrays the remarkable growth of the Methodists with this observation: "At mid-century, American Methodism was almost ten times the size of the Congregationalists, America's largest denomination in 1776."[20] Salter states, "In fact, from 1800 to 1810, Methodist's population increased 168 percent, while America's population increased 36 percent."[21]

CIRCUIT RIDERS

As American settlers began leaving the eastern seaboard journeying toward new land in the West, church leaders were confronted with a key question: How was the growing territory to the West to be reached with the gospel message? Asbury had the answer: circuit riding preachers. Wigger notes the milieu: "In this era, most Americans lived on widely scattered farms or in tiny, often remote villages. . . . Itinerant ministry provided preaching . . . to communities that would not otherwise have been able to attract or afford a minister."[22]

Where other groups' strategies involved a "settled ministry" (a pastor being assigned to one congregation in a village or town), Methodist

---

17   Smith, *Life and Labors of Francis Asbury*, 298.

18   I have not dealt with Camp Meetings here as another chapter in this book covers that topic. Asbury strongly supported camp meetings, referring to them as "fishing with a large net." See "Letter to Thornton Fleming, December 2, 1802," in *The Journal and Letters of Francis Asbury*, III:251, cited in Rudolph, *Francis Asbury*, 120.

19   Ludwig, *Francis Asbury*, xii.

20   John H. Wigger, "Holy, 'Knock-'Em-Down' Preachers," *Christian History* 45, no. 1 (1995): 22.

21   Darius Salter, *American Evangelism: Its Theology and Practice* (Grand Rapids: Baker, 1996), 90.

22   Wigger, "Holy, 'Knock-'Em-Down' Preachers," 22.

circuit riders had multiple preaching points they served, i.e. their circuit. Thus, the name "circuit riders" or "saddlebag preachers" was given these men. Wigger notes, "A typical Methodist itinerant was responsible for a predominantly rural circuit, two hundred to five hundred miles in circumference. He was expected to complete his circuit every two to six weeks, with the standard being a four weeks' circuit."[23] In addition to traveling and preaching, the circuit riders would meet with the Methodist classes (weekly small group gatherings for fellowship and accountability), as well as spend personal time with individuals and families. This ministry was not for the lazy or faint of heart.

This strategy of multiple preaching points was reflected in the low numbers of designated Methodist chapels. Wigger observes, "By 1785, only sixty Methodist chapels had been purchased or built, but there were more than eight hundred recognized preaching places. Meetings were held in homes, courthouses, schoolhouses, the meeting houses of other denominations, barns, or in the open."[24]

The growing Methodist Church aggressively enlisted circuit riders. Peter Cartwright said when he moved to Lewiston County, Kentucky, he asked his presiding elder for a letter of transfer as a Methodist member. What he received was a preacher's license and a commission to organize a new circuit.[25] Tuttle claims, "Once the appointment was given at the annual conference, it took the average itinerant about five minutes to pack, in ten he was on his way to a new circuit—sometimes as big as a state."[26] The farther west the circuit

23 Wigger, "Holy, 'Knock-'Em-Down' Preachers," 23. Unlike the men in "settled" parishes, circuit riders were constantly on the move. Peter Cartwright's observations concerning this difference in strategy are clear and pointed: "The Presbyterians, and other Calvinistic branches of the Protestant Church, used to contend for an educated ministry, for pews, for instrumental music, for a congregational or stated salaried ministry. The Methodists universally opposed these ideas; and the illiterate Methodist preachers actually set the world on fire, (the American world at least,) while they were lighting their matches!" See Peter Cartwright, *Autobiography of Peter Cartwright,* edited by W.P. Strickland (New York: The Methodist Book Concern, n.d.), 79.
24 Wigger, "Holy, 'Knock-'Em-Down' Preachers," 24.
25 Cartwright, *Autobiography of Peter Cartwright,* 59.
26 Robert G. Tuttle, Jr., *The Story of Evangelism: A History of the Witness to the Gospel* (Nashville: Abingdon Press, 2006), 302.

riders went, the less evidence they found of the Christian faith. There
was a common frontier saying that there was no law west of Kansas
City, and west of Fort Scott, no God.[27]

Except for Sundays, preaching services were held at noon in
rural areas. There were few clocks in the backwoods, but everyone
knew that when the sun was directly overhead it was time to hear
the preacher.[28] These traveling preachers were a welcome respite from
the rigors of frontier life, and when the circuit rider came to town
many people would drop what they were doing to come and hear
him preach. The subject of the sermon was the Lord Jesus Christ and
the gospel of grace, preached first to convert and then to sanctify by
the power of the Holy Spirit. Every preacher was to be an evangelist
and a preacher of holiness. Horace Bishop's experiences were typical
of most circuit riders:

> I preached twenty-eight times a month. I never took break-
> fast and dinner at the same place except on Friday, which was
> laundry day in the country. . . . My wardrobe was one end of
> my saddlebags; my bookcase the other end. . . . My "study"
> was the shade of any tree on the way to my appointments,
> where there was grass for my horse. . . . I slept wherever it
> was convenient, on a sheepskin or my Mexican blanket,
> occasionally on a dirt or a puncheon floor.[29]

The Methodist circuit riders were tireless in their pursuit of souls.
A discouraged Kentucky Presbyterian once was ambitious to find a
family whose cabin had not been visited by a Methodist preacher.
He lamented, "In several days I travelled from settlement to settlement . . . but into every hovel I entered I learned that the Methodist

---

27 Ross Phares, *Bible in Pocket, Gun in Hand: The Story of Frontier Religion* (New York:
     Doubleday, 1964), 3.
28 Ludwig, *Francis Asbury*, 160.
29 Phares, *Bible in Pocket, Gun in Hand*, 156, cited in Mark Terry, *Evangelism: A Concise
     History* (Nashville: Broadman & Holman, 1994), 128. A puncheon floor consisted of
     slabs hewn from logs.

missionary had been there before me."[30] Another contemporary noted that "not infrequently a Methodist circuit-rider called at the cabin of a settler before the mud in his stick chimney was dry or before the weight poles were on the roof."[31] Methodist circuit riders seemed to be everywhere, leading one New Yorker to exclaim in 1788, "I know not from whence they all come, unless from the clouds."[32] Mike Atnip summarized their tenacity:

> And hardly had such a pioneer gotten settled in his new clearing before a Methodist preacher would show up. This is illustrated by the incident reports by one of the itinerants in Mississippi. Following a pair of wagon tracks through the woods, he found they ended where a man was making camp in a little clearing. They began to talk, and upon finding out that his visitor was a Methodist preacher, the man exclaimed, "I left Virginia to get away from those Methodists, and went to Georgia. There they got my wife and daughter in the church. Now I have come here to escape them, and before I get my wagon unloaded, here they come!"[33]

Circuit riders were so relentless in their ministry that on stormy days there was a proverbial saying: "Nobody was out but crows and Methodist preachers."[34]

Asbury took good care of his horses and expected his circuit riders to do the same. The *First Discipline* had strong words about the care

---

30   Albert H. Redford, *The History of Methodism in Kentucky* (Nashville: Southern Methodist Publishing House, 1868–76), III:530, cited in Charles A. Johnson, *The Frontier Camp Meeting: Religion's Harvest Time* (Dallas: Southern Methodist University Press, 1955), 19.

31   Phares, *Bible in Pocket, Gun in Hand*, 11–12. See also William W. Sweet, *The Story of Religion in America* (Grand Rapids: Baker, 1973 reprint), 218–219.

32   Wigger, "Holy, 'Knock-'Em-Down' Preachers," 25.

33   Mike Atnip, *How the Methodists Saved America* (Newmanstown, PA: Primitive Christianity Publishers, 2003), 33.

34   Bernard A. Weisberger, *They Gathered at the River* (Boston: Little, Brown & Co., 1958), 45–6.

of one's mount: "Be merciful to your Beast. Not only ride moderately, but see with your own eyes that your horse is rubbed and fed."[35] James Gilruth, a circuit rider in Ohio, Michigan, and Illinois, was so large he needed two horses to carry him on his journeys. He would ride the horses alternately, allowing the worn out horse to follow behind.[36]

Asbury believed circuit riders should remain single due to the necessity of being away from home most of the year. Observing that marriage caused most circuit riders to "locate" or "settle" in a single local church, he lamented, "I believe the devil and the women will get all my preachers."[37]

Most country trails became seas of mud during heavy rains. Circuit riders learned how to veer their horses off the road to the right or left just far enough to find firm bottom beneath the mud but not far enough to get trapped or lost in the heavy timber.[38] Exhaustion, illness, animal attacks, and unfriendly encounters with outlaws or Indians in some regions were constant threats. Nights were often spent outdoors in the elements, and food was oftentimes what wild game they could shoot or what wild crops they could gather. Sometimes they were invited into people's homes; other times they slept in the barn. The circuit rider's staple food was beef or venison jerky, cured strips of meat that would not spoil easily.[39]

Circuit riders, following their "mentor" John Wesley, would take advantage of the long hours spent in the saddle between preaching engagements to read and prepare their messages.[40] Many of the early circuit riders were not ordained and therefore could not administer the sacraments or perform marriage ceremonies.[41] While most circuit riders had little or no education, that condition was not universally true. James B. Finley, a lifelong circuit rider, was a classical scholar who

---

35 Ludwig, *Francis Asbury*, 176.
36 William P. Strickland, ed., *The Life of Jacob Gruber* (New York, 1860), iii, 18.
37 William W. Bennett, *Memorials of Methodism in Virginia* (Richmond, VA: Published by the author, 1871), 184, cited in Rudolph, *Francis Asbury*, 107.
38 Rudolph, *Francis Asbury*, 75.
39 Johnson, *The Frontier Camp Meeting*, 155.
40 Johnson, *The Frontier Camp Meeting*, 166.
41 George T. Ashley, *Reminiscences of a Circuit Rider* (self-published, 1941), 12.

also served as professor of languages at Augusta College in Kentucky. Thomas S. Hinde was a doctor, compiler of a popular western camp meeting hymnal, and prominent church historian.[42]

Peter Cartwright's *Autobiography*,[43] first published in 1856, serves as a valuable primary source for understanding the life of a circuit rider. Cartwright, long-time circuit rider in Illinois, was twice elected to the Illinois legislature. His one defeat was in the Congressional race of 1846 when he lost to none other than Abraham Lincoln.[44] Cartwright's observations, shaped as they were through his own Methodist eyes, are worth noting at length:

> But it must be remembered that many of us early traveling preachers, who entered the vast wilderness of the West at an early day, had little or no education; no books, and no time to read or study them if we could have had them. We had no colleges, nor even a respectable common school, within hundreds of miles of us. Old *Dyke* or *Dilworth* was our spelling book; and what little we did learn, as we grew up, and the means of education increased among us, we found, to our hearts' content, that we had to unlearn, and this was the hardest work of all.[45]

And in this lengthy quote he reflects on the impact made by Methodist circuit riders:

> Right here I wish to say, (I hope without the charge of egotism,) when I consider the insurmountable disadvantages and difficulties that the early pioneer Methodist preachers labored under in spreading the Gospel in these Western wilds in the great valley of the Mississippi, and contrast the

---

42 Johnson, *The Frontier Camp Meeting*, 153.
43 Peter Cartwright, *Autobiography of Peter Cartwright,* edited by W. P. Strickland (New York: The Methodist Book Concern, n.d.).
44 Johnson, *The Frontier Camp Meeting*, 154.
45 Cartwright, *Autobiography*, 4.

disabilities which surrounded them on every hand, with the glorious human advantages that are enjoyed by their present successors, it is confoundingly miraculous to me that our modern preachers cannot preach better, and do more good than they do. Many nights, in early times, the itinerant had to camp out, without fire or food for man or beast. Our pocket Bible, Hymn Book, and Discipline constituted our library. It is true we could not, many of us, conjugate a verb or parse a sentence, and murdered the king's English almost every lick. But there was a Divine unction attended the word preached, and thousands fell under the mighty power of God, and thus the Methodist Episcopal Church was planted firmly in this Western wilderness, and many glorious signs have followed, and will follow, to the end of time. [46]

Riding a circuit was a demanding task. Statistics show of those who rode before 1800, half died before they were thirty. Those who rode up to 1844 had a slightly longer life span, with half living to be thirty-three. Yet some ministers thrived on the rigors of the circuit. Peter Cartwright had seventy-one years as an itinerant, Henry Smith sixty-five, and James B. Finley more than thirty-four years. [47]

Methodist circuit riders were also book distributors. Their commission on sales provided some of them with the only cash they ever saw. This practice helped spread Bibles, hymnbooks, and other religious literature throughout the frontier. Peter Cartwright wondered if he had done more good by distributing religious literature than he had by his preaching. [48] While Methodists relied on circuit riders to reach persons in the West, Baptists utilized farmer-preachers who spread out through the South in great numbers. By the 1830s these groups had replaced the Congregationalists and Presbyterians as the

---

46 Cartwright, *Autobiography*, 6–7.
47 Ludwig, *Francis Asbury*, 158. See also Johnson, *The Frontier Camp Meeting*, 159.
48 See *History of American Methodism*, I:281–87, cited in Rudolph, *Francis Asbury*, 135.

largest denominations, not only in the South but in the whole United States.[49]

The evangelistic spirit of John Wesley ("the world is my parish") had permeated the American world through the leadership and example of Francis Asbury and his Methodist circuit riders. Asbury's passion did not dim as he neared the end. He wrote this entry in his *Journal* less than a year before his death, exhorting himself as well as others:

> Tell this rebellious generation they are already condemned, and will be shortly damned; preach to them like Moses from Mount Sinai and Ebal, like David—"The wicked shall be turned into hell, and all the nations that forget God"; like Isaiah—"Who amongst you shall dwell with everlasting burnings?"; like Ezekiel—"O, wicked men! thou shall surely die!" Pronounce the eight woes uttered by the Son of God near the close of his ministry, and ask with him—"Ye serpents, ye generation of vipers, how can ye escape the damnation of hell?" Preach as if you had seen heaven and its celestial inhabitants and had hovered over the bottomless pit and beheld the tortures and heard the groans of the damned.[50]

Francis Asbury and his circuit riding preachers changed the religious landscape of America. Their passion for saving souls was clear. Darius Salter summarizes their heritage succinctly: "The early Methodist heritage is a story of men and women in love with Christ and His gospel."[51] May the same be said of us as Christ followers today.

---

49   J. Edwin Orr, *The Eager Feet: Evangelical Awakenings, 1790–1830* (Chicago: Moody Press, 1975), 63. See also Noll, *A History of Christianity in the U.S. and Canada*, 167.

50   Francis Asbury, "July 9, 1815," *Journal and Letters*, 2:784–785, cited in *Robert Coleman, Nothing to do but Save Souls: John Wesley's Charge to His Preachers* (Grand Rapids: Francis Asbury Press, 1990), 54–55.

51   Salter, *American Evangelism*, 91.

CHAPTER 7

CANE RIDGE *and the* CAMP MEETING REVIVAL MOVEMENT

....

....

D. Scott Hildreth

August 6, 1801, serves as one of the most significant dates in American revival history. Vanderbilt historian, Paul Conkin argued that the revival at Cane Ridge is, "the most important religious gathering in all of American history, both for what it symbolized and for the effects that flowed from it."[1] On this date, in rural Kentucky, about twenty miles from Lexington, men and women started gathering at the Cane Ridge church for an extended preaching, worship, and communion service. The resulting event left such an impression on the American religious landscape that many other gatherings opened with prayers of, "Lord, make it like Cane Ridge."

The final attendance numbered at close to twenty thousand, by far the largest religious gathering any had experienced. Those who took part report mighty works of the Holy Spirit as people fell under great conviction of sin and were converted, healed, and were swept away with various emotional outbursts.[2] The impact of this gathering was so great that the image of camp meeting revivals became the defining

---

1   Paul K. Conkin, *Cane Ridge: America's Pentecost* (Madison: University of Wisconsin Press, 1990), 3.

2   It is well documented that the events at Cane Ridge included emotional excesses.

symbol of the Second Great Awakening throughout rural America. Even today, over two centuries later, the long shadow of camp meeting evangelism shapes southern religion. This chapter will briefly trace the history of camp meeting evangelism with special focus on the largest and most influential camp meeting of all, the Cane Ridge Revival.

THE CONTEXT

As one looks back on the revival at Cane Ridge, and the movement that followed, it is perhaps important to note that there were very few cultural indicators that a spiritual awakening was on the horizon. Iain Murray has noted, "The decline of Christian influence before a revival has sometimes been exaggerated in order to emphasize the scale of subsequence transformation. The Second Great Awakening . . . requires no such distortion of history in order to justify its title."[3] The spiritual influence of the First Great Awakening had long since disappeared across the United States. The fledgling country struggled to create an identity, politicians clashed, and the social fabric showed little interest in religion. Most churches were small; the general attendance hovered at less than 20 percent of the population. William McLoughlin notes that the Calvinistic doctrine that had fueled the preaching of men like Jonathan Edwards and provided the foundation for the First Great Awakening had given way to non-Christian expressions of Deism, Universalism, and Unitarianism on the one hand, or sliding into hyper-Calvinism and lethargy on the other.[4] Methodist evangelist James Smith, who had traveled near Lexington in the autumn of 1795, feared that "the universalists, joining with the Deists, had given Christianity a deadly stab at hereabouts."[5]

---

3   Iain H. Murray, *Revival and Revivalism: The Making of American Evangelicalism, 1750–1858* (Edinburgh, England and Carlisle, PA: Banner of Truth Press, 1994), 116.

4   William G. McLoughlin, *Revivals, Awakenings, and Reform: An Essay on Religion and Social Change in America, 1670–1977* (Chicago: University of Chicago Press, 1978), 100–101.

5   Mark Galli, "Revival at Cane Ridge," *Christian History* (1995), accessed August 25, 2020, https://christianhistoryinstitute.org/magazine/article/revival-at-cane-ridge.

Along with this religious apathy, the moral compass of the nation also languished. Finke and Stark have observed, "It is important to realize that most colonial settlements . . . were part of an untamed frontier . . . not filled with God-fearing, Sunday-go-to-meeting folks, but were wide open, lawless capitals of vice and violence. . . . As a result, frontiers will be short on churches, and long on crime and vice."[6] Francis Asbury, writing about those who settled across the southern frontier, observed: "Not one in a hundred came here to get religion, but rather to get plenty of good land, I think it will be well if some or many do not eventually lose their souls."[7] At the beginning of a new century, the country found itself in a dark spiritual state and there seemed to be little anticipation that this would change. If the adage is true, "the darker the soil, the richer the harvest," then the American frontier was ripe for revival. It seems few in the area expected what would soon take place.

JAMES MCGREADY AND REGIONAL COMMUNION GATHERINGS

Even though the exact origins of camp meeting revival remain a matter of debate, many historians trace the most important stream through the influence of James McGready (or the alternate spelling, James M'Gready). McGready grew up in the Presbyterian church and began training for ministry at a young age. During his studies, McGready grew concerned with the reality that, despite his efforts to maintain orthodox theology, his heart remained cold to the things of the Lord. This conviction not only led him to repent of dead orthodoxy, but it also transformed his vision and hope for ministry. One man who sat under his preaching described it this way:

> Such earnestness, such zeal, such powerful persuasion, en-
> forced by the joys of heaven and the miseries of hell, I had

---

6   Roger Finke and Rodney Stark, *The Churching of America: Winners and Losers in Our Religious Economy* (New Brunswick, NJ, Rutgers University Press, 2008), 35–35.
7   Galli, *Revival at Cane Ridge*.

never witnessed before. . . . His concluding remarks were addressed to the sinner to flee the wrath to come without delay. Never before had I comparatively felt the force of the truth. Such was my excitement that, had I been standing, I should have probably sunk to the floor under the impression.[8]

Along with his renewed preaching, McGready also implemented a different type of religious assembly, the regional communion service. These gatherings provided the structure and opportunity for what would eventually become the camp meeting revival.

The camp meeting movement did not originate as an attempt at spiritual awakening. Instead, the large gatherings resulted from the restriction that only an ordained minister could oversee the Lord's Supper. At the turn of the century, there were few ordained clergy serving across the southern frontier of the United States. Even though smaller churches gathered regularly for worship services, their celebration of communion needed to be coordinated to coincide with the arrival of the minister. Because of the infrequency of these celebrations, they were usually more than a single service or event. It was not uncommon for the service to be planned as an extended worship service attended by surrounding congregations. As news spread, these communion gatherings became more regional and included other denominations and religious traditions. Preachers and congregants alike joined the celebration; it became a multidenominational event. As one might expect, the numbers exceeded the capacity of the church building and these services were move outside. To accommodate the crowd, people arrived prepared to camp in wagons and tents.

In 1800, McGready organized a communion gathering at the Red River church. He scheduled the event to take place over four days. He planned for the first two days, Friday and Saturday, to be preaching services that would include several preachers. Sunday was the communion service. Some groups participated in this Lord's

---

8   John B. Boles, *The Great Revival* (Lexington: The University of Kentucky Press, 1972), 39–40.

Supper together, while others felt compelled to restrict communion within their own denominational tradition. Monday was another day of preaching. McGready hoped that the extended time of preaching and the emotional appeal would stir up revival in the area. Many historians look at this as the original camp meeting event. For the first time, the purpose of the gathering was more than communion.

By all accounts, the service was a success; attendance was great, and the leaders reported a number of conversions, and evidences of the outpouring of the Spirit. John McGhee, one of the preachers, described it as follows:

> A power that caused me to tremble was upon me. There was a solemn weeping all over the house, wishing to preach. . . . At length I rose up and told the people I was appointed to preach, but there was a greater than I preaching; I exhorted them to let the Lord God Omnipotent reign in their hearts, and to submit to him, and their souls should live. Many broke silence; a woman shouted tremendously. I left the pulpit to go to her period as I went along through the people, it was suggested to me: "you know these people are much for order; They will not bear this confusion; Go back and be quiet!" I turned to go back, and was near falling. The power of God was strong upon me, I turned and losing sight of the fear of man, I went through the house shouting and exhorting with all possible energy and ecstasy, and the floor was soon covered with the slain; Their screams for mercy pierced the heavens, and mercy came down. Some found forgiveness, and many went away feeling unutterable agonies of souls for redemption in the blood of Jesus. This was the beginning of that glorious revival of religion in this country, which was so great of blessing to thousands; and from this occasion camp-meetings took their rise.[9]

---

9   Z. F. Smith, "The Great Revival of 1800: The First Camp Meeting," in *Register of Kentucky State Historical Society*, vol. 7, no. 20 (May 1909), 26.

On the heels of this Red River revival, McGready planned similar gatherings for the other churches that fell within his ministry responsibility. To prepare for these gatherings, he circulated word and invited people to "come prepared to camp on the ground, thus attracting an assemblage of six or seven thousand people."[10] Taylor notes that, "People came from a radius of 100 miles of the church. They could not possibly take their place inside the church. It was decided that the services would run continuously from dusk to dawn. . . . Simultaneously, and the preachers rotated from time to time."[11]

BARTON STONE AND THE CANE RIDGE REVIVAL

Through the rest of 1800, revivals and outdoor camp meetings sprang up across the Kentucky and Tennessee frontier. One of the revival preachers, John McGee, reported, "Many thousands of people attended. The mighty power and mercy of God was manifested. The people fell before the Word, like corn before a storm of wind, and many rose from the dust with divine glory shining in their countenances."[12] It seemed clear to many that God was moving through the region. The reports of these meetings attracted the attention of a young Presbyterian minister, Barton Stone.

Most historians believe that Stone first heard about McGready and the outdoor meetings during his studies for ministry. Paul Conkin claims that Stone arrived at college "just in time for him to become caught up in the revival that swept the school under the effective preaching of McGready."[13] Soon after his graduation, Stone became pastor of the Cane Ridge church in rural Kentucky. Then in late 1801, he attended to a meeting in order to investigate the possibility of holding similar open-air service for his congregation. He recorded his experiences as follows:

---

10   Smith, "Great Revival of 1800," 28.
11   Mendell Taylor, *Exploring Evangelism* (Kansas City. MO: Beacon Hill Press, 1964), 410.
12   Galli, *Revival at Cane Ridge*.
13   Conkin, *Cane Ridge: America's Pentecost*, 74.

Having heard of a remarkable religious excitement in the South of Kentucky . . . I was very anxious to be among them, and early in the spring of 1801, I went there to attend a camp meeting. There, on the edge of a prairie in Logan County, Kentucky, the multitudes came together, and continued a number of days and nights encamped on the grounds, during which time worship was carried on. . . . The scene to me was new and passing strange. It baffled description. Many, very many, fell down, as men slain in battle, and continued for hours together in an apparently breathless and emotionless state—sometimes for a few moments reviving, and exhibiting symptoms of life by a deep groan, or piercing shriek, or by a prayer for mercy most fervently uttered. After lying thus for hours, they obtained deliverance. The gloomy cloud, which had covered their faces, seemed gradually and visibly to disappear, and hope in smiles brightened into joy—they would arise shouting deliverance and then would address the surrounding multitudes.[14]

This experience convinced Stone that his church and his community needed a similar experience. When he returned, he started promoting a camp meeting at the Cane Ridge church. "The primary concern would be the gathering of people by the thousands, the continuity of services around the clock, and the coming of people on the grounds for six days."[15]

They set the date for the meeting to begin on Friday, August 6, 1801. The church made preparations for a large crowd. They sent invitations to Presbyterian and Methodist ministers; however, the attendees also included Baptists, several African American churches, and other denominations. Cane Ridge members made their homes

---

14 James R. Rogers, *The Cane Ridge Meeting House*, 2nd ed. (Cincinnati: Standard Publishing Company, 1910), 153–154.

15 Taylor, 411. The meeting lasted from August 6–12/13, 1801; the original plan was for the meeting to stop on Monday, August 9.

ready to receive guests, farmers cleared land, and even left grain on the ground to feed the horses. The congregation expected the crowd would be greater than its church building would hold, so they erected a tent—this too proved inadequate. Lexington, the largest city in the state, boasted a population of around two thousand. No one could have anticipated the throng of people who attended the services.

People began arriving on Friday, one report claims that wagons, carriages, horsemen, and people on foot crowded all the roads into the city. Every person in the county seemed to be making their way toward Cane Ridge.

Friday evening, the meeting began with Barton Stone welcoming the crowd from inside the church house. Despite the rain, the atmosphere was expectant; however, nothing extraordinary seems to have happened that that first evening. In response to the lack of movement, several attendees remained in prayer through the evening.

Saturday was a different story. By the afternoon session, the whole encampment buzzed with excitement and people were visibly moved; ecstatic, unrestrained emotional outbursts swept through the camp. Men, women, and children shrieked and shouted. Some fell to the ground while others stood in place, seeming to sway in the breeze. Of those who fell, some remained conscious, but many took the form of someone in a coma or even in the grips of a grand mal seizure. One eyewitness reported, "The noise was like the roar of Niagara, at one time I saw at least five hundred swept down in a moment as if a battery of a thousand guns had been opened upon them, and then immediately followed shrieks and shouts that rent the very heavens."[16]

One of the more notable phenomena that swept through the camp were the "jerks." These were the spasmodic twitching of the entire body as the person fell under conviction of sin. One eyewitness observed, "Their heads would jerk back suddenly, frequently causing them to yelp, or make some other involuntary noise. . . . Sometimes

---

16   From the firsthand account of James Finley, cited by Peter Smith, "Cane Ridge Meeting House 1801: Revival Reverberates Today Seminal Event's Bicentennial Celebrated," *The Courier Journal*, July 31, 2001.

the head would fly every way so quickly that their features could not be recognized . . . their heads fly back and forward so quickly that the hair of females would be made to crack like a carriage whip, but not very loud."[17] Richard McNemar described the jerks as follows:

> Still more demeaning and mortifying were the *jerks*. Nothing in nature could better represent this strange and unaccountable operation than for one to goad another, alternately on every side, with a piece of hot iron this exercise commonly began in the head which would fly backward and forward and from side to side with a quick jolt. . . . And the more anyone labored to stay himself and be sober, the more staggered, and the more rapid his twitches increased. He must necessarily go as he was stimulated, whether with a violent dash on the ground and bounce from place to place like a football, or hop around with head, limbs and trunk, twitching and jolting in every direction, as if they must inevitably fly asunder. And how such could escape without injury was no small wonder to spectators.[18]

Throughout the weekend, all manner of emotional outbursts accompanied these fallings and the jerks—barking, laughing, dancing, and singing. Rather than attempt to restrain these excesses, the preachers seemed to encourage them further, believing each signaled the work of the Holy Spirit as he brought conviction of sin or bliss of conversion in the lives of the attendees.

These emotional excesses and spiritual exuberance remain one of the most notable elements of the Cane Ridge revival. Johnson claimed that Cane Ridge was, "in all probability, the most disorderly, the most hysterical, and the largest revival ever held in the early day America." However, he suggests that this lack of order should not come as a

---

17   Galli, "Revival at Cane Ridge."

18   Robert R. Mathisen, *Critical Issues in American Religious History* (Waco, TX: Baylor University Press, 2006), 227.

surprise when one considers that "every shade of religious option was represented. There were many visitors whose religious convictions were nebulous. Tumult and Disorder were inevitable when a heterogeneous group of such large proportions assembled, especially since the occasion for social companionship was so rare on the frontier."[19] The multidenominational factor seems to have contributed to the feeling of freedom experienced by attendees.

Singing, praying, moaning, and shouting lasted through Saturday night, but by Sunday things seemed to have calmed considerably as Barton and the other ministers prepared for communion. However, as different denominational groups separated, spontaneous preaching broke out across the camp. Both pastors and laypeople, men and women, preached to various groups of people. Galli writes about a seven-year-old girl who climbed on a man's shoulders and preached until she was completely fatigued. When she lay her head on his as if to sleep, someone in the audience suggested "the poor thing" had better be laid down to rest. The girl roused and said, 'Don't call me poor, for Christ is my brother, God my father, and I have a kingdom to inherit, and therefore do not call me poor, for I am rich in the blood of the Lamb!'"[20] By all accounts, Sunday was more intense than Saturday; the preachers could hardly be heard above the shouting, and by the end of the day they were exhausted from ministering to the crowd.

They had scheduled the meeting to end on Monday, but as reports about the meeting spread through the county, people continued to arrive. In order to minister to the new arrivals, the leaders extended the service for several more days. In the end, the Cane Ridge revival lasted four more days. They continued to meet until most of the food for men and animals was gone. The number of attendees was estimated at twenty thousand. Of this group, about three thousand took part in the communion services and another three thousand were converted. Countless others were swept up in the more ecstatic elements associated with the revival. Finke and Stark write:

---

19   Johnson, *The Frontier Camp Meeting*, 61–63.
20   Galli, "Revival at Cane Ridge".

Cane Ridge holds such a central place in histories of American religion because it, unlike previous meetings that may have been large and that certainly produced as much emotional response, came to the attention of the eastern press. These press reports . . . [were] everywhere hailed as a miracle and the "greatest outpouring of the Spirit since Pentecost."[21]

IMPACT OF CANE RIDGE

The success and reputation of the Cane Ridge revival spurred a movement that swept through the American frontier. Along with the urban ministry of men like Charles Finney, camp meetings formed a key element of the Second Great Awakening. Bernard Weisberger noted, "the Frontiersman was different. He lived, worked, and died hard. It was natural that he should convert hard; that he should cry aloud in wrestling with his guilt; and that he should leap and twist and shout in rejoicing over his forgiveness."[22] Finke and Stark have noted that 94 percent of all Americans lived in rural areas. Therefore, these camp meetings were even more important for the growth of the church and the shaping of American religion than the urban revival movements.[23] Camp meetings provided the perfect place for rugged individualists to gather, worship, and meet God.

Despite the success of camp meetings, many condemned the methods and outcome. The more formal city churchmen criticized this method as too crude and too emotional. They expressed concern about men and women praying together and taking part in public worship. Many of the critics of the camp meeting movement claimed that these large, riotous gatherings reduced the inhibitions of that attendees and as a result, more babies were conceived than souls converted during meetings.[24]

---

21 Finke and Stark, *The Churching of America, 94.*
22 Bernard A. Weisberger, *They Gathered at the River: The Story of the Great Revivalists and Their Impact upon Religion in America* (Boston and Toronto: Little, Brown, and Company. 1958), 29.
23 Finke and Stark, *The Churching of America,* 107.
24 Smith, "Cane Ridge Meeting House 1801," claims a bumper crop of babies followed nine months after the Cane Ridge Revival. It is also reported that Francis Asbury

Not only did Cane Ridge spark a movement that transformed the American frontier, it also impacted American religious denominations. Soon afterward, Presbyterians expelled Barton Stone, along with several other revivalists. This created a split in the denomination between those who embraced revival tactics and those who rejected them. Eventually, Stone grew more frustrated with Presbyterian government and doctrine. He and his followers created the Christian Church or Disciples of Christ Church. Finke and Stark have observed: "Thus did the old mainline cease participating in the camp meetings, thereby surrendering all of the pulpit time to Baptists and Methodists."[25] This, they note, determined the growth of these denominations across the southern United States.

Mendell Taylor has noted four unique benefits of the camp meeting and their impact on the culture.[26]

1. Served as a Social Institution
   Camp meetings provided relief from the difficulties of frontier life. For men and women who lived in relative isolation, these gatherings presented them with the opportunity for socializing, catching up on latest gossip, worship, and Christian fellowship. "The farmer and his family considered going to camp meetings the high point on the social calendar. . . . Thus, the camp meeting was relevant to the lives of frontier settlers by filling a social vacuum."

2. Served as an Institution for Law and Morality
   Finke and Stark remind us that frontier towns like Dodge City, Tombstone, and Deadwood were mostly filled with "male drifters, gamblers, confidence tricksters, whores, and saloon keepers, and [were] without churches, schools, or

---

employed watchmen who wandered through the camps at night with sticks, breaking up any mischief they discovered.

25   Finke and Stark, *The Churching of America*, 112.

26   Taylor, *Exploring Evangelism*, 420–21.

respectable women."[27] Camp meeting preachers addressed these sins head-on as well as reminded the congregations about the reality and danger of God's judgment. They preached against "immorality, intemperance, tobacco, blasphemy, dueling, card playing, horse racing, and gambling." Those who attended received warnings about God's expectations for right living and the consequences for those who rebelled.

3. Served as a Promoter of Denominational Cooperation
As noted earlier in this chapter, camp meetings sprang directly from their multidenominational emphasis. As ministers from different churches preached from behind the same pulpit and occupied the same platforms, people mingled and worshiped together. Peter Cartwright wrote "the number of churchmen of different denominations who joined forces . . . might reach ten, twenty, and sometimes thirty."[28] These men preached together, prayed together, and ministered to those who attended the meetings.

4. Served as Growth Factor for the Churches
The success of the camp meeting caused churches across the frontier to grow. Taylor writes:

> In Kentucky alone, between 1800 and 1803, "the Baptists gained ten thousand members, the Methodists about an equal number, the Presbyterians also added large numbers to their congregations." For the nine-year period between 1802 and 1811, Methodists had an increase of almost 100,000 members.[29]

---

27 Finke and Stark, *The Churching of America*, 36.
28 Taylor, *Exploring Evangelism*, 421, citing Henry K. Rowe, *History of the Christian People* (New York: The McMillian Company, 1931) 52.
29 Taylor, *Exploring Evangelism*, 421.

No doubt these same increases can be see across the region. The camp meeting proved to be the right evangelistic event at the right time to reach men and women across the Southern frontier of the United States.

CONCLUSION

Camp meeting evangelism swept across the country at the turn of the century and left an indelible mark on the religious landscape of America. The reaction to seemingly unrestrained experiences and the emphasis on emotional responses attracted fans and critics alike. Traditional denominations were divided between pro-revivalists and anti-revivalists, while some adherents abandoned the existing institutions and formed new religious groups.

Camp meetings, despite the excesses, seemed well suited to bring the Christian message the rough and isolated population on the American frontier. Hard living seemed to demand hard preaching and a hard encounter with God. These outdoor meetings provided thousands of men and women entrance into the kingdom of God. Even today, the long shadow of the camp meeting can be seen across southern religion throughout the United States.

CHAPTER 8

BIBLE SOCIETIES *in* AMERICA *and* BIBLE DISTRIBUTION EVANGELISM

···

···

Thomas P. Johnston

Evangelism and Bible colportage have gone hand-in-hand since the evangelism of the Alpine Waldensians before the Protestant Reformation. It is no surprise that on American soil, evangelism sparked and fueled the formation of the American Bible Society (ABS) in 1816. One person who molded these methods as one was the leader of the Haystack Revival, Samuel J. Mills (1783–1818).

Samuel J. Mills provided the revived evangelistic fervor as necessary fuel for the founding of the ABS. Mills conflated the revivalist spirit of the Second Great Awakening with an urgency for evangelism and a heart for Bible distribution. This chapter will show that "Bible Work" has been a prominent feature in North America Evangelicalism, especially after the Second Great Awakening. It will begin by examining the circumstances around the founding of the ABS, then will describe methods of evangelistic Bible work. The chapter will draw lessons for the future related to Bible dissemination and evangelism. Lastly, it will provide tips for the use of the Bible in evangelism.

Mills was born in 1783 in Connecticut, a pastor's son.[1] When Mills was eighteen years old he came under the influence of the revival movement that was spreading across the United States, and experienced conversion. He was overcome by his sinfulness and turned to Jesus for forgiveness. Mills was converted. His newfound faith led Mills to sacrifice his life for his Savior. He soon felt convicted that he should be a missionary, so in 1801 he entered Williams College in Williamstown, Massachusetts.[2] At Williams he brought together a group of likeminded students who also felt called to foreign missions, to gather for prayer. At one of these prayer gatherings, a rainstorm caused the group to find shelter under a haystack, lending its name to the famed 1806 Haystack Prayer Meeting. This group of students eventually sparked the establishment of the society for the support of first United States foreign missionaries. The five young men meeting that day were James Richards, Francis Robbins, Harvey Loomis, Byron Green, and Samuel Mills. They devoted themselves to praying that they would be sent out as foreign missionaries.

By 1810 the groundwork was laid for Samuel Mills to plead with local pastors to form the "American Board of Commissioners for Foreign Missions." The group was formed, but as it turns out Mills was never sent out as a missionary with that agency. He later died in 1818 while serving as an agent of the American Colonization Society, on a return trip from Africa to secure land for the country of Liberia for the repatriation of American slaves.[3] It was, however, the efforts of Mills between 1810 and 1816 that led to the forming of the ABS. Before telling that story, we must move across the ocean to consider the work of God in Great Britain.

To set Mills in his context, it is helpful to understand the organizational momentum that began on the British Isles and moved across the Atlantic to the United States. Great Britain had a Bible

1   Kenneth Scott Latourette, *The Great Century: Europe and the United States, 1800 A.D. to 1914 A.D.*, A History of the Expansion of Christianity, vol. 4 (Grand Rapids: Zondervan, 1870), 79.

2   Williams College was founded just eight years prior in 1793.

3   Randall Balmer, "Samuel J. Mills (Jr) (1783–1818)," in *Encyclopedia of Evangelicalism* (Louisville: Westminster John Knox, 2002), 383–84; Latourette, *The Great Century,* 4:85.

society movement preceding that in the United States. The following organizations below had already been formed, each of which playing a role in the founding of the British and Foreign Bible Society (BFBS):

- **1698:** Society for Promoting Christian Knowledge (SPCK) in London; the SPCK began printing Bibles as a part of its overall ministry.
- **1701:** Society for the Propagation of the Gospel to Foreign Parts
- **1750:** Scottish Society for Promoting Christian Knowledge among the Poor
- **1780:** The Bible Society, to supply Bibles to soldiers and sailors of Great Britain
- **1785:** Society for the Support and Encouragement of Sunday Schools
- **1792:** French Bible Society was formed in London to "furnish destitute persons of the French nation copies of the Scriptures in their native tongue."
- **1795:** London Missionary Society was formed
- **1799:** Religious Tract Society (RTS) was formed[4]

On December 7, 1802, in the Board Room of the RTS, when discussing the need for Welsh Bibles, Baptist pastor Joseph Hughes was heard to say: "But if for Wales, why not for the Kingdom? Why not for the world?" These men of the RTS soon went on to form the organizational grandparent of a vast number of Bible Societies worldwide, the BFBS. The BFBS was founded in 1804.[5] By its sixteenth annual report, the London-born organization explained: "The Auxiliaries of the Society itself amount to 265, and the Branch Societies to 364; forming together a total as of last year, of 629."[6]

---

4   William Canton, *The Story of the Bible Society* (London: John Murray, 1904), 5, 13.
5   Canton, *Story of the Bible Society,* 13–15.
6   "British and Foreign Bible Society, Abstract of Sixteenth Report," *Christian Watchman & Baptist Register,* Vol 2, New Series No. 7 (January 27, 1821): 1.

This growth was a true spiritual movement. Auxiliaries grew by 16.5 per year in the first sixteen years, and societies grew by just under 23 new branch societies per year. The BFBS had ignited in the hearts of evangelical Christians everywhere a new and worthy cause. They felt compelled to provide Bibles to the spiritually hungry peoples of the world. Along with handing out Bibles, persons needed to learn how to read. Hence, in its wake Sunday schools were formed, and public schools prospered. The Bible Society Movement tracked alongside the Restorationist Movement (churches going back to the Bible as the norm for church order), the Second Great Awakening, and an array of evangelistic, educational, philanthropic, and missionary societies in Germany, Great Britain, and the United States.[7]

The dynamo of this Religious Movement in England began stirring across the Atlantic. In the United States it produced an unusual organizational impetus:[8]

- **1800:** Massachusetts Missionary Society
- **1803:** Massachusetts Society for the Promotion of Christian Knowledge among the Indians
- **1804:** New Hampshire Missionary Society
- **1807:** Connecticut Religious Tract Society
- **1808:** Philadelphia Bible Society
- **1809:** Connecticut, Massachusetts, New York, and New Jersey Bible Societies
- **1810:** American Board of Commissioners for Foreign Missions

---

7 Paulus Scharpff, *History of Evangelism: Three Hundred Years of Evangelism in Germany, Great Britain, and the Unites States of America,* Helga Bender Henry, trans. (1964; Grand Rapids: Eerdmans, 1966).

8 This organizational tendency impacted denominational groupings, such as the organization of Baptist state conventions and schools: "Seventeen theological schools came into existence between 1807 and 1927, among them Princeton Theological Seminary, 1812; Yale Divinity School, 1822; and Union Theological Seminary in New York, 1824. . . . Of 180 denominational colleges in the West in 1860, 144 or so were founded and maintained by the more evangelistic denominations. Led by teachers with strong convictions, it is not surprising that religious awakenings recurred" (J. Edwin Orr, *Campus Aflame* [Glendale, CA: Regal, 1971], 36–37).

- **1814:** More than one hundred Bible Societies were organized in the United States, all "with the purpose of providing Bibles."[9]
- **1816:** One hundred thirty Bible Societies already existed in the United States.
- **1816:** ABS was born.

During the same year the ABS was formed, "Forty-three [Bible Societies] at once joined the national organization; forty-one new societies were formed for the express purpose of co-operating in its labours." [10] The founding document of the ABS acknowledged this sovereign impetus: "An excitement, as extraordinary as it is powerful, has roused the nations to the importance of spreading the knowledge of the one living and true God, as revealed in his Son, the Mediator between God and men, Christ Jesus."[11]

The founders of this society understood that God was doing a new work among them in "the [new] age of Bibles":

> We would fly to the aid of all that is holy, against all that is profane; of the purest interest of the community, the family, and the individual, against the conspiracy of darkness, disaster, and death—to help on the mighty work of Christian charity—to claim our place in the age of Bibles.[12]

The BFBS drove the passion of the age of Bibles across the world, and Samuel Mills brought an evangelistic fervor for the Bible in the nascent United States of America.

Between 1810 and 1814 Samuel Mills was a key figure in forming some of these early U.S. Bible Societies. The "Haystack Prayer Meeting"

---

9   Henry Otis Dwight, *The Centennial History of the American Bible Society* (New York: MacMillan, 1916), 7–9.
10   Canton, *Story of the Bible Society,* 70.
11   *Constitution for the American Bible Society formed by a Convention of Delegates, Held in the City of New York, May, 1816* (New York: American Bible Society, 1816), 13.
12   *Constitution for the American Bible Society*, 13.

moved from its original Alma Mater (Williams College) 132 miles to the newly founded Andover Seminary in Newton, Massachusetts.[13] As the prayer meetings gathered momentum, they were joined by other students. Luther Rice became a part of this prayer movement. Adoniram Judson joined the group at Andover Seminary. Mills was a key instigator in the formation of the American Board of Commissioners for Foreign Missions in 1810, though they never appointed him as a missionary; a door of ministry finally opened to him two years later.

In 1812, the Massachusetts and Connecticut Missionary Societies joined forces to commission J. M. Schermerhorn to explore the missionary possibilities in the newly acquired territory of the Louisiana Purchase. Samuel Mills was selected to join Schermerhorn for this five-month journey. The men were furnished with Bibles by the Philadelphia and New York Bible Societies. The trip made a profound impact on Mills, as he found a ministry niche that fit his evangelistic and organizational skills:

> Mr. Mills was so moved by the prevailing destitution that at every opportunity he gathered people together and induced them to form a local Bible Society; for there were plenty of good people who, when brought together, found that they could work with some prospect of success. In this way the Ohio State Bible Society, the Indiana Bible Society, the Illinois Bible Society, and the Nashville, Tennessee, Bible Society were formed.[14]

Also formed by Mills on that trip were the Kentucky Bible Society at Lexington; the Natchez, Mississippi, Bible Society; and the New Orleans Bible Society. As a result of his efforts, in five months, Mills was instrumental in the founding of seven Bible societies.

In 1814 Mills wrote an impassioned plea for a half mission copies of the Bible to be sent to the destitute of the United States. His appeal

---

13   Randall Balmer, "Haystack Prayer Meeting," in *Encyclopedia of Evangelicalism*, 275.
14   Dwight, *The Centennial History*, 12.

was published in a prominent newspaper of that day, the *Panoplist*: "It is thought by judicious people that half of a million of Bibles are necessary for the supply of the destitute in the United States. It is a foul blot on the national character. Christian America must arise to wipe it away."[15]

Mills's vision was large. None of the individual Bible societies had the financing to accomplish such a feat. This published call for a half of a million Bibles to meet the needs in the U.S. was the ultimate spark that spurred the vast organizational engine of the ABS.

Gathering more than one hundred Bible societies and auxiliaries dispersed among the colonies and territories of the United States to work as one Bible society was a monumental feat. For this challenge, Mills received the expert help of one of the Founding Fathers of the United States, Dr. Elias Boudinot (1740–1821). Boudinot had been president of the U.S. Continental Congress from 1782–1783, U.S. congressman from New Jersey, and director of the U.S. Mint from 1795–1805. Boudinot provided his administrative expertise, his network of contacts, and his understanding of the organization of the American Colonies. On January 31, 1816, Boudinot called together a Bible society convention. It was at this convention that the ABS was born, its constitution being published on May 16, 1816, after its first annual meeting. Boudinot himself served as the first president of the ABS until his death in 1821.

While Elias Boudinot loaned his sterling reputation and infused his administrative savvy of 76 years to the founding of the American Bible Society (ABS), it was the youthful evangelistic zeal of the thirty-three-year-old Samuel Mills that sparked the passion of the Bible Society Movement within the United States. To Mills belonged the evangelistic vision of the ABS. Mills exemplified the unusual spiritual fervency of Colonial America which swept across the United States in the founding of Christian colleges and multitudinous evangelistic societies: "The Christianity which had been planted in colonial days had taken root and flourished in a fashion never surpassed and but

---

15   Dwight, *The Centennial History*, 15; from *Panoplist* (Oct 1813), 357.

seldom equaled in the entire history of Christianity, or, indeed, of any other religion."[16]

Along with the birth of the ABS, it early pioneers developed evangelistic methods and encountered administrative quandaries. To this end, this chapter will turn, first, to evangelistic methods of the early Bible Society practitioners. Second, it will discuss some of the issues with which the ABS wrestled as it sought to deliver the Word of God to the U.S. and the world. Third, this chapter will conclude with some tips for the use of the Bible in evangelism. The amazing work of God called the Bible Society Movement brought new opportunities in evangelism.

EVANGELISTIC METHODS

Evangelism as Bible distribution necessitated a robust administrative workflow. First, Bibles needed to be made available to churches and distributors at the lowest cost possible. The first and primary driving force behind the Bible society movement was to provide a Bible for every American household. The ownership of books was quite sparce at the turn of the nineteenth century. Further, impoverished Americans often did not know how to read. The ownership of a Bible could change that deficit. Pierre Samuel Du Pont de Nemours explained: "In America, a great number of people read the Bible, and all the people read a newspaper. The fathers read aloud to their children, while breakfast is being prepared—a task which occupies the mothers for three quarters of an hour every morning."[17]

Correspondingly, the literacy rate was tied directly to the reading of the Bible: "England, Holland, the Protestant Cantons of Switzerland more nearly approach the standard of the United States, because in those countries the Bible is read; it is considered a duty to read it to children; and in that form of religion the sermons and liturgy in

---

16   Latourette, *The Great Century,* 4:222.
17   Pierre Samuel Du Pont de Nemours, *National Education in the United States of America* (1812), accessed October 29, 2020, https://www.dailykos.com/stories/2003/12/5/4379.

the language of the people tend to increase and formulate ideas of responsibility."[18]

As owning a Bible enhanced literacy, so the absence of a Bible diminished literacy. Bibles were also fairly expensive. One scholar suggested that purchasing a Bible in America in 1816 may have cost as much as 1 pound, 1 shilling, or $600–800 today.[19] Acquiring a Bible may have been comparable to purchasing a computer today—it required a week's wages for the common worker. Low-cost Bibles were necessary for the spiritual, educational, and economic benefit of impoverished Americans. Printing low-cost Bibles drove the business model of the ABS.

Second, what version of Bibles were they to make available? The first article of the Constitution of the ABS made it clear: "I. The Society shall be known by the name of THE AMERICAN BIBLE SOCIETY, of which the sole object shall be, to encourage a wider circulation of the Holy Scriptures without note or comment. The only copies in the English language to be circulated by the Society, shall be the version now in common use."[20] Hence, the 1769 "Oxford Standard Text," a stylistic revision of the 1611 King James Bible, was the Bible made available through the early publishing efforts of the ABS. Printing and disseminating this common-use Bible allowed the ABS to maintain broad denominational support.

Third, the ABS developed avenues of Bible distribution. Scripture dissemination needed to cover both the physical and spiritual geography of the nation. Bible Houses were needed in major cities across the United States, to be used by all cooperating local denominations. For the physical geography of the nation, the Bible Convention held in January 1816 in New York City gathered forty-eight delegates representing twenty-nine regional Bible societies and auxiliaries. In addition, eight persons were admitted representing four other

---

18   Du Pont de Nemours, *National Education.*
19   Ken Eckert, "Was the Bible Available/Affordable for Common People in the 17th Century in Europe?" accessed October 28, 2020, https://www.quora.com/Was-the-Bible-available-affordable-for-common-people-in-the-17th-Century-in-Europe.
20   *Constitution for the American Bible Society*, 2.

regional Bible societies, and four persons were received as members. Thirty-six men (all from NYC) were appointed as managers of the affairs of the ABS. The twenty-three vice-presidents of the ABS were from seventeen states and the District of Columbia. From its very start nearly a hundred prominent leaders from all parts of the U.S. cooperated to found the ABS. These leaders served as conduits for funding and Bible distribution channels for their localities, regional Bible Societies, and denominations.

For the spiritual geography of the United States, the ABS called on Christians of all denominations to participate in its efforts. Boudinot hailed the example of the BFBS in his call for cooperation and the exclusion of party prejudices:

> The impulse which that institution, ten thousand times more glorious than all the exploits of the sword, have given the conscience of Europe, and to the slumbering hope of millions in the region and shadow of death, demonstrates to Christians of every country what they *cannot* do by insulated zeal; and what they *can* do by co-operation. . . .
>
> Under such impressions, and with such views, fathers, brethren, fellow-citizens, the *American Bible Society* has been formed. Local feelings, party prejudices, sectarian jealousies, are excluded in its very nature. Its members are leagued in that, and that alone, which calls up every hallowed, and puts down every unhallowed, principle—the dissemination of the Scriptures in the received versions where they exist, and in the most faithful where they may be required.[21]

His plea was heeded, and as a result gathered were "Presbyterians, Episcopalians, Baptists, Reformed Dutch, Congregationalists, Friends."[22] Of the founding, Dwight wrote: "These sixty men for the Master's sake set aside strong personal preferences. Under divine guidance at

---

21 *Constitution for the American Bible Society*, 14–15.
22 Canton, *Story of the Bible Society*, 69.

a crisis in the national growth they had called into being an institution suited to the emergency, which would provide the nation with Scriptures and make many souls glad forever."[23]

Fourth, Bibles were distributed by church members and Bible colporteurs.[24] It was at this stage that the evangelistic spirit roused the Bible societies and auxiliaries. Bible salesmen went door-to-door throughout the United States selling Bibles. Along with selling Bibles, they would read Scripture and explain the gospel to those whom they sought to reach through their sales. Many Bible colporteurs planted churches in this fashion. Often, they would become pastors of the churches they planted. The door-to-door sale of Bibles became an important recruiting and training tool for future pastors and evangelists.

Fifth, Bibles were given away to impoverished families who could not afford them. As in the case of Samuel Mills, Bibles were given at low cost or even free to those who would read them. Likewise, in France Victor de Pressensé, president of the French and Foreign Bible Society, employed between 280–300 colporteurs "to sell Bibles and Testaments at a low price."[25]

As the battle for souls is real, so is the battle for the Bible is evident. These are Siamese twins of the same conflict, with the forces Satan arrayed against the gospel of Christ. Without the Bible there is no message, no weapon to pierce the heart. It comes as no surprise that this chapter on evangelism in North America addresses wounds and wars, skirmishes, and scars. These are lessons to be learned from the Bible Society Movement.

ISSUES IN BIBLE PUBLICATION AND DISSEMINATION

While a cross-section of issues assails and complicates the distribution of the Bible, the first and greatest lesson is the grace of God. The Bible Society Movement and the early decisions of the ABS left

23   Dwight, *The Centennial History*, 24–25.
24   A French Protestant term designating Bible distributors as carriers (*porteur*) of a package (*un colis*) of Bibles which they carried around their neck (*col* or *cou*).
25   Canton, *Story of the Bible Society,* 125–126.

their imprint on American Evangelicalism. For 148 years the ABS stood firm on the values of its founders. It is a miracle of God for any parachurch ministry to remain anchored to its founding principles for one and a half centuries. It speaks to wise leadership early on, and God's providential mercies in the intervening years.

Second, even as the "good seed" is spread, so also the enemy comingles tares into the harvest field (Matt 13:25). Three examples of tares being sown among the good seed in North America after the distribution of Bibles are:

- The Church of Jesus Christ of the Latter-Day Saints (A.D. 1830), aka Mormons, and their proselytizing efforts.
- Jehovah's Witnesses (A.D. 1870) with their massive printing operation and door-to-door distribution.
- Christian Science (A.D. 1887) and its many KJV Bible Reading Rooms.

Each of these examples and more modeled their efforts in the wake of the "Bible work" of the ABS Bible colporteurs.

Second, inherent in multidenominational effort, there exist complexities in Bible publication. For example, one big issue faced especially on the continent of Europe was the battle over including the apocryphal books when printing the Bible. Many state-churches desired the apocryphal books included in their Bibles and did not appreciate Bible distribution in their areas if the apocryphal books were not included. However, in the United States the situation was different. The Board of Managers of the ABS made the following recommendation in 1828: "That without deeming it expedient to detail the reasons which have influenced the decision of the Committee, they have unanimously agreed that the Apocrypha ought not to be printed and circulated with the canonical Scriptures by the Managers of the American Bible Society."[26] In doing so, North American evangelicalism was shielded from the issue of the apocryphal books for a time.

---

26   Robert T. Taylor, *Wings for the Word* (Plainfield, NJ: Logos International, 1978), 26.

The situation was different in the rest of the world. In England in 1831 the BFBS began including the apocryphal books in some of publications of the Bible. This action resulted in the founding of the Trinitarian Bible Society. Likewise, in France, in 1863 there were four French Protestant Bible societies, two of them merging in 1864.[27] They all responded differently to the following three questions:

- What translation should we print?
- Shall we include the apocryphal books to accommodate Catholic sensibilities?
- Should we work with Catholics in Scripture distribution?[28]

These issues were not easily resolved.

The ABS printed only the King James Bible. They determined in 1828 not to include the apocryphal books. It was not until 1964 that the ABS approach to the second [and third] questions above were altered: "The Society's translation committee recommended to the board 'that translation of the Old Testament Apocrypha which meets the translation standards of the Society be recommended for publication.'"[29]

The ABS also faced other cooperative issues. There was a battle over the translation of the verb "baptize." William Carey, a Baptist, used "to dip" rather than "to baptize" in Bengali. This same translation was used by Baptist missionaries in a total of thirty-one languages, including Chinese and Sanskrit, languages spoken by one half the world population.[30] In 1836 the BFBS refused to print any Bibles with the Carey translation of "dip" until they be changed to read the loan word from the Greek, "baptize." Biting explained: "For twenty-six years the society (BFBS), without question, continued to appropriate for printing and circulating the very versions that they rejected in 1836 on account

---

27   Daniel Lortsch, *Histoire de la Bible en France*, accessed March 5, 2005, http://www.bibliquest.org/Lortsch/Lortsch-Histoire_Bible_France-3.htm.

28   Lortsch, *Histoire de la Bible*.

29   Taylor, *Wings for the Word*, 27.

30   C. C. Biting, *Bible Societies and the Baptists* (1883; Philadelphia: American Baptist Publications, 1897), 15–16.

of prejudice and clamor."[31] The result of this battle was the eventual forming of the Baptist "American and Foreign Bible Society," which later dissolved.

The ABS began to face disagreements over the Greek New Testament texts used in translation. This ongoing debate has morphed into two camps. One adhered to the use of the Textus Receptus, Byzantine Text, or Greek Orthodox Text. This first camp includes King James–only advocates. The second camp prefers the use of the Nestle-Aland Text, UBS Text, Critical Edition Text, or Eclectic Text. Twentieth-century debates and scholarship seem to have shifted evangelicalism from the first camp to the second camp, although there seems to be a resurgence of interest in the first camp in the beginning of the twenty-first century.

The twentieth century could rightly be called the century of ecumenism. The ABS has not been immune to these pressures. The call for interchurch cooperation has moved even beyond Christianity to interreligious cooperation in some circles. Meanwhile 1968[32] and 1987[33] mark a new day for interchurch relationship for the United Bible Society (formed in 1946 by the BFBS, ABS, National Bible Society of Scotland, and the Netherlands Bible Society). The impact of these ecumenical decisions on the ministry of the ABS will be felt in years to come.

Third, the work of the BFBS was met by antagonism from the Roman Catholic Church as early as 1816. Pope Pius VII warned the Archbishop of Mogilev in Belarus of the dangers of heretics editing Bibles in the vulgar tongue in an 1816 letter, "Magno et Acerbo":

---

31   Biting, *Bible Societies and the Baptists*, 17.
32   "Guiding Principles for Interconfessional Cooperation in Translating the Bible." In Thomas F. Stransky, C.S.P., and John B. Sheerin, C.S.B., eds. *Doing the Truth in Charity: Statements of Pope Paul VI, Popes John Paul I, John Paul II, and the Secretariat for Promoting Christian Unity 1964–1980.* (New York: Paulist, 1982), 159–69.
33   "Guidelines for Interconfessional Cooperation in Translating the Bible. The New Revised Edition Rome," accessed October 29, 2020, http://www.vatican.va/roman_curia/pontifical_councils/chrstuni/general-docs/rc_pc_chrstuni_doc_19871116_guidelines-bible_en.html.

This is why the heretics with their biased and abominable machinations had the custom, in editing Bibles in vulgare tongue (of which the astonishing diversity and contradictions results that they accuse and tear each one the other), to seek to insidiously impose their respective errors by wrapping them of the magnificence of the most holy divine Word.[34]

Pius IX continued in the same vein:

IV. SOCIALISM, COMMUNISM, SECRET SOCI-ETIES, BIBLICAL SOCIETIES, CLERICO-LIBERAL SOCIETIES: Pests of this kind are frequently reprobated in the severest terms in the Encyclical 'Qui pluribus,' Nov. 9, 1846, Allocution 'Quibus quantisque,' April 20, 1849, Encyclical 'Noscitis et nobiscum,' Dec. 8, 1849, Allocution 'Singulari quadam,' Dec. 9, 1854, Encyclical 'Quanto conficiamur,' Aug. 10, 1863.[35]

This antagonism was never felt to the same degree in the U.S. because of the early founders of the ABS. Their decisions sheltered U.S. evangelicalism from the difficulties encountered in Catholic lands across the world.

Meanwhile, even with all these problems encountered and ongoing, the Bible remains the only spiritual weapon available to the evangelist. The ABS was a supernatural gift to the United States as it grew from seventeen states to fifty. The chapter will end with some practical tips on the use of the Bible in evangelism.

USE OF THE BIBLE IN EVANGELISM

The Word of God is truly "lively and mighty in operation" (Heb. 4:12, English Geneva). It alone convicts of sin, righteousness, and judgment.

---

34 Pius VII, Letter "*Magno et Acerbo*" (1816) to the Archibishop of Mogilev [Belarus]; DS 2711.

35 Pius IX, "Syllabus of Errors" (Rome, 1864); accessed October 21, 2005, http://www.papalencyclicals.net/Pius09/p9syll.htm.

In fact, it is not too much to say that outside of the power of the Scriptures exerted upon the soul of man, no divine work can be accomplished. Here follows several principles related to the Bible in evangelism—these principles were and are the heartbeat of the early Bible Society Movement.

First, use the words of the Bible in gospel conversations. This brings God into the discussion. His Holy Spirit works in, with, and by God's words (in a mother tongue translation). When the sentences and phrases from the Bible are used in witness and preaching the Holy Spirit is invited to do his work in the hearts of the hearers.

Second, God's primary work through the word is described by Jesus as "convicting." The Holy Spirit delves deeply below the surface of the rational mind. He works on the inner heart of man. "When He comes," said Jesus, "He will convict the world of sin, and of righteousness, and of judgment" (John 16:8 NKJV). God's Spirit dwells within God's words and he does his work.

Third, God prepares some people for a "hearing of faith" (Gal. 3:2, 5). The evangelist naturally desires that all people to whom he speaks would be saved—which is also the revealed will of God (2 Peter 3:8–9). The truth is that only some will be saved. Paul wrote, "I have become all things to all men, that I might by all means save some" (1 Cor. 9:22 NKJV). When God's Word is used in witness, some are prepared for a hearing of faith.

Fourth, God allows others to persist in a carnal hearing. God uses his Word as a winnowing fork. It separates the wheat from the chaff. Some have a carnal hearing of the gospel and their response is to mock, or remain disinterested, preoccupied with other things, and nonchalant. Yet God is not idle. He is at work!

The powerful Word of God has truly made an impact on this nation. The United States has been called a land of Bibles. Samuel Mills, Elias Boudinot, and the ABS played a pivotal role in accomplishing this result. There have been problems. The enemy has sown tares among the wheat. But the result of the Bible Society Movement and the evangelism that followed in its wake have led to abundant spiritual prosperity.

CHAPTER 9

THE REVIVAL *of* 1800 *on the* AMERICAN FRONTIER

Robert Matz

While revivals in the colleges and churches of the east spread, the spiritual state of the newly settled western states declined. Following the American Revolution, twelve states were added to the original thirteen. As the land west of the Appalachian Mountains was opened to settlers, the territories of Kentucky and Tennessee exploded with people. Yet religion was obviously not a priority for these settlers. Between 1790 and 1800, Kentucky grew by 300 percent or nearly 150,000 people; yet the few Methodist, Baptist, and Presbyterian preachers in the region were largely ineffective. Their churches and memberships were all either stagnant or in decline.[1]

Additionally, as the population of the United States shifted westward, those who had something to get away from led the way. Kentucky struggled under the weight of a growing populace, of whom few were members of organized religion. Many in Kentucky were escaped convicts from the east. Perhaps the most lawless location in the state was Logan County. Orthodox Christianity had largely been forsaken. The few ministers in the county were either of a poor

---

1 John B. Boles, *The Great Revival: Beginnings of the Bible Belt* (Lexington: The University Press of Kentucky, 1996), 43.

quality or advocated universalism.[2] The county soon became known as "Rogue's Harbor." Peter Cartwright, who grew up in the area during this time, describes what it was like:

> Here many refugees, from almost all parts of the Union fled to escape justice or punishment; for although there was law, yet it could not be executed, and it was a desperate state of society. Murderers, horse thieves, highway robbers, and counterfeiters fled here until they combined and actually formed a majority. The honest and civil part of the citizens would prosecute these wretched bandits, but they would swear each other clear; and they really put all law at defiance, and carried on such desperate violence and outrage that the honest part of the citizens seemed to be driven to the necessity of uniting and combining together, and taking the law into their own hands, under the name of Regulators (sic). [3]

While man's depravity was fully visible on the western frontier, it is important to note that most of these settlers had not forsaken God entirely. They were, by and large, the descendants of Scottish-Presbyterians. Most had moved west to find a better life on the open land. While they had relegated God to a lower place of importance, their basic conception of God was still unmistakably Protestant. Indeed, "the common view of religion held by most settlers paralleled that of early Puritan immigrants. Deeply affected by their environment, they were not about to discard a source of strength and comfort. They felt themselves deeply affected by the direct sovereignty of God, who had somehow slipped out of the bonds of covenant and moral government to meet them face to face."[4] As a result, the people of Rogue's Harbor were open to the preaching of revival.

---

2   Boles, *The Great Revival.*
3   Peter Cartwright. *Autobiography of Peter Cartwright, the Backwoods Preacher* (New York: Carlton and Porter, 1856), 29–30.
4   John Opie Jr., *Conversion and Revivalism: An Internal History from Jonathan Edwards through Charles Grandinson Finney* (Ph.D. diss., The University of Chicago, 1963), 168.

CAUSES OF REVIVAL AND
METHODOLOGIES EMPLOYED

Many factors have been blamed for the failure of religion in the West to keep pace with the rapid growth of the populace. Some have contended that the interdenominational infighting over issues such as foot-washing, baptism, and hymns had hindered revival. Additionally, poor preaching and an overreliance on Calvinistic doctrine about God's sovereignty were blamed for standing in the way of genuine evangelistic work.[5] Yet while there is a consensus about the theological causes of the decline of religion, the actual cause of the revival is disputed.

Secular historian John Boles argues that the revival "was an unusual combination of personality, theology, time, society, and coincidence." He notes that around 1796, one county in Kentucky— Logan County—had been bombarded with evangelistic Presbyterian ministers. [6] Opie supplements this idea with his commentary on what the people of Kentucky were like. He states that despite having wandered from their faith they still viewed the world through a lens where "God constantly intervened in the affairs of the frontiersman, breaking men down or raising them up according to his seemingly arbitrary will." As a result, "The directness, quickness and extensiveness of revivalist conversion did not seem an unusual experience, but fitting to the conditions of existence on the frontier."[7] Despite this fact, Boles must still concede that these revivals and their ministers were committed to prayer and that it was within these times of prayer that God seemed most active.[8]

While the religious heritage of the frontiersmen certainly made revival easier, simply dismissing any supernatural elements to it, as Boles and Opie seem to do, is presumptuous. Indeed, the list of convenient coincidences needed for this Western Revival to occur

---

5   Boles, *The Great Revival*, 45.
6   Boles, *The Great Revival*, 38, 47–48.
7   Opie Jr., *Conversion and Revivalism*, 168.
8   Boles, *The Great Revival*, 38, 47–48.

is beyond the pale. For example, the Western revival could not have occurred without the eastern revival predating it by a couple of years. Specifically, William Warren Sweet points to the close connection between the college revivals of the east and the ministers of the west. He notes that the revivals at Hampden-Sydney and Washington colleges led these schools to "train a ministry for the new west."[9] Thus, the revivalists of the West were educated men from the schools of the east.

Additionally, numerous new methodologies were employed throughout the Western phase of the Revival of 1800. Historian Paulus Scharpff notes that the Methodists had just developed a particularly effective method in spreading the revival westward. Their newly organized system of circuit riding between churches was an excellent technique on the frontier where people lived far apart. As a result, several small churches were able to function with a single pastor even when separated by a great number of miles. The pastor would ride between the churches and preach in each church once per month. As a result, Methodists were able to spread out over a great swath of land and spread the revival message.[10]

KEY LEADER IN THE REVIVAL MOVEMENT

Returning to Rogue's Harbor, one man was used to turn the county. Boles notes, "the leading personality in this particular beginning [of revival] was James McGready."[11] McGready was a product of the "Log College" movement of the first Great Awakening. He was a Presbyterian, but only mildly so. Specifically, he rejected high Calvinism's understanding of election. For him, election meant that God knew who would eventually achieve salvation.[12] For this reason, McGready advocated the use "of every possible means to alarm and awaken

---

9   Sweet, *Revivalism in America*, 119.
10 Paulus Scharpff, *History of Evangelism: Three Hundred Years of Evangelism in Germany, Great Britain, and the United States of America*, trans. Helga Henry (Grand Rapids: Wm. B. Eerdmans Publishing Co., 1966).
11 Boles, *The Great Revival*, 36.
12 Boles, *The Great Revival*, 41.

Christless sinners from their security." His motivation was clear; while acknowledging that his denominational brethren may mock him, McGready argues powerfully "do this we must, or we will be the worst murders; the blood of sinners will be required at our hands—their damnation will lie at our door."[13]

He migrated to Kentucky from the Carolinas after leading a growing (although controversial) ministry there. While being doctrinally astute and homiletically gifted, McGready was physical ugly. In fact, he was so ugly, according to Orr, that he attracted attention. People would listen to what McGready said simply because they thought someone that ugly must have something interesting to say.[14] Despite the interest he could generate with his looks, over the course of his first four years in ministry he saw little fruit. Therefore, he committed himself and his churches to regular prayer.[15] He would bring his three churches together every summer to pray and prepare for revival. They did this for three straight years before anything happened.[16]

THE REVIVAL EXPERIENCE:
WHAT ACTUALLY HAPPENED?

In July 1800, the revival began in earnest in the West with a "remarkable outbreak of religious eruption in Logan County."[17] The distinguishing event of this revival was the camp meeting. McGready called together the several hundred members of his three churches. On the fourth and final day of the meeting, two visiting brothers—one Methodist, one Presbyterian—rose to speak after the sermon concluded. An emotional outbreak overtook the service and

---

13   James McGready, *The Posthumous Works of the Reverend and Pious James M'gready: Late Minister of the Gospel in Henderson, Ky.* (Nashville: J. Smith's Steam Press, 1831), 316–317.

14   J. Edwin Orr, "Prayer and Revival" (lecture, National Prayer Congress, Dallas, TX, Oct. 26–29, 1976), accessed March 28, 2012, http://www.jedwinorr.com/prayer_revival.htm.

15   McGready, *The Posthumous Works*, xvi.

16   Boles, *The Great Revival*, 53.

17   Boles, *The Great Revival*, 36.

it quickly became clear to all that God was at work.[18] McGready describes the scene as follows:

> After sermon Mr. Rankin gave a solemn exhortation—the congregation was then dismissed; but the people all kept their seats for a considerable space, whilst awful solemnity appeared in the countenances of a large majority. Presently several persons under deep convictions broke forth in a loud outcry—many fell to the ground and lay powerless, groaning, praying and crying for mercy. As I passed through the multitude, a woman, lying in awful distress, called me to her. Said she, "I lived in your congregation in Carolina; I was a professor, and often went to the communion; but I was deceived; I have no religion; I am going to hell." In another place an old grey headed man lay in an agony of distress, addressing his weeping wife and children in such language as this: "We are all going to hell together; we have lived prayerless, ungodly lives; the work of our souls is yet to begin; we must get religion, or we will all be damned. But time would fail me to mention every instance of this kind."[19]

After the meeting dismissed, McGready immediately began making plans for a second one. Crowds massed outside one of McGready's churches. People came from more than one hundred miles away to attend the meeting and see what was happening.[20] Multiple denominations were represented. Within a few months, camp meetings had sprung up all over Tennessee and Kentucky.

The camp meetings themselves actually were a product of lowland Presbyterianism. Presbyterians rarely took communion, but when they did, they had:

---

18   Boles, *The Great Revival*, 54.
19   McGready, *The Posthumous Works*, xi–xii.
20   Boles, *The Great Revival*, 55–56; and Malcolm McDow and Alvin L. Reid, *Firefall: How God Shaped History through Revivals* (Nashville: Broadman & Holman, 1997), 237.

a sacramental meeting consist of several successive days, including a Sabbath. At this meeting it is common to have a plurality of ministers. . . . The meeting begins either Friday or Saturday, and closes Monday; Sabbath is the communion. Preaching everyday is at the same place, which is either a meeting-house, or a stand in some piece of woods; and often where there is a meeting-house, the house is so small, and the assembly so large, that they have to go to the woods. The congregation consists of the people of the congregation, where the meeting is held, and numbers, from others round about. . . . Some of these come 25, and others 30 miles, purposely to attend the meeting.[21]

This communion meal would frequently bring about significant change in the attitude of the people. Schmidt notes that after taking communion on Sunday, the group would experience deeper and more powerful meetings on the following closing day of the revivals. The sacramental element was frequently cited as the reason for such.[22] With Baptists[23] and Methodists joining in, the word quickly spread about the unusual occurrences taking place at these meetings. It must be noted, however, that these meetings were prone to excess. John Christian states that common occurrences at these meetings included different psychological or physical manifestations, known as "the falling, jerking, rolling, running, dancing, barking, and visions and trances."[24]

---

21   Isaac Reed, *The Christian Traveller in Five Parts Including Nine Years and Eighteen Thousand Miles* (New York: J. & J. Harper, 1828), 212. as quoted in Leigh Eric Schmidt, *Holy Fairs: Scottish Communions and American Revivals in the Early Modern Period* (Princeton, NJ: Princeton University Press, 1990), n.p.

22   Leigh Eric Schmidt, *Holy Fairs: Scotland and the Making of American Revivalism*, 2nd ed. (Grand Rapids: Wm. B. Eerdmans Publishing Co., 2001), Chapter 2.

23   Although, Baptists would often go off and have communion at a separate gathering.

24   John T. Christian, "Chapter IV: The Revival of 1800," in *Of the United States From the First Settlement of the Country to the Year 1845*, vol. 2 of A History of the Baptists: Together with Some Account of Their Principles and Practices (Nashville: Sunday School Board of the Southern Baptist Convention, 1922), chapter 3.

RESULTS OF THE REVIVAL OF 1800 IN THE WEST

From the Revival of 1800, modern southern evangelicalism was birthed.[25] The number of Baptists, Methodists, and Presbyterians skyrocketed.[26] Hundreds of thousands became Christians. The revival would spread throughout the South into Georgia. Indeed, many attribute the modern Bible Belt to the Revival of 1800 on the Western Frontier.[27]

Not only were churches transformed numerically, they also saw a significant shift in their theology. Prior to the revival, most had an understanding of salvation closely tied to Scottish Calvinism. The revival ushered in a hybrid form of theology that affirmed both Calvinistic and Arminian tenets. Whereas the Calvinism held by the Presbyterians only offered salvation to a few, the Methodist view of free grace[28] was more hopeful because the sinner was part of the conversion process. Charles Johnson summarizes the shift taking place when he states:

> If conversion did take place, it had to be the result of each individual's personal consciousness and should be visibly demonstrated. The democratic nature of the dogma appealed to the frontiersman, who could understand an idea if he could feel it emotionally. At the mourner's bench he would experience complete repentance and thus at a definite time and place be cleansed of his taint of sin, "washed clean in the blood of the Lamb." While an integral

---

25 Dickson D Bruce, Jr., *And They All Sang Hallelujah: Plain-Folk Camp-Meeting Religion, 1800–1845* (Knoxville: University of Tennessee Press, 1974).

26 Ellen Eslinger, *Citizens of Zion: The Social Origins of Camp Meeting Revivalism* (Knoxville: University of Tennessee Press, 1999), 182.

27 W. L. Muncy, Jr., *A History of Evangelism in the United States* (Kansas City, KS: Central Seminary, 1945), 84.

28 Of particular note at this point is the shift that occurred amongst the Calvinistic denominations. While a Presbyterian, McGready recognized that his theology had turned its back on classic Calvinism. He even admitted as much, then stated that he didn't care if he was called a Methodist. See Boles, *The Great Revival*, 41.

component of this seeming miracle was the factor of man's active role of choice, "justification by faith" was considered an act of God, the sinner himself having no control over the process.[29]

Another significant theological shift that occurred along the Western frontier was the newfound emphasis on Christian experience. Prior to the Revival of 1800 in the West, revival meetings had been characterized more by intellectual assent than by emotional response. For example, leaders of the eastern revival which predated the revival on the frontier by only a few years discouraged emotional response.[30] This emotionalism on the frontier has led some to challenge the genuineness of this revival movement.[31]

Closely tied to the emotional outburst that occurred were the unusual phenomena that accompanied them. For nearly a century, some scholars have been working to discredit the legitimacy of these phenomena. Catherine Cleveland attempts to explain what occurred. She argues that some those of those gripped by these strange phenomena were actually experiencing seizures as a result of the protracted nature of the meetings in the excessive summer heat. Others, desiring to touched by the Spirit, faked it. Still others were hypnotized by the meeting as a whole. [32]

While it would be simple to reject the revival as God's work because of these excesses, such a position is unwarranted. Note that the experiential excesses of the Western Frontier stand in stark contrast to the methodical removal of sin within the Eastern colleges. This contrast serves to rebut pointedly the idea that the Revival of 1800 was nothing

---

29 Charles Albert Johnson, *The Frontier Camp Meeting: Religion's Harvest Time* (Dallas: Southern Methodist University Press, 1955), 175–76.

30 For example, Yale president and revival leader Timothy Dwight emphasized emotional restraint through academic reflection during the revivals of Yale from 1795–1802. McDow and Reid, *Firefall 2.0,* 231.

31 See McDow and Reid, *Firefall 2.0,* 245 for a more comprehensive discussion of this factor.

32 Catherine C. Cleveland, *The Great Revival in the West, 1797–1805* (Chicago: University of Chicago Press, 1916), 115–127.

more than purely an emotional experience. As Orr notes, while "Anti-evangelical sociologists seem to delight in stressing the emotional extravagances of the awakenings on the far frontiers . . . ignoring the fact that the frontiersmen were generally illiterate and that at the same time in the college towns there were occurring deep and thorough religious revivals without any extravagance whatsoever. To this day, the emotional response of people is affected by temperament and education."[33]

Additionally, as Sweet notes, the argument that the Western Revival can simply be dismissed as an exercise in emotional excesses is far too simplistic. Methodist circuit riders frequently sold catechisms, religious books, and Bibles. Presbyterian evangelists moonlighted as school teachers.[34] Christian education and not simply emotional response stood at the center of this revival movement.

WHY DOES REVIVAL END?

In one sense, the Revival of 1800 would continue on for another fifty years[35]; yet in another sense the revival would be over within a few years. In the West, the meetings themselves became more sectarian in nature and would wind down and lose their initial fervency by as early as 1804. By the time of the War of 1812 the nation was entering a new, albeit brief, period of spiritual decline.

In studying the cause of the decline, a few final observations will be made about the causes of revival. For the participants of the Revival of 1800, prayer obviously played a key role. The movement was birthed in the camp prayer meetings mentioned above. The parishioners attending these revival meetings were genuinely seeking their God and seeking to discern His will.

---

33 J. Edwin Orr, *Campus Aflame: A History of Evangelical Awakenings in Collegiate Communities*, new and rev. ed., ed. Richard Owen Roberts (Wheaton, IL.: International Awakening Press, 1994), 40.

34 Sweet, *Revivalism in America,* 134.

35 Well-attended protracted revival meetings still occurred throughout the West well into the 1840s. Awakenings continued at the colleges throughout the presidencies of the leaders mentioned above. Further, Finney's revival ministry of the 1820s and '30s is an outgrowth of these revivals.

Another cause of the revival was interdenominational coopera-tion. The peak of denominational cooperation was reached in 1802. Presbyterians and Methodists held communion services together, while the Baptists only separated themselves during "sacramental seasons." By 1804, theological and ecclesiastical differences, together with complaints over proselytizing, separated the churches. The Great Revival declined by 1805.[36]

Further, a strong emphasis on personal holiness came out of these revivals. Whereas prior to the revivals, religion was seen as the enemy of the state, after the revival the church became a friend of the state, bringing about social reforms. Yet once opposition to Christianity declined, there seemed to be a corresponding decline of religious fervency. Other issues began to take precedence, such as the looming war with Britain.[37] As a result Christian revival, at least for a season, was pushed to the side.

Fourth, the leaders who were raised up stood up for revival. They risked personal safety in order to make sure the gospel message was proclaimed and protected from its critics. Once these leaders faded from roles of prominence, the revival itself began to fade.

---

36 Opie, *Conversion and Revivalism*.
37 J. Edwin Orr, *The Eager Feet: Evangelical Awakenings, 1790–1830* (Chicago: Moody Press, 1975), 76–77.

CHAPTER 10

J. WILBUR CHAPMAN: EVANGELIST *and* PASTOR

Jeff Farmer

No study of the history of evangelism in the twentieth century United States of America would be complete without an examination of John Wilbur Chapman. Chapman has been described as "the pastor evangelist."[1] He was an urban pastor and evangelist who refined revival techniques to such an extent, D. L. Moody described him as "the greatest evangelist in the country"[2]; and Billy Graham noted, "the last great revival meeting held in this queen city of the Green Mountain State took place when the famed J. Wilbur Chapman preached here in 1908."[3]

Chapman was born June 17, 1859 in Richmond, Indiana, to middle-class parents. He attended churches and Sunday schools throughout his childhood. Chapman stated that he was unsure of the exact date of his conversion, and that the clearest moment he could recall occurred at Grace Methodist Church in Richmond. A guest speaker in his Sunday school offered an invitation. Though Chapman was reticent to stand, he was prompted when "Mrs. Binkley, his teacher,

---

1 Frank Beardsley, *Heralds of Salvation* (New York: American Tract Society, 1939), 9.
2 Dwight L. Moody, *The Family Call* (November 23, 1896), 8.
3 Billy Graham, *Boston Post*, Saturday, April 8, 1950.

put her hand under my elbow . . . and I stood up with the others. I do not know if this was the day of my conversion, but I do know it was the day of my acknowledgment of Christ."[4]

Chapman would later enroll in Oberlin College due to the influence of Charles Finney,[5] the second president of Oberlin College and a significant revivalist preacher. Finney died the year before Chapman matriculated at Oberlin, but his influence on Chapman was significant. Chapman wrote in his book, *Revivals and Missions*, "There can be nothing better said along this line than what Mr. Finney records in his Lectures on Revivals of Religion."[6] In fact, Chapman devoted an entire chapter of this book to Finney and called Finney "The Prince of Modern Revivalists."[7]

Chapman transferred to Lake Forest University in Chicago in 1877, where he became a colleague and collaborator with the evangelist B. Fay Mills. Chapman and Mills partnered for several years, seeking to find the most effective ways to bring people to "personal repentance and conversion."[8] While Mills later strayed into Unitarianism, his influence on Chapman is undeniable. Mills was instrumental in providing the framework for the simultaneous meeting for which Chapman later became famous.[9]

It was while at Lake Forest that Chapman first heard Moody preach. During one of Moody's meetings in Chicago, Chapman decided to go to the inquiry room to settle his concern of eternal security. Chapman noted:

> When the great evangelist called for the after-meeting I was one of the first to enter the room and to my great joy Mr. Moody came and sat down beside me. I confessed that I was

---

4   John C. Ramsay, *John Wilbur Chapman* (Boston: The Christopher Publishing House, 1962), 25.

5   Ramsay, *John Wilbur Chapman*.

6   J. Wilbur Chapman, *Revivals and Missions* (New York: Lentilhon & Company, 1900), 69.

7   Chapman, *Revivals and Missions*, 39.

8   William G. McLoughlin, Jr. *Modern Revivalism* (New York: The Ronald Press Company, 1959), 336.

9   John Junkin Francis and Charles B. Morrell, *Mill's Meetings Memorial Volume* (Cincinnati: Standard Publication Company, 1892), 180.

not quite sure I was saved. He handed me his opened Bible and asked me to read John 5:24. . . . He said to me: "Do you believe this?" I answered: "Certainly." He said: "Are you a Christian?" I replied: "Sometimes I think I am and again I am fearful." "Read it again," he said. Then he repeated his two questions and I had to answer as before. Then Mr. Moody seemed—it was an only time—to lose patience, and he spoke sharply: "Whom are you doubting?" and then it all came to me with startling suddenness. "Read it again," said Moody, and for the third time he asked: "Do you believe it?" I said: "Yes. Indeed I do." "Well are you a Christian?"—and I answered: "Yes Mr. Moody, I am." From that day to this I have never questioned my acceptance with God.[10]

Chapman later went to Lane Seminary, and served as pastor of a two-church pastorate in Liberty, IN and College Corner, OH. Next, he served the Old Dutch Reformed Church in Schuylerville, NY. Here Chapman's leadership in evangelism began to come forth. This was described in minutes of the church as "in those early days his evangelistic methods would arouse such a religious fervor that the membership in and the attendance at the church would show an immediate increase."[11] Chapman's success in Schuylerville led to the First Reformed Church of Albany, New York to extend a call to Chapman. Chapman then served in the urban setting of Albany, where the minutes of the church record the church experienced more than one hundred additions each year, regular evangelistic evening services, and special collections for the poor at each communion service.[12]

During his pastorate in Albany, Chapman began to spend significant time with Moody.[13] Based on Moody's recommendation,

---

10 Ford C. Ottman, *J. Wilbur Chapman* (New York: Doubleday, Page & Co., 1920), 29–30.
11 Ottman, *J. Wilbur Chapman*, 48.
12 Addison J. Hinman, *Our 250 Years, A Historical Sketch, First Reformed Church, Albany, N.Y.* (Albany, NY: C. F. Williams Press, 1899), 40–41.
13 Ottman, *J. Wilbur Chapman*, 56.

Chapman was named the director of the Winona Bible Conference at
Winona, IN. He served in this role for the next fourteen years. As the
director at Winona Lake, Chapman hosted many notable evangelists
including Sam Jones, R. A. Torrey, W. E. Biederwolf, Samuel Hadley,
Evangeline Booth, and Billy Sunday.[14]

In 1890, Chapman accepted a call to serve from Bethany Presbyterian Church in Philadelphia. During his first month at Bethany,
440 new members were brought into the church.[15] During this time,
he also worked with Moody and Mills as an associate evangelist. In
1892, Chapman sensed the call to "full-time" evangelistic work and
resigned from Bethany.[16] Two years later, Bethany issued a call to
Chapman. During his second pastorate at Bethany, the total Sunday
attendance in all departments was 12,000 people.[17]

The Fourth Presbyterian Church of New York offered a call to
Chapman in 1899. Chapman served as pastor until December 1903.
During this pastorate, Chapman was appointed to the position of
Presbyterian General Secretary of the Assembly's Committee on
Evangelism.[18] Fourth Presbyterian Church grew from 230 members
to 781 members during Chapman's pastorate. Once his workload
became too much, Chapman felt obliged to terminate his connection
with Fourth Presbyterian.[19]

From 1903 to 1910, Chapman organized and carried out a plan
of evangelism with the aid of fifty-six evangelists and various other
workers. This effort saw Chapman and his team conduct 10,597
evangelistic services in 470 cities. Chapman was forced to deny approximately one thousand requests for evangelistic meetings for lack
of evangelists.[20]

---

14   Ramsay, *John Wilbur Chapman*, 39–40.
15   Ramsay, *John Wilbur Chapman*, 42.
16   Ottman, *J. Wilbur Chapman*, 65.
17   Ottman, *J. Wilbur Chapman*, 67.
18   Ottman, *J. Wilbur Chapman*, 76. The original title for the position was Correspond-
     ing Secretary, but the name changed as the department grew. The duties were essen-
     tially the same.
19   Ottman, *J. Wilbur Chapman*, 76.
20   Ottman, *J. Wilbur Chapman*, 124–125.

During the years of 1904–1909, Chapman organized and developed the simultaneous method of evangelism.[21] In 1904, in Pittsburgh, Chapman conducted the first completely organized simultaneous revival. Thirteen denominations participated, representing five hundred churches, and more than two thousand made professions of faith.[22] Following this successful campaign, Chapman assembled his own evangelistic team, which crossed denominational lines. At the same time, Chapman continued his denominational service on the Presbyterian board.[23]

While conducting the simultaneous meetings, Chapman met Charles Alexander, a music evangelist. Alexander was asked to lead the music services of the Winona Lake Bible Conference in 1907. In 1908, he joined Chapman's evangelism team. Chapman and Alexander worked together conducting revivals around the globe for the next eleven years.[24]

Chapman died on Christmas Day, 1918, and was buried in Woodlawn Cemetery in New York City. On a plaque placed in the Fourth Presbyterian Church in Chapman's memory, an inscription sums up the ministry of J. Wilbur Chapman: "He that winneth souls is wise" (Proverbs 11:30).[25]

PASTORAL EVANGELISM

Chapman is significant in the history of evangelism in North America due to the contributions he made to modern revivalism. Chapman was one of many evangelists who followed Moody, and innovated revivalism to great effect into the twentieth century. He was very successful at implementing the simultaneous revival method. He promoted evangelism through his denomination in such a way that

---

21   Ottman, *J. Wilbur Chapman*, 311–313.
22   Macfarlane, "The Reviver of Revivalism," 19; J. Kennedy Maclean, *Chapman and Alexander* (New York: Revell and Company, 1915), 37.
23   Ramsay, *John Wilbur Chapman*, 52.
24   Mrs. Charles M. Alexander and J. Kennedy Maclean, *Charles M. Alexander* (London: Marshall Brothers, Ltd., 1920), 136.
25   Ramsay, *John Wilbur Chapman*, 210.

the evangelistic "movement swept like a tide beyond the area of the Presbyterian church."[26] He promoted evangelism in his denomination's seminaries and desired evangelism training in the seminary to prepare pastors and professional evangelists.[27]

Chapman was both a model of pastoral evangelism and a proponent for pastors to be evangelists. Chapman wrote, "To be an evangelistic minister . . . is to choose the best in this finest of all callings."[28] He continued:

> There is no greater need today than that the message of the minister should be evangelistic. . . . But if he is narrow in his views, selfish in his spirit, neglectful of his personal appeals for others to come to Christ, and if, with it all he does not in his preaching impress his hearers with the fact that he concerned that they should accept Christ and order their lives according to His teaching, then his experience will be sad indeed; for the door of opportunity will open, and he will fail to enter, the hour of crisis will strike, and he be deaf to its appeal.[29]

Ephesians 4 is an essential chapter for pastors to understand their calling. Specifically, Ephesians 4:11–13 (CSB) provides guidance: "And he himself gave some to be apostles, some prophets, some evangelists, some pastors and teachers, to equip the saints for the work of ministry, to build up the body of Christ, until we all reach unity in the faith and in the knowledge of God's Son, growing into maturity with a stature measured by Christ's fullness." Essentially, the calling of the pastor is to equip the body (the church) to do the work of ministry. Pastors do that by teaching, modeling, and providing the

---

26 Ottman, *J. Wilbur Chapman*, 124–125.
27 J. Wilbur Chapman, "The Limitations of Professional Evangelism," *The Homiletic Review*, vol. 35 (April 1898), 312.
28 J. Wilbur Chapman, *The Minister's Handicap*, second edition (New York: American Tract Society, 1918), 56.
29 Chapman, *The Minister's Handicap*, 57.

opportunities for the church to do ministry. Pastors set the direction and the pace for evangelism in the local church. No one else in the church will be more evangelistic than the pastor. Therefore, the pastor must be intentional in personal and church evangelism.

INTENTIONALITY

A recent study of the personal evangelism practices of smaller membership church pastors was conducted by the Caskey Center for Church Excellence and the Billy Graham Center for Evangelism,[30] in partnership with about a dozen denominations. The results provide a snapshot of the personal evangelism habits of smaller membership church pastors. A comparison between the top 20 percent of churches that retained new commitments with the bottom 50 percent of churches reveal the key to reaching a community with the gospel through intentionality in personal evangelism, creating a climate of evangelism within the church, and leading members to make disciples.

Intentionally evangelistic pastors (top 20%) are more likely to see an increase in the numbers of attenders in the worship services and are also more likely to see new commitments to serve Jesus Christ as Savior. In Matthew 9:37–38 (ESV), Jesus said, "The harvest is plentiful, but the laborers are few; therefore pray earnestly to the Lord of the harvest to send out laborers into his harvest." Missional Christians who see their very lives as mission fields are the laborers the Lord sends in answer to this prayer. Pastors must lead their congregations to be diligent in this endeavor. As pastors are intentional in personal evangelism, God provides the harvest.

Perhaps the greatest indicator of a pastor's effectiveness in personal evangelism is intentionality. A pastor can very easily get caught up in addressing the needs of the congregation. "One-stop-shop" pastors

---

30   Jeffrey Farmer, et al., "Personal Evangelism in the Small Church: A Sample of 1500 of Pastors in Smaller-Membership Evangelical Churches," Caskey Center for Church Excellence, Billy Graham Center for Evangelism at Wheaton, and Lifeway Research. Presented at the Southern Baptist Research Fellowship, New Orleans Baptist Theological Seminary, New Orleans, September 21, 2017.

already feel overwhelmed, overworked, and underresourced. In larger churches, the pastor fights the urge to delegate as much responsibility to associate pastors. For all pastors (and believers for that matter), the need to prioritize often leads to the pastor prioritizing those things that keep him employed rather than what is most important.

Intentionally evangelistic pastors have developed the discipline of sharing the gospel on a weekly basis. In the Caskey study, three out of four pastors responded that they attempted to share their faith at least once a week, but the difference in the most evangelistic and least was clear. Among those who were most evangelistic, 87.3 percent of the pastors intentionally shared their faith at least once a week, and 97.9 percent attempted to share the gospel at least once a month. Those who were least evangelistic were not nearly as intentional. Of the lowest 50 percent of churches, 65.9 percent reported weekly attempts to share their faith, and 91.6 percent made a monthly attempt.

Pastors who are bold, especially around other members of the congregation, model for others what it looks like to witness. It could be as simple as asking someone how you can pray for them, but looking and engaging with opportunities for spiritual dialogue is critical. A pastor must think about where to frequently meet with lay leaders and volunteers. It helps to choose places where you can model boldness for the gospel so others can see you do it, and thus be inspired to boldness themselves.

Pastors who are intentionally evangelistic also invest in relationships with non-Christians throughout their lives. In the survey, Caskey found it encouraging that eight out of ten pastors spent time with non-Christians in order to make friends and share the gospel at least once a month. Nearly 60 percent of pastors intentionally blocked out time in their calendars to be outside the church office to share their faith with non-Christians. But those who were seeing the greatest conversions said they made time to be in their community at a rate of 71.3 percent. The bottom 50 percent of churches reported making time only 49.6 percent of the time.

John Manning, former pastor of Spindle City Vineyard Church in Cohoes, NY, described how he led his church members to set up chairs in the community and offer prayers for people. In one instance, a man named Patrick had asked for prayer, and through that prayer, God revealed himself and Patrick made a commitment to Christ.

Another way to be intentional in personal evangelism is to actively consider the mission field right outside your own door. Pastors who openly invest in relationships with those in proximity to them and their family are modeling to their congregation what being missional looks like every day. Loving and caring for local schools, sports teams, and neighborhood needs are all ways to purposefully invest in those whom God has placed in proximity to pastors and will have lasting impacts on small church congregations. It is hard for small church pastors to hide!

Intentionally evangelistic pastors are intentional about asking the non-Christian to commit to Christ after hearing the gospel, but they don't necessarily do it every time. While 75 percent of pastors shared their faith once a week, only 48 percent asked someone to commit to Christ after hearing the gospel once a week. When adding in the "once a month" frequency, the percentage of pastors grew to 75 percent. For those with the most effective evangelism, 88.3 percent of the intentionally evangelistic pastors reported asking a person to commit to Christ at least monthly, compared to 66.5 percent of the pastors in the bottom 50 percent of churches.

The Bible tells us to be bold with our witness, and pastors who exemplify boldness to their people will see it multiplied in their context. Doing this intentionally in front of lay leaders and new believers will also solidify and form a culture of mission and evangelism.

PRAYER

The most productive witnesses for Christ are those who devote significant attention to prayer. I often tell my students, "If evangelism is a car, prayer is the fuel." Prayer is so important for the believer who is engaged in gospel conversations. It aligns our hearts and minds with God. It makes us receptive to the Holy Spirit, who speaks through us to proclaim the gospel message. Believers can have all the evangelistic training, skill, and opportunity at hand, but without prayer, the power just will not be there. Ken Hemphill cautioned, "Prayer is in no way a squeaky wheel designed to manipulate God into remembering us. . . . [P]rayer is not about answers. Prayer is about reward."[31] The reward is being brought into the Father's presence.

What is prayer evangelism? It is praying for the souls of the lost people in the world. What is church prayer evangelism? It is a group of believers gathered in unity (Matt. 18:19–20), being taught how to pray (Luke 11:1), and praying in faith (Matt. 21:22; Mark 11:24) for the lost (Rom. 10:1–3; 1 Tim. 2:1–8)—who are their "neighbors" (Luke 10:25–37)—lovingly by name (Exod. 33:17; Isa. 43:1), regularly and persistently (Luke 18:1–8), and recording the answers and building faith (1 Chron. 16:4).

Why does prayer evangelism work? Because prayer aligns our hearts with the heart and mind of God. We do not pray so that God would know what we want or need. We pray so that we might know God. Prayer wrestles against the powers and principalities (Eph. 6:10–20) that keep people in spiritual bondage (Eph. 2:1–4; 4:17–19), and which can deceive them away from the truth (1 Tim. 4:1–4). Prayer also opens people's spiritual eyes (Eph. 1:17–19; Col. 1:9) and assists with the Holy Spirit's work of convicting them of sin, righteousness, and judgment (John 16:8). We are instructed to pray in faith and expect answers (Matt. 21:22; Mark 11:24). The Scriptures tell us to pray "believing we have received" (1 John 5:14–15). Faith and holy expectation reach heaven. Finally, we are to pray lovingly by name for people. Names are important to God who knows us by name and redeems us by name (Exod. 33:17; Isa. 43:1), and for some reason have great power in the spiritual realm. Prayer that is directed personally and lovingly, in faith, on the basis of redemption of a soul, is powerful.

Instruction in prayer is often neglected in the church. Perhaps church leaders believe that prayer is a discipline that should be caught rather than taught. I believe that both modeling and instruction

---

31   Ken Hemphill, *The Prayer of Jesus: The Promise and Power of Living in the Lord's Prayer* (Nashville: Broadman & Holman, 2001), 10.

should be pursued. Kirk Hadaway, a noted church growth expert, noted, "Growing congregations are not only evangelistic and outreach oriented. They also place a greater emphasis on prayer."[32] Essentially, evangelistic and growing churches emphasize prayer as much or more than evangelism training or outreach efforts. Hemphill indicts the modern church's lack of prayer as an indication for declining churches: "We spend more time praying to keep dying saints who are prepared to die out of heaven than we do to keep sinners out of hell. There is little passion to our praying and little confidence that it really does matter."[33] In order for the church to accomplish its purpose, it must help its members be more effective prayers.

In addition to preaching on the topic of prayer or teaching a Bible study on prayer, church leaders should schedule prayer times and events. These can include prayer chains, prayer partners, prayer groups, seasons of prayer for certain occasions, the development of prayer rooms, prayer retreats, prayer request cards, and prayer walking. The goal is to create an environment of prayer within the church to enable the church to reach out to the world.

Personal Prayer Evangelism Strategies

While praying within the context of the local church is highly important, all believers own the commission to make disciples. Therefore, all believers should develop a personal strategy of evangelistic prayer. Two strategies covered in the chapter are the *Oikos* Prayer Strategy and the Lighthouse of Prayer Strategy.

Oikos *Prayer Strategy*

The *Oikos* Prayer Strategy is a simple approach to develop a prayer list of those people within one's sphere of influence who are not Christ-followers. *Oikos* is the Greek term for "household." For the purpose of this prayer strategy, *oikos* refers to all the people within a person's sphere of influence. The steps to develop an *Oikos* Prayer list are simple.

---

32   C. Kirk Hadaway, *Church Growth Priniciples* (Nashville: Broadman Press, 1991), 163.
33   Ken Hemphill, *The Antioch Effect* (Nashville: Broadman & Holman, 1994), 61.

Begin by setting aside approximately two hours to prayerfully develop your list. Pray that God would bring people to mind who are within your sphere of influence—people you know but are not sure whether they are believers or not. Spend the next two hours writing down the names of everyone who comes to mind. The only people to exclude from your list are those people of whom you are absolutely certain of their testimonies. If you end up having a Christ-follower on your list, that is fine. I doubt any believer would be upset that you are praying for their walk with Christ. Strive to have at least one hundred names on your list.

Once you have your list of one hundred or more people, pray for the people on the list each day. You do not have to pray for the entire list each day; pray for as many as you feel led. I tend to pray for about ten people per day. Pray that God would reveal himself to these people, and that they would be receptive to hearing and believing the gospel of Jesus Christ. Pray for the Christ-followers who interact with these people every day.

The next step is to select three to five people each week and find an opportunity to have a gospel conversation with them. Then, boldly proclaim the gospel to these people. If you find that one of the people on your list professes to be a Christian, ask him/her to share his/her testimony with you. Christ-followers learn to share the gospel across contexts when they are familiar with different testimonies. As you listen to the testimony, pray for discernment. Many times, people profess to be Christian but they do not have an appropriate understanding of what that means. Sometimes, some will say they are Christian because they grew up attending a church. Once I had someone tell me he was a Christian because he was an American citizen. If the person is legitimately a believer, celebrate his/her story and encourage one another to faithfully proclaim the gospel. If not, share the gospel.

As people on your list become Christ-followers, note the date and the circumstances in your prayer journal. This is always a good practice so that you can read back over the answered prayers at a later date. Whenever I am discouraged, there is great comfort in reading my personal accounts of God answering my prayers.

Finally, as you pray through your list, share the gospel, and meet people, keep adding to the list. The *Oikos* Prayer List is not a static, one-time document. It is dynamic. Add people as you meet them; remove people once they are saved.

Lighthouse of Prayer Strategy[34]

In Matthew 5:14–16 (NASB), Jesus said, "You are the light of the world. A city set on a hill cannot be hidden; nor do people light a lamp and put it under a basket, but on the lampstand, and it gives light to all who are in the house. Your light must shine before people in such a way that they may see your good works, and glorify your Father who is in heaven." The Lighthouse of Prayer Strategy is based on your house being a gospel light in your neighborhood. Begin by praying for your neighbors: across the street, to the right, to the left, and directly behind you. Pray that God will reveal himself to them, that they would be receptive to the gospel, and that you would have the opportunity to present the gospel and a Christ-honoring witness to them.

As you pray for these neighbors, look for opportunities to show God's love to them. Find ways to show that you care for them. Perhaps you could mow their lawn if they've been too busy to do so. Maybe you can take care of a pet or collect their mail. Bringing a hot meal when your neighbor is sick is a possibility. There are infinite ways to show that you care.

By praying and caring for your neighbors, you are building relationships and creating opportunities to have gospel conversations. Following the Prayer-Care-Share formula is a simple reminder to be incarnational with your neighbors. As those immediate neighbors become Christ-followers, expand your efforts to the next house out. As the light from the lighthouse penetrates further into the darkness, let your prayer efforts do the same.

---

34 Developed by Richard Krejcir and other staff members of Campus Crusade for Christ ©1985, 2004, www.intothyword.org.

OUTREACH

There are many ways for a pastor to lead his church to be evangelistic. A systematic outreach strategy must be implemented if the church is going to have sustained success at discipling the church to be evangelistic. One-on-one training is highly effective, but outreach allows the church members to see the body of Christ working together to reach the community with the gospel.

Outreach is the process by which a church connects with non-churched people in the community for the purpose of bringing those non-churched people into a relationship with Christ and active participation in discipleship in the church. Outreach includes evangelism with the lost, and the encouraging of believers who are not involved in a local church to begin to fellowship. Many churches use outreach as their front door, or as a marketing approach. Certainly, outreach should include those aspects, but I think the church would be better positioned by thinking of outreach as hospitality.

Hospitality is the relationship between a guest and a host. It entails the host receiving the guest with goodwill. Jesus's parable of the banquet in Luke 14 is a good place to think of church hospitality and outreach. In verses 21b–23 (NASB1995), Jesus shared, "Then the head of the household became angry and said to his slave, 'Go out at once into the streets and lanes of the city and bring in here the poor and crippled and blind and lame.' And the slave said, 'Master, what you commanded has been done, and still there is room.' And the master said to the slave, 'Go out into the highways and along the hedges, and compel them to come in, so that my house may be filled.'" Jesus wants his church to compel the people in the community to fill his house. Outreach is the response of the church to the Master's command to "go out into the highways and along the hedges."

There are numerous ways to engage in outreach. Common amongst most of these is to develop a list of prospects, devise a systematic approach to contact the prospects, prepare your members to show hospitality for the prospects who attend (either a worship service or a special evangelistic event like a block party), and a plan a time to clearly present the gospel message to the prospects.

DEVELOPMENT OF A PROSPECT LIST

The development of a prospect list can be accomplished in a variety of ways. In fact, the church should not rely on only one method, but use a combination of methods. For instance, to maximize the influence of relationships, church members can be asked to submit a list of their friends and family who are not currently involved in a local church. Included with the list of names would be contact information. Another approach would be to audit the church's membership/attendance rolls. Anyone in the database who is not currently participating would then be considered a prospect. An approach that garners many names but is not based on a prior relationship would be to target neighborhoods, and gather prospect names as church members go from house to house.

SYSTEMATIC APPROACHES TO CONTACT PROSPECTS

As the pastor and church leadership develop the prospect list for outreach, it is imperative that they also devise an approach to systematically contact the prospects on the list. Computer programs and membership software make the management of the prospect list very simple. The key is to record who is contacted, when they are contacted, and by whom. This will enable the leadership to focus on effective outreach rather than contacting the same people over and over again. Contacts should be by email/text, traditional mail, phone calls, and personal visits.

HOSPITALITY INSTRUCTION

Just as essential of contacting people in the community and inviting them to participate in the church is the need to train church members to be welcoming and loving. Every local church perceives themselves to be "friendly," but they often are not friendly to outsiders. It is not because they are mean or hard-hearted. Rather, human nature is to be friendly and focused on those within the group.

One of the questions asked in the Caskey study was, "How often do you specifically teach your congregation to be friendly to non-Christian people?" Seventy-six percent of pastors in the top 20 percent churches reported weekly lessons while only 56 percent of the bottom fifty percent churches.[35] Just as Christ-followers must be intentional in engaging in personal evangelism, we must also be intentional in making friends for the purpose of having gospel conversations.

CONCLUSION

Pastors have the divine privilege of modeling and mentoring the local church into being disciples who make disciples. This is accomplished best by engaging in evangelism. As this chapter has emphasized the role of the pastor in evangelism as evidenced by J. Wilbur Chapman, I would like to give the final word of encouragement to Chapman himself. In his book, *The Minister's Handicap*, Chapman stated:

> If one is to be an evangelistic minister, let him keep in mind
> the following thoughts:
>
> 1. All ministers have the evangelistic gift, and they have only to
>   exercise it in order to be as God intended they should be.
>
> 2. Christ is the only hope; men are saved not by character alone,
>   but by Calvary and character; not by what they themselves
>   can do for themselves, but what Christ has done for them and
>   their personal acceptance of Him.
>
> 3. The preacher himself must be right if God is to use him, for
>   God will speak only through clean lips, testify only by means

---

35   Farmer, et al., "Personal Evangelism."

of a consistent life, and entrust His power only to the one who is wholly yielded to Him.

4. Evangelism is never to be separated from prayer. When Edwards prayed, the people trembled. When Livingstone prayed, five hundred turned to Christ in a day. When Moody prayed, they took knowledge of him that he had been with Jesus.

5. The evangelistic minister must ever remember that preaching is a passion, and not a profession. If it is the former, it is great. If it is the latter, it is like sounding brass or a tinkling cymbal.

6. There must be unquestioned loyalty to Jesus Christ. To question His deity, or to allow others to do so, is to make the salvation of the sinner quite impossible.

7. There must be absolute confidence in God's word, for if the preacher is not sure, he cannot satisfy his anxious hearer nor lead the troubled one to Christ.[36]

Let us follow in his footsteps, and lead our churches on his mission.

---

36 Chapman, *The Minister's Handicap*, 62–63.

CHAPTER 11

JOHN MASON PECK *and* ROCK SPRINGS SEMINARY

· ·

· ·

Doug Munton

Few stories of missions and evangelism are more intriguing or more forgotten than the life and ministry of the incredible man named John Mason Peck and his founding of the Rock Springs Seminary. One of the earliest home missionaries sent out by Baptists and starting one of the first colleges west of the Alleghenies, Peck has been largely overlooked by history. But his story is a fascinating tale of adventure and faith and perseverance. God used him to accomplish great and lasting things in what was then the Wild West of Illinois and Missouri and the surrounding regions. In his day, Peck was broadly involved in preaching, evangelism, church planting, encouraging the Sunday school movement, distribution of Bibles, support for overseas missions, political activities such as the abolition of slavery and other vices, editing a newspaper, writing on issues of faith and other subjects and, of course, education. His was an active life given to the service of the Lord and spread of the gospel. Famed historian William Warren Sweet said, "No other man in the early history of Illinois exercised a larger influence than did Peck."[1]

---

1   William Warren Sweet, *The Story of Religion in America* (New York: Harper & Brothers Publishers, 1930), 249.

Such were the accomplishments of Peck's life that he was widely recognized for this work in the pioneer region of the country. Not only did he record much of the history of the state of Illinois, he helped make it. His preaching was credited with helping Illinois governor Edward Cole defeat efforts to revise the constitution to permit slavery. It was estimated that he contributed to the establishment of nine hundred Baptist churches and the ordination of six hundred Baptist pastors during his lifetime of ministry. He wrote biographies of Daniel Boone, John Clark, and John Berry Meachum, the pioneer black minister in Missouri. He was later tasked with writing the first history of the state of Illinois. Peck was awarded an honorary master's degree from Brown University in 1835. In 1852, Harvard University granted him an honorary doctorate in recognition of his influence and accomplishments.

That Peck could accomplish so much without a great deal of education and with chronic shortages of finances is amazing. He faced numerous difficulties and tragedies in his life. Out of necessity he spent a great deal of time laboring as a farmer and postmaster to provide for the needs of his family and the work of the churches, the seminary, and fellow Christians. But Peck serves as an example of what God can do with a person who fully commits to following the Lord's purpose and plan for life.

THE LIFE OF AND MINISTRY OF JOHN MASON PECK

John Mason Peck was born on October 31, 1789 in Connecticut. He gained rather limited education due to both the lack of adequate opportunity and his need to work on the family farm. He did accomplish enough in his early education to qualify as a country school teacher by the age of eighteen. He attended church regularly but was not converted until he was eighteen. At that time, he attended a revival meeting "where the work of God's converting grace was progressing in a most remarkable manner."[2] Peck recognized his sinfulness and

---

2   John Mason Peck and Rufus Babcock, *Forty Years of Pioneer Life: Memoir of John Mason Peck D.D.* (Philadelphia: American Baptist Publication Society, 1864; reprinted, 2010), 16.

he trusted Jesus Christ as his Savior. Not long after, he felt called to ministry but felt inadequate academically for the task and was unable financially to bear the burden of further education.

In 1809, Peck married Sarah Paine and the two began life together. When their eldest son was born, they were expected, as members of the Congregationalist Church, to have him baptized within a month or two. But both parents harbored doubts about the scriptural authority of infant baptism. Not even their pastor, the esteemed Lyman Beecher, could persuade them otherwise. This led them down the path that culminated in the young couple being baptized into the Baptist church.

Soon thereafter, John Mason Peck revisited his sense of call to preach the gospel. In late 1811, Peck preached his first sermon from the text Mark 16:15, which records Jesus's command to go into all the world and preach the gospel. A missionary heart was born.

Peck was ordained a Baptist minister in 1813, and pastored and taught in New York. But an interest in missionary work was kindled in his heart. Reading articles in missionary magazines fueled this passion. But meeting and conversing with famed mission enthusiast Luther Rice brought that interest to another level. By 1816, he had moved with his family to Philadelphia in order to gain more education under the tutelage of William Staughton who operated a ministerial academy there. Peck hoped to give himself to missions in America noting, "A large part of the American continent is . . . in darkness. Yes, (even in these) United States, there is an abundant field for missionary labor. How I should rejoice if Providence would open a door for my usefulness and labors in this way."[3] Soon that door would swing wide open.

The Triennial Convention of Baptists met in May 1817. Among their most momentous decisions was to commission John Mason Peck and fellow minister, James E. Welch to open a mission work together in the West. By June, the Peck family was beginning the journey of

---

3   Myron D. Dillow, *Harvesttime on the Prairie* (Franklin, TN: Providence House Publishers, 1996), 60.

more than 1,200 miles to St. Louis, Missouri. They arrived on the
first day of December at the outpost town to begin the mission work
that would consume the rest of Peck's life.

Peck and Welch set out immediately to organize a church and a
school for children in the rough-and-tumble town that was St. Louis.
Not long after, they began to organize for a wider outreach to areas
beyond. But adversity came in both opposition to the "new" mission
methods and in lack of funding from the mission board back East.
Peck, without continued financial support from his original sending
agency back East, determined to remain in this region which teemed
with spiritual needs. By 1822, some limited support for his ministry
resumed through the Massachusetts Baptist Missionary Society. But
Peck would struggle with financial shortages for the rest of his life
and ministry, and traveled back to the East on several occasions to
raise funds for his ministry endeavors.

In April of 1822, Peck moved his home and the center of his
missionary work across the Mississippi River to Rock Spring, IL.[4]
There he would farm to support his family. Peck remained there for
the rest of his life. From his home in Illinois, Peck continued his
life's work of preaching and starting churches while his farm helped
to feed and provide for his growing family. He would even serve as
the postmaster for the region, as his farm was next to the Vincennes
Trail and therefore convenient as a place to send and receive mail.

The next years for Peck were filled with activity. He preached and
wrote and travelled extensively. The focus of Peck's ministry in these
years followed this basic formula: First, he preached the gospel (often
with great evangelistic results) and established churches among those
who professed faith. Then, he disseminated Bibles among the people,
using Bible societies as a means of publishing and providing them to
the population. He followed that with the establishment of Sunday
schools where he taught the children and willing adults to read and

4   Rock Springs is today part of O'Fallon, IL. The original location of Peck's home and
the Rock Springs Seminary is less than a mile due east of First Baptist Church, O'Fallon, IL and about eighteen miles from downtown St. Louis, MO.

to appreciate the Scriptures. Then, he made plans to start a seminary which would prepare teachers for future schools and help ministers of the gospel to become more effective. This would all be aided by religious newspapers which would disseminate information and encourage the spread of the faith and better understanding of truth.[5]

Through these efforts, Baptist work slowly spread and began to flourish throughout Missouri and Illinois. Peck saw slow but steady increases in the numbers of believers and churches. But controversy spread as well.

Perhaps the most vexing of problems for Peck and others like him, was the opposition to missions among many pastors and churches in the West. Missionary opposition in the region was often born out of Hyper-Calvinistic theology and a belief that any organizations outside of the local church were inherently wrong.[6] Certainly, a sense of sectionalism and mistrust of the East played a role. Some pastors opposed an educated and paid ministry. Peck spent innumerable hours dealing with this anti-missions subject which vexed local associations and churches for a number of years and even decades. Some opposed sending missionaries of any kind while there were some who opposed any organization outside of the local church, including Sunday schools and Bible societies. The anti-mission controversy overlapped with the Campbellism controversy[7] which led some churches to leave the Baptist denomination altogether.

Peck believed much of the problem lay with a lack of sound biblical understanding. He organized numerous Bible societies throughout the region to print and distribute Bibles, believing this could help to eventually settle the problem. Bible distribution and the need for additional education among pastors and lay leaders alike became a major issue for Peck. And, organizing Sunday schools where people could learn the Bible in the local church (and sometimes be used as a means of teaching children to read) remained a major theme.

---

5   Peck, *Memoirs*, 240.
6   Daniel Parker, a Baptist pastor, was a leader in this anti-missions movement.
7   This name comes from Alexander Campbell, who was a Baptist pastor in his early ministry until breaking away.

He believed these efforts would "silently undermine the prejudices against missions."

These problems, challenges, and difficulties played a role in helping Peck see the need for further educational opportunities among the pastors and believers in this frontier region. He believed education could be an aid in spreading the gospel message and establishing churches that would continue to evangelize and make disciples. And, his own love for learning and the understanding of the benefits this brought to his life led Peck to consider further educational opportunities for the people of the region. He began to make plans for a major ministry focus that would culminate in the founding of one of the first colleges west of the Alleghenies.

ROCK SPRINGS SEMINARY

John Mason Peck, despite his limited educational start, was always a committed learner. He read extensively, often reading and writing while riding his horse to various assignments, always seeking to improve his mind and to learn. A contemporary thought him the most learned and best-informed man in the entire Mississippi Valley. But that was not as high a compliment as it might sound given the low level of education among most of Peck's associates.

Many of the pastors of the region lacked even the most rudimentary form of education. Those raised in the area often lacked any opportunity to attend school at any level. For those fortunate enough to attend school, it had often been limited. Schools almost universally lacked reading materials. Peck noted that a pioneer preacher was fortunate if he owned a library that included a Bible, a copy of Isaac Watts's *Psalms and Hymns* and Robert Russell's *Seven Sermons*. One contemporary preacher noted that the only books he owned were an English Bible, a German New Testament, and a small hymn book.[8] Winthrop Hudson, in his influential book *Religion in America*, quoted Peck and said he had declared that one-third of the preachers in this

---

8   Dillow, *Harvesttime on the Prairie*, 161.

region were "doing positive injury to religion" while another third were able to render no more than "minor service."[9] Such was the state of education and Bible knowledge among many of the churches and pastors in the pioneer regions of the United States.

John Mason Peck determined to do something about the lack of education among the preachers and the spiritual leaders of his day. He began to make plans to open a school that would allow the next generation of clergy, especially Baptists, to know more about the Bible and theology. But he also wanted it to train them to be more effective in combating practical issues they would face. It would prepare them to preach, teach, and evangelize. While the school would help in broader ways to educate those who attended (including training those who would become teachers in what we know as elementary schools), Peck wanted it specifically to teach and train those who would propagate the spread of the gospel.

As early as 1818, Peck and his original missionary partner, James Welch, began to lay the foundation that would lead to Rock Springs Seminary. They stated, "We agree that our sole object on earth is to promote the religion of Christ in the western parts of America." They determined to do that with all peoples, black, white, and Indian. And they considered the means of doing this which included preaching, Bible distribution, and starting a school.[10] The path that led to the establishment of Rock Springs was formed in the very earliest stages of this mission endeavor.

As he was considering the founding of the school years later, Peck said in a letter that "the theological school has been an object in my mind for years as a very necessary part of that system of measures which I have attempted to carry forward." He stated that he "cannot bear that our preachers in Illinois and Missouri should continue as ignorant as some of them now are." He believed young men who are called to preach "will avail themselves of such a school, with immense

---

9   Winthrop S. Hudson, *Religion in America*, 3d edition (New York: Charles Scribner's Sons, 1965), 149.

10   Dillow, *Harvesttime on the Prairie*, 160.

benefits to themselves and the cause." After noting how much he had sacrificed to "promote the interests of religion" in the West, Peck said, "I cannot bear the thoughts of living and dying without an attempt to establish (such) an institution."[11]

In 1826, Peck travelled back East to raise the necessary funds for the establishment of the school and met with some limited success. In 1827, Rock Springs Theological and High School (more commonly called Rock Springs Seminary) was established and located just a few hundred yards from Peck's home. A group of trustees was formed which included James Lemen, a dear friend and a Baptist pastor and farmer who saw a large number of sons join him in the same calling. Peck was to be the first theology professor. The school included a theological seminary exclusively for preachers and a literary and scientific department designed for students of high school standing. A building was built (largely through the personal physical efforts of Peck himself) to house students and provide classroom space. Twenty-five students enrolled and by the end of the year there were fifty students.

For the next four years, the school remained at the Rock Springs location. Enrollment slowly increased but there were constant struggles. Getting a charter from the state proved to be surprisingly difficult. The initial charter was denied through the efforts of anti-missions pastors and legislators. Financial difficulties were a constant and pervasive issue that caused Peck to work, write, and pray without ceasing.

Peck went back to the East to attempt to raise money among Baptists there. But he also decided the school needed a location that was more accessible to larger numbers of people, including those who might wish to attend from Missouri. A site in Alton, IL was found and purchased, and plans were formed to move the school while another small school in the region consolidated with them. Coupled with some additional funds from Baptists and other friends back East, hope for the future was better secured. The school gained a new name with the move in 1832 and became Alton Seminary, and then later

---

11   Peck, *Memoirs*, 221.

Alton College. A large gift of $10,000 in cash, and that much again in pledges, was provided for the school by a sympathetic Baptist from Boston named Dr. Benjamin Shurtleff and the school was renamed once again in his honor as Shurtleff College in 1836. By 1839, the school was finally flourishing.[12]

Peck did not move to Alton with the college. He certainly considered it and even looked into parcels of land there on which he might build a home. But circumstances did not allow him to leave Rock Springs and so he remained there. While he was often at the college and continued to serve as a guiding influence, his direct involvement began to wane due to difficulties with travel and with health. But Peck never lost interest in the fate of the school he had founded by his own vision, fundraising, and arduous toil. He remained as active in the affairs of the school as circumstances would allow until the end of his life in 1858.

Shurtleff College would remain known by this designation for well over a century. It reached a peak of seven hundred students in 1950 with ninety-nine graduates that year. In 1957, with a declining enrollment, it folded into the Southern Illinois University system and became part of Southern Illinois University at Edwardsville (SIUE). Though one of the large buildings at SIUE is named Peck Hall, his name and his mission has largely been forgotten by that secular institution. The original campus site is now the dental school for the university.

Nevertheless, the training that began at Rock Springs Seminary lasted for 130 years. Large numbers of students were educated, and many pastors gained valuable teaching through the ministry of that school. Peck believed Rock Springs Seminary "exerted an influence over this whole field and was a prompter to others in the same work."[13] While Peck would undoubtedly be sad to know of its ultimate demise, he would certainly exult in the long influence it had in service to the cause of Christ for well over a century.

---

12 L. H. Moore, *Southern Baptists in Illinois* (Nashville: Benson, 1957), 38–9.
13 Quoted in Dillow, *Harvesttime on the Prairie*, 165.

THE ROLE OF EDUCATION IN TRAINING AND ENCOURAGING EVANGELISM

Rock Springs Seminary was the first college in Illinois and the first to be both west of the Alleghenies and east of the Mississippi River. It had a lasting influence in the region and beyond. But it was certainly not the only Christian institution of higher education formed to propagate the gospel of Jesus Christ.

George Whitefield was instrumental in the forming of the University of Pennsylvania. Gilbert Tennent started the influential Log Cabin School that trained large numbers of pastors in the early days of American history. R. A. Torrey formed what would become the Moody Bible Institute. Numerous other schools were formed for the purpose of spreading the message of the gospel to their region and beyond to the ends of the earth. Evangelicals as a whole, and Baptists in particular, have been actively involved in higher education for the purpose of spreading the gospel throughout the history of the United States. Large numbers of these schools give testimony to that fact to this very day.

The formation of these schools in the early days of our nation's history had a lasting impact in several ways. One impact of education was training pastors to know the message of the Bible more thoroughly than ever before. Much of the curriculum for Rock Springs Seminary revolved around teaching the Bible in systematic ways. The study of the text in the original languages forced these young pastors to grapple with the issues raised in the Bible in ways they had never done before.

A second benefit of this theological training was preparing pastors and church leaders for practical issues of church leadership. There, the next generation of pastors and missionaries could learn to preach and teach effectively. They learned to share the message of the gospel clearly. They dealt with some of the practical issues of church governance and administration. The goal of seminary education was more than just knowledge. It was to provide biblical and practical knowledge that could be used in the real-life ministries to which these young leaders would one day find themselves placed.

This purpose matched the ideals of Peck. He believed evangelism and missions should be at the heart of the churches and institutions. In forming the Edwardsville Baptist Association in 1830, Peck departed from the usual practice of the associational body. This association would not be primarily for fellowship, but for missionary purposes. This was the spirit of the founding of Rock Springs Seminary. Evangelistic principles were at the heart of the institution. One writer saw Peck's motives for starting Rock Springs Seminary as follows, "With an educated ministry to serve the churches, the missionary objective of his heart could be reached."[14] Rock Springs Seminary was not just an educational institution, but also a means of fulfilling the purposes of evangelism and missions. This has often been the case in the history of North America. The great historian of revivals in history, J. Edwin Orr, noted this when speaking of the connection of evangelism and education in the early days of the United States: "Far from being anti-intellectual, evangelism provoked educational enterprise."[15] Such was the nature of Rock Spring Seminary.

Education and evangelism can and should remain lifelong friends. The purpose of education should always be more than the mere accumulation of knowledge. Knowing more about God should always lead us to want to be more effective in obeying God in his commission to us to "make disciples of all nations." And, our love for evangelism should lead us to desire to increase our commitment to education so that we can be more effective in understanding and communicating the truth to people. Rightly understood, education and evangelism are linked together forever in the cause of Christ.

When John Mason Peck was called by God to leave his home and travel to the faraway west, he could not have fully known the impact his life and ministry would leave. But God used him in great ways to impact what is now known as the Midwest for the sake of God's kingdom. Because of the work of his life and ministry, thousands of

---

14   Moore, *Southern Baptists in Illinois*, 34.
15   J. Edwin Orr, *Campus Aflame: Dynamics of Student Religious Revolution* (Glendale, CA: Regal Books, 1971), 13.

people were saved by the truth of the gospel, hundreds of churches were started, and generations of preachers and teachers were trained to lead them.

God used a man who was fully committed to him to make an impact that lasts to this day. The amazing story of John Mason Peck and Rock Springs Seminary is a story that needs to be remembered and retold. It is a story of missions. It is a story of church planting. It is a story of evangelism. It is a story of Christian education. It is a story of God at work in ways that changed countless lives for generations to come right up to our own day. It is a story of the history of North American evangelism.

CHAPTER 12

HENRIETTA MEARS *and* SUNDAY SCHOOL EVANGELISM

....

....

Kristen Ferguson

Hollywood, CA, in 1928, was a small town with a big future. "Talkies" had just broken out on the big screen, but many doubted that the innovation of voice narration would become popular. Glamor, risk, and innovation were the burgeoning city hallmarks perpetuated by individuals pursuing the new movie industry's limelight and fame. As if on cue, Henrietta Mears stepped into the scene, into the city, and the lives of thousands through her incredible Sunday school program at First Presbyterian Church of Hollywood.

Her impact in the kingdom was a big as her eccentric hats and bold personality. Over her thirty-five years of ministry, Mears saw more than six thousand enrolled in her Sunday school at one time, more than four hundred sent off to ministry leadership and missions, and countless leaders such as Bill Bright and Billy Graham directly influenced by her ministry.[1]

Foundational to her strategy was multiplication. Although she won countless souls to Christ, she did not consider her job complete

---

1 Arlin C. Migliazzo, *Mother of Modern Evangelicalism: The Life & Legacy of Henrietta Mears* (Grand Rapids: Eerdmans, 2020), 2–3, 138.

until they were likewise making disciples. In a day and place when many pursued the glory of self, Mears single-mindedly pursued the glory of Christ by multiplying her teaching, leadership, and publications so that many beyond her direct influence would know Jesus.

EARLY LIFE: A LOVE FOR LEARNING AND THE LORD

Henrietta Mears was born on October 23, 1890, in Fargo, North Dakota. Although born into wealth, her family quickly entered into a time of struggle and tragedy.[2] Enduring the death of children and a depression that affected the family finances, these tragedies cultivated the soil by which Mears's mother would accept Christ and, through shepherding her children, indirectly affect so many lives with the gospel of Jesus Christ.

Margaret and Elisha Ashley Mears fostered a spiritually rich home for Mears. Her father provided an atmosphere of wit and humor, both of which Mears used later in life to draw people to Christ in a winsome manner. Her mother, though, was the spiritual force in the home. The family attended First Baptist in Minneapolis under Rev. William Bell Riley's teaching, known for fundamentalist convictions. However, it was in her home that Mears saw the impact of faith firsthand. Mears recounted how her mother would spend an hour praying each day. When attempting to replicate this discipline herself, Mears set a timer and prayed for as long as possible, only to realize that she had only prayed a minute.[3] Margaret allowed her daughter to accompany her as she served others, encouraged her spiritual questions and growth, and modeled to her a faithful follower of Christ. It is no wonder that when Mears was only ten years old, she took it upon herself to inform her mother that it was about time that she be baptized, having been fully convinced of the gospel and her need of a Savior.[4]

Mears's home likewise cultivated in her a love for learning that she carried throughout life. Her mother played an active role in

---

2   Marcus Brotherton, *Teacher: The Henrietta Mears Story* (Ventura, CA: Regal Books, 2006), 33.

3   Brotherton, *Teacher*, 34.

4   Migliazzo, *Mother of Modern Evangelicalism*, 28.

Mears's education, constantly asking her what she had read and how it impacted her.[5] For Mears, learning was an essential part of life that should be taken seriously. Even kindergarten was mildly disappointing, as young Mears relayed to her mother that the first day of school was merely games, not education.[6] Her zeal for education would continue throughout her life as she pursued a formal education, became a chemistry teacher and principal, and then in her role at First Presbyterian Church.

As her love for the Lord and learning continued to develop, Mears carried a deep burden about what God would have her do in life. Near the end of high school, Mears and her friend, Evalyn Camp, received a clear call to Christian service. Evalyn believed God wanted her on the mission field and eventually ended up in Japan as a missionary.[7] Burdened for the lost and committed to Christian service, Mears prayed and sought God's direction for her future but never felt that international missions was his plan for her. After her mother passed away, Rev. Riley turned to Mears and said, "Henrietta, I am praying that your mother's spiritual mantle will fall upon you."[8] Sensing an unbearable weight of that burden, she struggled to discern what that would mean for her life, resolving that if God had something for her to do that it would have to be done in his power, not hers.[9] Although she finally resolved that missions was not her destiny, her calling did become more evident over time as she continued to pursue excellence in teaching, leading, and serving both in the church and in the community.

PREPARATION AND CALLING: CHOOSING THE LORD

As Mears began to implement her love for the Lord and learning, she often found herself beginning or renovating ministry with

---

5   Earl O. Roe, ed. *Dream Big: The Henrietta Mears Story* (Ventura, CA: Regal Books, 1990), 66.

6   Roe, *Dream Big*, 60.

7   Migliazzo, *Mother of Modern Evangelicalism*, 29.

8   Brotherton, *Teacher*, 41.

9   Migliazzo, *Mother of Modern Evangelicalism*, 30–31.

a large and lasting impact. These experiences and a few personal events led Mears to conclude that educational ministry was God's calling. He prepared her and opened the door for her to serve him in incredible ways.

After college, Mears had a series of public educational experiences in North Branch, Beardsley, and Minneapolis, MN. Her skill in teaching was evident from the beginning as she gained favor among both students and administrators. She had an apparent gift for classroom management, using both her humor and holistic approach to students' well-being. Furthermore, her administrative skills blossomed throughout these placements. She organized fundraisers, social events, teacher training, plays, graduations, trade workshop opportunities, and so much more.[10]

Throughout her public-school vocational settings, God gave her opportunities to have a spiritual impact in her community. In her public-school assignment at Beardsley, Mears started the football team for her school. After they attended her Bible study at the Methodist church, they requested her to teach a special Bible study for them. Her one condition was that they invite other students to the study.[11] Attendance for her Bible studies for young people multiplied so much that they had to open the house's windows so students could stand outside and attend. These were among the first indications that her teaching and leadership could have a significant influence for Christ.

Although she did have two romantic relationships in her lifetime, she ultimately would use her singleness for the Lord, giving countless hours, efforts, passions, and energy to his service. Never frustrated that God did not have her marry, she would typically comment that the apostle Paul was the only man she could have married.[12] She lived with the resolve that God gave her "a beautiful home" and "thousands of children" through her ministry.[13]

---

10 Summaries of her public-school career can be found in Migliazzo, *Mother of Modern Evangelicalism*, 33–53; and Brotherton, *Teacher*, 45–56.
11 Brotherton, *Teacher*, 48.
12 Brotherton, *Teacher*, 52.
13 Roe, *Dream Big*, 82.

During her ten-year public-school assignment in Minneapolis, her spiritual impact deepened to an even greater degree, finally leading to her vocational transition to full-time ministry in Hollywood. Upon her arrival at her post in Minneapolis, Mears moved in with her sister Margaret, whom she would live with until Margaret died in 1951. They were active members of First Baptist Church, the church of their childhood, under Rev. Riley. Knowing Mears's previous success with leading Bible studies, Margaret turned her dysfunctional class of young ladies over to her sister, who would revolutionize it from top to bottom.

Soon after taking over the class, Mears led the two or three ladies in attendance to visit all the ladies on the roster. The next Sunday, the class had forty-four in attendance, and it would not stop there.[14] Through her constant imploring to reach more young women for Christ and achieve a greater number of members in their newly named Fidelis class, the ladies saw an ever-increasing attendance that mounted to more than 530 in 1925.[15] Throughout the time Mears led the Fidelis class, young women engaged in "Bible study, Christian growth, evangelism, and service."[16] These emphases were to become hallmarks of Mears's future ministry endeavors. The Fidelis class indicated God's favor on her leadership and demonstrated her gift for full-time service. Reflecting on her initial call and struggle with a ministry direction, Mears would ultimately resolve her call to ministry:

> She had been called to train leaders and to nurture the spiritual growth of thousands who could go in her place to penetrate the world with the Gospel of Christ. Only one Henrietta could have gone to Japan—or to anywhere else. Instead of sending her, God was asking her to multiply herself in the lives of the many others whom He would then send out in her place.[17]

---

14 Migliazzo, *Mother of Modern Evangelicalism*, 61–62.
15 Migliazzo, *Mother of Modern Evangelicalism*, 64.
16 Migliazzo, *Mother of Modern Evangelicalism*, 67.
17 Roe, *Dream Big*, 91.

After fourteen years in her public-school career, Mears became unsettled and sought discernment about God's call to full-time ministry leadership. Learning of her angst regarding her future, Rev. Riley encouraged her to take a sabbatical to travel with her sister. Upon returning from their travels in Europe, the sisters entertained a visiting preacher, Rev. Stewart P. MacLennan of Hollywood. He was so impressed with Mears's knowledge and leadership that he eventually invited her to visit California, which she did during her sabbatical. Shortly after, he would call her to be the director of Christian education at First Presbyterian. After much prayer, insight, and clear affirmation, she accepted.[18]

INFLUENCE AND MULTIPLICATION: SUNDAY SCHOOL EVANGELISM

Henrietta Mears began serving as director of Christian education at First Presbyterian Church of Hollywood in 1928. Her primary responsibility was the Sunday school department, but her administrative genius would soon launch into leadership development, curriculum publishing, and so much more. Over the thirty-five years of her ministry there, she dedicated her efforts to influencing others for Christ and multiplying her fervor for gospel service in them.

Sunday School

While some had already written off Sunday school as a thing of the past, Mears brought new purpose, rigor, and enthusiasm to the education department of First Presbyterian Church. She paired her education experience with her passion for the Bible as she approached her new ministry assignment. Marked by quality, age-appropriate learning, trained teachers, and a commitment to the Bible, the Sunday school program grew from 1,624 to more than six thousand,

---

18   A thorough summary of her sabbatical, searching, and call to First Presbyterian can be found in Migliazzo, *Mother of Modern Evangelicalism*, 70–76.

becoming one of the largest in the country under her leadership.[19] Her constant focus on evangelistic outreach drove her decisions and leadership throughout her ministry, resulting in dramatic, numerical increase, and spiritual growth.

Mears was committed to quality in her education department at First Presbyterian. A few years earlier, the infamous Scopes trial meant evolution could be taught in public school. As a response, many church education programs, including Mears's, felt that their responsibility was to ensure students received education to counter this unbiblical worldview.[20] Thus, Mears often promoted that the quality of the education in Sunday school needed to be on par with public schools' quality.[21] She felt that if students were to follow Christ and commit themselves to his service truly, they would need a place to get their questions answered from Scripture. She provided just that through strong biblical teaching, open dialogue, social activities, and constant investment into their lives in a personal way.

Part of offering quality church education was to ensure that the materials and lessons taught were age-appropriate. Mears advocated, "As a child grows from infancy to adulthood, there are three distinct periods of development that are passed—childhood, youth and adult—that have characteristics so definite that they may be easily marked. All are part of the sowing field of our Sunday school."[22] While still prioritizing the Bible's authority, Mears was an integrationist as she used the most up-to-date theories of education and childhood developmental psychology in her instructional methodology. She organized and oversaw classes for every age from infancy to adulthood. Mears wanted strong relationships to be formed in the church and encouraged cohorts to move through classes together as they grew into adulthood.[23]

19 Migliazzo, *Mother of Modern Evangelicalism*, 79, 138.
20 Edward J. Larson, *Summer for the Gods: The Scopes Trial and America's Continuing Debate over Science and Religion* (New York: Basic Books, 1997), 233.
21 Henrietta Mears, *Sunday School Changes Everything: Your Church's Best Opportunity to Reach the Next Generation for Christ* (Ventura, CA: Regal Books, 2012), 32; Migliazzo, *Mother of Modern Evangelicalism*, 80.
22 Mears, *Sunday School Changes Everything*, 45.
23 Migliazzo, *Mother of Modern Evangelicalism*, 133.

Mears taught that "the most powerful part of a Sunday school lesson was the teacher behind it."[24] She rejected installing teachers in her classes who would just fill the position; instead, she often recruited volunteers whose profession was teaching or who felt strongly called to teach in Sunday school. Regardless of their background, Mears offered regular training that was eventually attended by more than five hundred teachers from various churches. The Sunday school ministry grew so large that in 1948 she oversaw 309 teachers at First Presbyterian.[25] She wanted her teachers to be confident in sharing the gospel with their students from each lesson and encouraged them to "take every opportunity to do so."[26]

Though many in Mears's time questioned the validity of the Bible, she stood firmly on the Bible as inerrant and held that it provided a unified message about God and his plan of salvation.[27] Her commitment to it was steadfast as she consistently guided students to it for their questions and concerns. She desperately wanted her students to understand the Bible's impact in their own lives and the culture around them. Her book *What the Bible Is All About* served that purpose by providing deep and detailed information on the contents of each book of the Bible and gospel story found throughout Scripture.[28] Mears knew that if her students were to meet Jesus, it would come from explicit encounter with his Word, both intriguing and relevant for every person.

Evangelism Training and Emphasis

Sharing the gospel was integrated into Mears's approach to Sunday school. However, she also deemed it necessary to have direct evangelism training and efforts as a primary program for her education

24 Migliazzo, *Mother of Modern Evangelicalism*, 132.
25 Migliazzo, *Mother of Modern Evangelicalism*, 138–140.
26 Migliazzo, *Mother of Modern Evangelicalism*, 86, 92.
27 Henrietta Mears, *God's Plan: Finding Yourself in His Grand Design* (Ventura, CA: Regel, 2008), 31.
28 Henrietta Mears, *What the Bible Is All About* (Carol Stream, IL: Tyndale, 2015) is found in various editions for multiple Bible translations. Handbooks, visual editions, and companion works can also be found.

department. She expected everyone to join in making visitations to share the gospel, especially those recently converted. In her book, *Sunday School Changes Everything*, she wrote, "It is our duty to Christianize every generation."[29] She believed that all Christians had the responsibility to help others know Christ and then grow in the knowledge of his Word through the church programs. Her evangelism training and emphasis were crucial in the growth of First Presbyterian in both regular membership and Sunday school attendance.

Before she arrived at First Presbyterian, the church grew under the leadership of Rev. MacLennan. However, most of those new additions were from transfers of membership. When Mears came on board, the addition of members primarily came from new converts rather than transfers.[30] This incredible growth in new believers continued to push her Sunday school attendance upward for most of her ministry.

Evangelism training was strategic for Mears. Even as far back as her time with the Fidelis class, she enlisted volunteers to call or visit individuals who did not attend the church functions or Sunday school meetings. She trained these volunteers to invite them to church, tell them that they were missed, and encourage them in their need for Christ.[31] Furthermore, at First Presbyterian, she would hold regular evangelism training. These classes would sometimes train as many as three hundred students. They were required each week to share the gospel and report on the outcome to the class. Memorizing key verses and learning the basics of the Christian faith was only part of the training experience. Mears wanted each person to resolve on a personal commitment to God and share about him in her evangelism training.[32] In her book *God's Plan*, she outlines a clear presentation of the gospel that she likely equipped these students to share:

> By [Christ's] death, we are saved from the penalty of sin, the power of sin and the presence of sin. We receive a new

---

29   Mears, *Sunday School Changes Everything*, 22.
30   Migliazzo, *Mother of Modern Evangelicalism*, 109.
31   Migliazzo, *Mother of Modern Evangelicalism*, 116.
32   Roe, *Dream Big*, 189.

life and a new heart. We are made into new creatures, a new
song is put into our mouths, we are given new minds, and
a new service opens before us. The new commandment of
love becomes the only commandment of our lives.[33]

Although visitations and direct evangelistic efforts were abundant in
Mears's Sunday school program, she also promoted a perspective about
the culture that was not entirely common among her contemporaries.
Though she indeed held that the Bible was inerrant, she did not adopt
the sectarian disposition that was gaining prominence among fundamentalists. Instead, Mears found it necessary to engage with culture
from a biblical perspective so that some might come to know Christ.[34]
To do so, she opted for holistic experiences for her students such as
plays, musical performances, college campus engagement, and various
other social activities, providing a bridge to the lost wherever possible.

Curriculum and Publishing
As if establishing a rigorous Sunday school program was not enough,
God created a need and opportunity for Mears to publish her curriculum. Frustrated with the curriculum available, Mears would
soon develop her passion for teaching the Word into a full-fledged
international publishing company.

Mears's commitment to quality in her Sunday school program
meant a reassessment of the curriculum in 1930. Upon thorough
review of the available materials at the time, Mears was less than impressed. Some did not support the historicity of miracles. Some were
not age-appropriate, and still others jumped around the Bible in such
a way that Mears felt would entirely confuse children.[35] Unrelenting
in her pursuit of biblical literacy in her students, Mears recruited a
friend, Esther Ellinghusen, to begin writing the curriculum. Without
a printer or access to professional printing funds, the ladies assembled

---

33   Henrietta Mears, *God's Plan: Finding Yourself in His Grand Design* (Ventura, CA: Re-
     gal books, 2008), 237.
34   Migliazzo, *Mother of Modern Evangelicalism*, 141.
35   Migliazzo, *Mother of Modern Evangelicalism*, 89–90.

the student and teacher books by hand, including activity sheets, crosswords, and pictures cut from old calendars.[36]

It did not take long for other churches to inquire about the curriculum that Mears's highly successful Sunday school program was using. When she indicated it was something "thrown together" by her and some of her staff, book requests came in. She refused to print them for financial reasons, but after being implored repeatedly by a Mr. Falconer at a nearby church, she found a printer who would charge after the copies sold.[37] Gospel Light Press was born.

Ten years later, Gospel Light Press "was recognized as one of the four largest independent publishers of Sunday school supplies in the U.S."[38] Their curriculum was used in 2,100 churches of all ages and grades.[39] These churches and affiliated ministries used the curriculum to teach essential Bible literacy with a Christocentric and evangelistic aim for each lesson. Mears's curriculum expanded to vacation Bible school, multimedia, and beyond. Her concern for quality curriculum eventually impacted international churches as she expanded her publishing efforts worldwide just before her death in 1961.

Leadership Development and Service Commitment

Being a leader of multiplication means multiplying leaders. Leadership was one of the most valued emphases in Mears's program. She stated, "The world needs Christian leaders today as never before—leadership of the highest type to meet the exigencies of the hour."[40] Her vision for leadership often included service project assignments, cabinet member enlistments, and mentorship opportunities. Through various means of influence, Mears's legacy of leadership development impacting millions beyond her direct reach.

As with many other aspects of her ministry, leadership had to be high-quality for Mears. She knew that developing leaders would

36 Roe, *Dream Big*, 134–135.
37 Roe, *Dream Big*, 136–137.
38 Migliazzo, *Mother of Modern Evangelicalism*, 128.
39 Migliazzo, *Mother of Modern Evangelicalism*, 128.
40 Mears, *Sunday School Changes Everything*, 27.

ultimately mean expanding God's kingdom as they were launched and mobilized to do his work in Hollywood and worldwide. She would not settle for poor leadership. In fact, after assessing the leadership potential of her students in the early days of her ministry, she decided that she needed to go outside of the church for high-quality leadership. After learning that the college student body president was not a believer, she arranged a time to share the gospel with him, won him to Christ, and assigned him to leadership in her college department.[41]

Mears often paired leadership opportunity with service projects and programs. She and her leadership organized what they called "deputation teams" that would do the ministry's work on behalf of the Sunday school program. These deputation teams put on conferences for youth and children, visited jails, supported mission endeavors, and served the community's needy. At one of the youth conferences organized by a deputation team, more than five thousand attended and one hundred committed their lives to Christ.[42] Through their efforts, many heard the gospel, attended the church, and were discipled. All the while, Mears was behind the scenes coaching the team leaders, evaluating with them failures and victories, and exhorting them toward deeper commitment to Christ.

Mears's constant exhortation of leaders impacted leaders who made a significant impact in the kingdom. Leaders like Bill Bright, Billy Graham, and Jim Rayburn all credit Henrietta Mears as playing a substantial role in their growth in Christ and as a leader.[43] Billy Graham credited her as a friend and sought her advice regarding Scripture's trustworthiness just before his revival work in Los Angeles

---

41 Migliazzo, *Mother of Modern Evangelicalism*, 114.
42 Migliazzo, *Mother of Modern Evangelicalism*, 94.
43 Mears has been attributed by one researcher as having had direct influence on these leaders in the modern discipleship movement, which though effective for evangelism, marginalized the necessity of the church in the process of discipleship. An excessive dependence on programs has been critiqued as delineating from historical ecclesial models here: Joseph Aaron Tombrella, "Mears Christianity: The Birth of the Modern Discipleship Movement," Southwestern Baptist Theological Seminary, 2017, https://gbtssbc.idm.oclc.org/login?url=https://www-proquest-com.gbtssbc.idm.oclc.org/docview/1990158377?accountid=11145.

in 1949.[44] When he heard of her passing in 1963, Graham reflected on Mears's multiplication impact: "Teacher's dead? Don't you believe it. She'll live this Sunday in thousands of classes where her lessons are taught . . . in the hundreds of pulpits across the United States and around the world."[45]

MULTIPLYING LIKE MEARS: A LEGACY

Christians in the twenty-first century would do well to remember the legacy of Henrietta Mears. Her continuous work to multiply believers who multiply believers reverberates into our present day. With so much gospel work still left to do, we can implement some tried-and-true principles that made Mears's Sunday school evangelism strategy a success. Among those multiplication principles are a commitment to the Bible, quality, discipleship, and the glory of God around the world.

Henrietta Mears trusted the Bible. She helped others trust the Bible. Moreover, she expected each person she influenced to search the Bible for themselves, convinced that the Holy Spirit would use it to transform lives. She taught it, modeled it, referred to it, and published curriculum so others could do the same. Her commitment to the Bible was the substance that gave vitality and conviction to all she did. From the Bible, she showed countless people the way to Christ.

Mears was likewise committed to quality and hard work. She knew that anything worth doing should be done with excellence. From this conviction, she expected others to rise to the challenges that she put before them, train thoroughly for the task at hand, and learn from failure to do better in the future. A commitment to quality led her to set rigorous standards, critique honestly, and pursue big things in the service of the gospel.

If Mears was anything, she was a disciple-maker. Her goal was to win students to the Lord and teach them his Word and send them back

---

44 Migliazzo, *Mother of Modern Evangelicalism*, 204–207.
45 Migliazzo, *Mother of Modern Evangelicalism*, 259.

out to make disciples. Evangelism detached from Bible knowledge and disciple-making was insufficient to Mears. She wanted them to be biblically literate and culturally engaged as they walked through each season that life had to offer them. All this was to make disciples as they continued their discipleship as followers of the Lord Jesus. This commitment resulted in millions hearing the gospel of Christ.

Finally, Mears did not stop at making Christ known in Hollywood or even California. Her commitment was to spread God's glory around the globe. Although she struggled for a time with whether or not she should go to the mission field, she finally concluded that she must multiply that desire by sending many on the field in her stead. Through her frequent travels, she was often burdened and changed by the lack of Bible teaching and evangelism she saw around her. On more than one occasion, those burdens would work their way back into her strategic planning in her Sunday school program in the way of a new emphasis or event. She had regular missions nights, collected missions funds, and equipped many young people to pursue missions. She ultimately fulfilled her calling in multiplying her missional impact through her Sunday school program.

CONCLUSION

A true gospel woman of her time, Henrietta Mears not only cultivated a deep love for Christ in her own heart but made it her life's work to multiply that love by influencing others. Beyond this chapter's mentions, her care for the disenfranchised, her international travels, and her camp ministries further her legacy today. Her quality Sunday school program focused on bringing up the next generation to know God and his Word would impact people and places beyond her immediate reach. Completely surrendered to God's leading and dependent on his power alone, Mears's legacy today is a lasting testimony of the vast impact one life can make in the kingdom.

CHAPTER 13

DAWSON TROTMAN: THE NAVIGATORS, *and the* DISCIPLESHIP MOVEMENT

···
···

Allan Karr

D o you remember a day in your life that is ingrained in your memory because from that day forward, your life was on a different trajectory, and your life today is different than it would have been otherwise? Each of us likely have several of those days in our memories, and one of those happened in my life in 1975, the day my parents sat me down in our living room and told me and my siblings that they were getting a divorce. Even though it was a tragic circumstance, the path of my life took a turn that day that allowed me to be the beneficiary of a legacy of faith and discipleship that has shaped my worldview and ministry until this day. Some faithful men in my church—mostly not in vocational ministry, but who were trained to be disciples of Jesus in the ministry of the Navigators—took an interest in me as a young man from a broken home and invested time and resources in me as a young teenager. My life was changed by God because of it. They modeled for me a godly lifestyle, discipled me in church and in their homes, and made it possible for me to travel year after year to Eagle Lake Camp in Colorado (the Navigators youth camp), and begin the journey of discipleship that is as old as the ministry of Jesus in the first century and was carried on by the evangelism and discipleship ministry started by Dawson Trotman in the twentieth century. The Navigator ministry directly impacted my life, and it has likely directly and indirectly influenced most evangelicals in the world today.

In the history of evangelism in America, the circumstances and global events of the twentieth century set the stage for a new emphasis on international missions and making disciples. America's involvement in the two world wars raised the consciousness of the need for the gospel to be shared to all people, and the need for those who were Christians to live empowered lives as followers of Christ.

In the first half of the twentieth century, one of the most influential men in his era or since was the Navigators founder Dawson Trotman (1906–1956). Fueled by a life transformed by the Holy Spirit, an eternal optimism, and an American entrepreneurial spirit, Trotman (and his contemporaries) helped to change the narrative of evangelism and discipleship—in America initially, but eventually the movement would change the landscape of evangelicals globally.

DAWSON TROTMAN'S LIFE

The impact of The Navigators in the history of evangelism and discipleship cannot be told without a summarized biographical history of Dawson Trotman. Both before and after his death, Trotman and The Navigators' ministry was inextricably intertwined. Dawson's father, Charles, was an idealistic and adventuring immigrant from England, and married Trotman's mother, Mildred, in Bisbee, Arizona in September 1902, when the west was still "wild." Dawson Earle Trotman was born on March 25, 1906, "in the home behind the general store from which Charles Trotman and a partner provided Bisbee with groceries, pack saddles, ladies wear, dynamite, and whiskey."[1] Dawson's parents were not in agreement regarding religion. Mildred was Pentecostal and part of a Foursquare

---

1   Betty Lee Skinner, *Daws: A Man Who Trusted God* (Colorado Springs: NavPress, 1974), 21.

church, and Charles had been christened in the Church of England but was a professed atheist.[2] The family moved to Lomita, California, outside of Los Angeles, and this was Dawson's childhood home.

Dawson Trotman was involved in a Presbyterian high school youth group called Christian Endeavor. He made a disingenuous profession of faith to get a reward that was offered. Even though he was a leader of everything he did in school and church, and was valedictorian of his class, he lived hypocritically, and on his graduation night got drunk and decided to "quit trying to live a double life."[3] He wasted the next three years of his life drinking, getting arrested, playing pool, and wandering and searching for meaning. His mother, as well as some friends and church ladies, prayed for him to return to God.

During this time, Dawson was arrested. He started attending church again, paying more attention, and memorizing Scripture. When Dawson was twenty years old, he was walking to his job at the lumberyard and remembered John 1:12: "But as many as received Him, to them gave he power to become the sons of God, even to them that believe on his name." Dawson prayed a very simple but sincere prayer to receive the gift of salvation, "whatever it means to receive Jesus, I want to do it right now."[4]

> If indeed one of those earlier occasions had been the time he passed from death to life, then this was the referee's whistle calling time on his living for self and turning him to follow Christ completely. One vital difference marked this decision: it sprang not from impulse, face-saving or self-effort to do right, but from the living Word planted in his heart. Whether the earlier or later time was his real conversion, the *prevenient grace*[5] of God had brought him to the point of commitment this June day in 1926 when

---

2   Skinner, *Daws*, 23.
3   Skinner, *Daws*, 26.
4   Skinner, *Daws*, 30.
5   *Emphasis* is mine. "Prevenient grace" is the divine grace of God that precedes human decision without reference to anything humans may have done. Ephesians 2:1–10 is a biblical example.

he yielded his autonomy to the lordship of Jesus Christ. He would be God's son and servant from that day forward.[6]

The significance of Dawson Trotman and his ministry in the history of evangelism in the United States of America was only possible and only had power because he was transformed by the power of the Holy Spirit, through the grace made possible by Jesus Christ. Dawson Trotman truly had new life in Christ, and the fruit of the Spirit became evident. From that special day forward, he read the Bible with a great passion to learn. His prayer life became legendary. The Holy Spirit began to clean up his bad habits and behavior. His worldly character was transformed. Dawson possessed and developed a passion to tell others about this life-giving relationship with Jesus, and his first person to convert to a life of Christ was his boss at the lumberyard.

This was the beginning of a man's life that God had prepared and called for a ministry that would have historical impact in the lives of so many people globally, and a ministry that would bear much fruit. Dawson Trotman did not try to appear polished and refined, but he resonated with so many in everyday life.

> The motorcycle, leather jacket, whipcord pants, boots, and studied casualness of grooming might have stamped Dawson Trotman as a member of the youth subculture a generation later. . . . He intentionally cultivated the rugged, he-man image to counter the idea that Christianity was suitable only for women and children.[7]

It was this man who would share Christ with the sailors and college students and regular people, many of whom were not from a Christian background. This young man was gifted before Jesus became his Lord, but in the power of a transformed life, empowered by the

---

6   Skinner, *Daws*, 30–31.
7   Skinner, *Daws*, 11–12.

Holy Spirit, Dawson Trotman lived a life that influenced and inspired future generations of evangelists and disciple-makers.

THE FOUNDING OF THE NAVIGATORS

After his life-transforming decision at age twenty, Dawson Trotman "began to tell everyone about how Christ rescued him. . . . Daws realized that he should be encouraging his new converts to read the word and pray. . . . While he developed this method of discipleship, he married Lila Clayton."[8] Dawson had led Lila to receive Christ when she was in junior high. He started courting her when she was fifteen. "On July 3, 1932, a month after Lila's high school graduation, they were married in the second-floor storefront of South Lomita Bible Church."[9] After his marriage to Lila, his faith continued to grow.

> Because they fed on the promises of Almighty God, they were able to feed others and to show them how to feed themselves. As Dawson's confidence and trust grew, he developed a pattern of "risk-taking," acting in faith before God had actually supplied the money, and this lifestyle began to become evident in the people associated with him in the ministry.[10]

Before he formally began The Navigators, an incident with a hitch-hiker shook up his idea of being a disciple. Dawson recognized this hitchhiker as a man that he had led to the Lord the previous year, but he was clearly not following Jesus.

> From that time on Dawson resolved to follow up anyone he led to Christ—a work more difficult than soul winning— and to encourage others to give their converts their rightful

---

8   Susan Fletcher, *Extraordinary Navigators: Dawson Trotman and the Beginning of the Navs* (Colorado Springs: Navigators History Department), 3–4.

9   Skinner, *Daws*, 72.

10 Robert D. Foster, *The Navigator: Dawson Trotman* (Colorado Springs: NavPress, 2012), 48.

opportunity to grow in Christ. The truth had come into focus, and he made an axiom of it: "You can lead a man to Christ in twenty minutes to a couple of hours, but it takes twenty weeks to a couple of years to adequately follow him up." The hitchhiker convert startled him into realigning his ministry—less emphasis on getting the decision and more on growing up in Christ.[11]

This holistic view of making disciples was a keystone of Dawson Trotman's life. The commission to "make disciples to all the nations" in Matthew 28 was not only evangelism and not only discipleship. In the institutional church, we have made evangelism and discipleship two different "programs," but truthfully it is not only two sides of the same coin but rather one holistic process of God in the life of a person. Dawson was passionate to make disciples in the holistic way.

Dawson had a love for the common person, and used his home and his dinner table as a platform for sharing Christ. This passion resulted in a lifestyle from which a ministry naturally evolved.

Dawson began teaching high school students and local Sunday school classes these principles. In 1933, he and his friends extended their work to sailors in the U.S. Navy. There, Dawson taught sailor Les Spencer the foundations of Christian growth. They spent many hours together praying, studying the Bible, and memorizing Scripture. When one of Spencer's shipmates asked him the secret of his changed life, Spencer brought the man to Trotman: "Teach him what you taught me," he said. "You teach him!" Trotman responded. And the 2 Timothy 2:2 vision was strengthened. Spencer did teach the sailor, and soon the two men were meeting with others. Eventually, 125 men on their ship, the U.S.S. West Virginia, were growing in Christ and actively sharing their faith. By the end of World War

---

11   Skinner, *Daws*, 70.

II, thousands of men on ships and bases around the world were learning the principles of spiritual multiplication by the person-to-person teaching of God's word.[12]

Dawson had met the sailors by working with The Minute Men church and the Fishermen Clubs where he was involved in evangelism. He eventually had moved to a new home, closer to where he could disciple the sailors, and regularly, almost daily, hosted Bible studies in his home and at his job at a gas station. "That was the start of spiritual multiplication; each person passing along what they know about the Christian life to a friend, and so on. The Bible Study grew quickly, and the sailors started calling themselves The Navigators."[13] In the telling of the history of The Navigators ministry, 1933 is known as the year that it was founded.

A significant milestone and miracle of God's providence of The Navigators ministry was the purchase of Glen Eyrie in 1953, the castle estate of Colorado Springs founder, General William Jackson Palmer. The castle was built in 1871 but had not been lived in since the death of General Palmer in 1909. Dawson had been introduced to Colorado Springs by his friendship with Young Life and started looking for property in Colorado Springs.

[I]n February 1953, Daws's realtor showed him the property, which had been optioned by Billy Graham for a future academy. Daws told Graham that if he didn't get it, The Navigators wanted it. Graham planned to make it an international home incorporating year-round training facility for The Navigators. However, that summer, Graham realized he wasn't meant to have the Glen—it seemed too separate from his evangelistic-focused campaigns. He believed God wanted The Navigators there.

---

12   The Navigators, "History of the Navigators," https://www.navigators.org/about/history, accessed February 29, 2020.
13   Fletcher, *Extraordinary Navigators,* 4.

Knowing Graham's decision, Daws felt called to attempt to purchase it. The Navigators presented their case to Graham and the sponsors and had 6 weeks to raise $100,000. The deadline was September 29th, 1953. People gave generously to help raise money. Staff members gave, as did the men and women they impacted through discipleship. . . . Nearing the deadline, a professional fundraiser came in and was amazed at the progress, but said they would need a large gift of $35,000. Later, Sanny reported that a $40,000 loan had been offered. In the last few hours, a businessman raised $8,000 for The Navigators campaign. This last gift was exactly what was needed for fire insurance and closing costs. The Lord provided everything—every gift counted. When Graham heard, he shouted, "The Lord did it!"[14]

The Navigators moved into Glen Eyrie in 1954, and it has been their headquarters ever since. Eagle Lake Camp is located nine miles up Queen's Canyon and is a vital part of The Navigators ministry. Many lives have been changed at Glen Eyrie (and Eagle Lake), and it is also the site of Dawson Trotman's gravesite.

TROTMAN'S INVESTMENT IN OTHERS

Dawson Trotman continually devised creative and innovative ways to communicate the principles which were the passion of his heart to make disciples globally. "The Wheel diagram, created by Navigator founder Dawson Trotman in the 1930s, is a simple, effective way to visually explain the structure of a God-glorifying life."[15] Billy Graham said, "The mechanical wheel that Daws designed to get his primary message across in effect became his logo. Christ was at the

---

14   The Navigators, "Glen Eyrie Purchase," https://www.navigators.org/history/glen-eyrie-purchase, accessed February 29, 2020.

15   The Navigators, "The Wheel Illustration," https://www.navigators.org/resource/the-wheel-illustration, accessed February 5, 2021.

hub in center of the wheel, then the spokes were The Word, Prayer, Obedience, and Witnessing."[16]

Additionally, Dawson developed the "Hand" illustration to teach a balanced prayer life. Dawson Trotman's prayer life was legendary and was a large part of what he focused on training to new disciples of Jesus. When giving an account of Dawson's life, a significant issue that could take chapters of text to describe is his prayer life and how it emboldened his faith, expanded his worldview and passion for the nations, and guided his daily decisions. This aspect of Dawson's ministry cannot be adequately expounded here.

Dawson Trotman and Billy Graham became close friends in the late 1940s, after Dawson had spoken to Graham's congregation. Billy Graham persistently asked Dawson to assist in the follow-up training of new converts in the Crusades where thousands made life-changing decisions:

> "Daws, we would like you to help with our follow-up. I've been studying the great evangelists and the great revivals, and I fail to see that there was much of a follow-up program. We need it." . . . At first, Daws protested that he had little experience with mass evangelism; his work had always been with individuals and small groups.[17]

Dawson struggled with this decision and prayed about it for weeks. He ultimately decided that God had called him to this opportunity, but it meant a great time investment, and some coworkers in The Navigators disagreed and even withdrew. In the famous Los Angeles Crusade of Billy Graham that was the first to receive national attention, Dawson Trotman joined the effort to counsel and follow up in the professions of faith that were made there and in many other crusades in the future. Graham later observed, "The very extensive follow-up system we now have, which I think is the most intensive and

---

16   Foster, *The Navigator,* 11.
17   Foster, *The Navigator,* 143.

extensive in the history of so-called 'mass-evangelism,' actually came from Dawson Trotman's heart and mind."[18] Graham also observed:

> Daws was developing The Navigators into some of the most highly skilled people in the use of Scripture, soul-winning, and discipleship to be found in the Christian world. He left thousands with principles of Christian growth to live by. . . . He was deeply dedicated to evangelism and follow-up.[19]

Years later, after his death, and only knowing his name without benefit of the significance of his impact, as a pre-teen I was given these tools Dawson had developed for spiritual growth. Scriptures were memorized from the Topical Memory System,[20] and the "Wheel" and "Hand" principles were part of my training. At Eagle Lake Camp, the Navigator wilderness camp in Colorado, a balanced life of growth was taught to many young people (including me from age eleven) based on Luke 2:52: "And Jesus increased in wisdom and stature, and in favour with God and man." This verse implied growth in four areas of life: intellectual, physical, spiritual, and social. That training is still the foundation of the life and ministry of this author. "He (Dawson Trotman) left no legacy except that held in trust in the lives of men. His investment in the countless lives of men and women throughout the world would be the evidence of his influence on his times."[21]

---

18   Foster, *The Navigator*, 12.

19   Foster, *The Navigator*, 10–11.

20   "The Topical Memory System (TMS) and Topical Memory System: Life Issues were developed by The Navigators as a simple, easy-to-use system to help believers memorize key verses that point to basic truths and important instruction. If you want to memorize Scripture but aren't sure what to memorize or how, this system is the perfect launching point to begin hiding God's Word in your heart. Below is a list of the 5 pivotal topics addressed in the original Topical Memory System." The Navigators, "Topic Memory System" (TMS)," https://www.navigators.org/resource/topical-memory-system, accessed February 29, 2020.

21   Skinner, *Daws*, 386.

REDISCOVERY OF THE MULTIPLICATION PRINCIPLE

In 1955, Trotman spoke to the staff of Back to the Bible. This speech was eventually titled "Born to Reproduce."[22] In this forty-seven-minute message, he articulated a multiplication process that was a passion of his heart. "[Another] contribution [of Trotman] is rediscovery of the multiplication principle. This, too, Dawson demonstrated in his own ministry, boldly claiming the Great Commission could be fulfilled, the world reached in a generation if the principle were taken seriously."[23] In this message, Trotman explained the idea, starting with one person leading someone to Jesus and then teaching that person to be ready to teach another, theoretically taking up to six months. After that, he explains the principle in the following way:

> So this first man at the end of six months has another man. Each man starts teaching another in the following six months. At the end of one year, there are just four of them. . . . So the four of them in the next six months each get a man. That makes eight at the end of a year and a half. They all go out after another, and at the end of two years there are sixteen men. At the end of three years there are sixty-four; the sixteen have doubled twice. At the end of five years there are 1,024. At the end of fifteen and a half years there are approximately 2,147,500,000. That is the present population of the world of persons over three years of age.[24]

Keep in mind this was 1955; today the population of the world is closing in on 8 billion, children included. But the principle Trotman argued for was that we should make disciples in a way that reproduces. Trotman's personal ministry was focused on men from his earliest days

---

22   Dawson Trotman, *Born to Reproduce* (Colorado Springs: NavPress, 2008).
23   Skinner, *Daws*, 388.
24   Trotman, *Born to Reproduce*, 23.

of working with sailors, but the reproductive principles work just as well when females are involved in evangelism and discipleship. Trotman said in his message, "Men, where is your man? Women, where is your woman? Where is the one whom you led to Christ and who is now going on with him?"[25] Most evangelicals today who have a heart to share the good news of Jesus have heard some version of this principle explained in their training. Later in this message, Trotman said that the principle is undermined by Satan keeping Christians busy with activity other than making disciples. Trotman said, "I believe that is why Satan puts all his efforts into getting the Christians busy, busy, busy, but not producing."[26]

Dawson Trotman was "an inventive genius combined with an inquiring mind that enabled him to devise methods any Christian could use to study and memorize the Word, to pray, to witness, to grow in Christ."[27] Trotman's life epitomized and reflected "the implied value and usefulness of every Christian, for in this ministry [of multiplication discipleship] every layman, talented or not, could participate."[28]

FURTHER IMPACT OF DAWSON TROTMAN'S LIFE

Another aspect of the impact that Dawson Trotman's life had on the history of evangelism was his passion to see new believers discipled into followers of Jesus that could grow and reproduce. This was true all the way back to the very beginning of his ministry when he was sharing Christ with sailors and then investing time in them so that they grew, and their faith became contagious. Trotman became friends with many of the influential evangelical history makers of the twentieth century, including Hubert Mitchell, missionary to India and Indonesia; Bob Evans, the visionary leader of Greater Europe Mission; and Billy Graham, who likely needs no introduction to the

---

25   Trotman, *Born to Reproduce*, 24.
26   Trotman, *Born to Reproduce*, 24.
27   Skinner, *Daws*, 386.
28   Skinner, *Daws*, 388.

reader. In the summer of 1948, representatives from all over the world gathered at Beatenberg, Switzerland for the first Youth for Christ World Conference on Evangelism. These four men—Trotman, Billy Graham, Hubert Mitchell, and Bob Evans—went off to a private place on the mountain to talk and pray together. Daws told the story:

> "Before we prayed, we had a confessional meeting. We all felt we wanted to have power in our lives, more quickening of God's Holy Spirit, a greater knowledge of His Word, and we just wanted to be earthen vessels that were clean and pure and strong to do the will of God. We made a covenant on that mountainside, and the four of us stood there like the four corners of the earth and we shook hands across, four pairs of hands, and we formed the cross and made a contract together that from that moment on we would give ourselves to the Word, prayer, and the preaching of the gospel to the ends of the earth!" God heard and answered their prayers. All four men have been used in significant ways of leadership for the kingdom of God.[29]

On July 9, 1956, Dawson Trotman's life on earth ended tragically. During a conference to train people to make disciples, Dawson was relaxing on a boat ride with some friends. The boat hit a wave and Dawson and a young lady were thrown into the water. As the young lady struggled, Dawson held the young lady up until she was rescued, but he then sank into the deep water after his heroic act and drowned. The tragic event rocked the Christian world.

> Many Christians now recognize that in his thirty years of service for God, Daws had been used to help bring back into focus for the Christian world some foundational truths which had been forgotten for years: the importance of personal follow-up of new Christian converts, the one-on-one

---

training of disciples, and the multiplication of disciples as a means of carrying out the Great Commission.[30]

Speaking at Dawson's memorial service in 1956, Billy Graham said that Dawson Trotman had personally impacted more people for Christ than anyone he knew. He said Dawson was always thinking up new schemes to bring people to Christ.[31]

SOME CRITIQUES OF TROTMAN

With ministry comes critiques, some with merit and some out of preference or opinion differences. Dawson Trotman was an amazing man of vision and enthusiasm, and this led him to innovate and break with tradition at times. "Controversial he was, as some detractors fervently attest. Loved, admired, sometimes followed blindly, resented bitterly he was also."[32] The historical realities of the United States in the 1930s and 1940s made the time ripe for a new theological movement. The stock market crash in 1929 brought the Great Depression. The political unrest because of the rise of power in Japan and Germany was a reality.

> Finally, there was a theological upheaval. The mainline denominations of that period were deeply institutionalized in their mission. The fundamentalists, those who insisted on a return to orthodoxy and the "fundamentals" of Christianity, began taking the offensive in church planting, youth work, and foreign missions. The "modernists" were considered the enemy of the gospel.[33]

Trotman was viewed as a "modernist." It was during this time of history in America that some of the most influential evangelicals

---

30 Foster, *The Navigator*, 15–16.
31 Jim Downing, *Living Legacy: Reflections of Dawson Trotman and Lorne Sanny* (Colorado Springs: NavPress, 2007), 1.
32 Skinner, *Daws*, 386.
33 Foster, *The Navigator*, 22.

were being cultivated for service to God. Trotman biographer Foster elegantly observes:

> While Dawson Trotman was being nurtured as a young sprout in Southern California, the heavenly horticulturist had his saplings springing up all over the continent. C. Stacey Woods was helping to organize the U.S. Branch of InterVarsity Christian Fellowship in Canada, an evangelistic and discipleship ministry to university students that was to become worldwide in its scope and influence. Jim Rayburn was in training in Dallas, Texas, for the leadership of Young Life Campaign, his ministry with high school students; Billy Graham had come off the farm in North Carolina to get his start as a pastor and radio evangelist; and later, out of the ranch land of central Oklahoma, came Bill Bright to get tooled up on the campus of UCLA near Los Angeles for his worldwide outreach with Campus Crusade. . . . Many of these men and women were close friends and comrades of Dawson Trotman.[34]

This new generation of untraditional Christians rocked the institutional Christian boat in the twentieth century in America. This unique era in American history between the two world wars gave rise to a new breed of Christian and a new vision for ministry.

> Dawson Trotman did not fit into the traditional "churchly" image of a saint. He was natural, fun-loving, and thoroughly unconventional. He was not a schoolman, deliberately avoided formal ordination to the ministry, had no homiletics to speak of, and possessed an instinctive distrust of tradition. . . . That a matter had always been dealt with in a certain way was no reason, he felt, why it should continue to be dealt with that way. It was, in fact, probably a good

---

34   Foster, *The Navigator*, 24–25.

reason for striking out in some new direction. He was unimpressed by established precedent and was not intimidated if his course of action did not receive the approval of traditionalists.[35]

One of the main critiques was that his ministry was "parachurch," and that many times it operated outside the traditional parameters of the local church, sometimes even substituting for some people their involvement in a local body of believers. "Question-and-answer Bible studies, popularized by Dawson along with card systems for Scripture memory, proliferated for church and home study and individual use. Some contend that these practical methods of follow-up helped stem the increasing drift away from the church."[36] It should be noted that my exposure to The Navigators happened almost entirely in the context of the local church, and that an entire branch of the ministry is devoted to making disciples in the local church context. Perhaps in some contexts of campus ministry, or military contexts, the link to the local church may not have been as strong, but the power of the discipleship which was the fruit cannot be denied. Besides, when you make disciples, "church" happens.[37] Local churches are stronger because of The Navigators' ministry.

Trotman was a breath of fresh air in a world of institutional religious organizations, in a season where this was needed. When faced with challenges, he was undaunted. "If he could not untie knots, he would cut them!"[38]

Such an approach quite naturally aroused criticism by the established church. Where the critics had a case, Dawson listened and sometimes changed his methods. But where his convictions were strong, or where the critics were

---

35   Foster, *The Navigator*, 29.
36   Skinner, *Daws*, 388.
37   Allan Karr and Linda Bergquist, *The Wholehearted Church Planter* (Atlanta: Chalice Press, 2013), 40.
38   Foster, *The Navigator*, 30.

misinformed, he first tried to convert the critics, and if that failed, he ignored them and maintained his course.[39]

Another critique is not enjoyable to highlight, but future generations of ministers and disciple-makers can glean wisdom from the merit of the issue. Dawson Trotman normally was known for having boundless energy, but toward the end of his life he was known to have struggled with burnout and lack of focus. If his life had not ended tragically, he would likely have had to have made some adjustments in his boundaries and schedule, as his ability to keep up with all that was happening had reached a limit. One of his best friends, Jim Downing, wrote about him:

> Like John the Baptist, he was not only a shining light but a *burning* light. During the last years of his life, Dawson's physical, emotional, and mental energy had peaked and was on the decline. . . . During his last months at Glen Eyrie, one of his assistants, Dottie Anderson, noticed that he could only muster the strength to spend an hour or so a day taking care of urgent and routine matters at his office. . . . There seems to be a common profile among entrepreneurial types like Dawson Trotman. They are visionary, are unrealistic about finances, and find it difficult to delegate.[40]

Two weeks before he died, Dawson had spoken to Lorne Sanny, saying if anything happened to him, Lorne should take the leadership of The Navigators. "Sanny, what if the Lord took me Home—would you be ready to take over?"[41] The day of his death stunned the Christian world. He was so influential, and had invested in so many people, and he was only fifty years old. His friend Jim Downing later reflected:

---

39   Foster, *The Navigator.*
40   Downing, *Living Legacy*, 47–48.
41   Skinner, *Daws*, 380.

Perhaps God was so determined that the Navigator ministry increase and multiply that He did not intervene in
the natural events on Schroon Lake that day in 1956. He
changed leadership according to His schedule. Soon The
Navigators would learn the meaning of "team leadership"
as discovered and implemented by Lorne Sanny. Lorne
knew how to exploit the strengths of strong men who were
driven by the Navigator vision. Under his leadership, The
Navigators would grow tenfold and then a hundredfold.[42]

It is not in the heart of God to have a ministry schedule that is so
busy that the minister's physical, emotional, and spiritual health is
jeopardized. In the aftermath of his death, quiet and respectful observations were voiced that the passion of ministry burns brightest
when the minister is the healthiest in a comprehensive way.

THE SIGNIFICANCE OF
THE NAVIGATORS, POST-TROTMAN

To say that The Navigators has grown into a global force for making
disciples among all the nations is completely understated. "Since its
founding in 1933, The Navigators has upheld the mission 'To know
Christ, make Him known, and help others do the same.'"[43] The
following realities are some of the highlights gleaned from the 2019
Annual Report of the Navigators.[44] There are currently more than
five thousand Navigator missionaries serving in the states and inter-
nationally, and more than 2,800 of those are from the United States.
There are more than 1,500 church discipleship ministries. Navigator
missionaries serve on 126 military instillations. Navigators serve in
112 countries worldwide. There are 175 Navigators campus ministry

---

42   Downing, *Living Legacy*, 48.
43   "The Navigators," https://www.navigators.org, accessed February 25, 2020.
44   The Navigators, "Navigators Annual Report 2019," https://www.navigators.org/
     wp-content/uploads/2020/01/The-Navigators-2019-Annual-Report.pdf,   accessed
     February 25, 2020.

locations in the United States. In 2019, almost 12,000 young people attended Eagle Lake Camps (where my life was changed). The 2019 budget for the Navigators last year was more than $137 million. Glen Eyrie is still the international headquarters and used all year round for retreats and training. These are some the highlights that are summarized but there are many other aspects of the ministry that represent the creative spirit that was part of the DNA of the ministry as it was birthed from the passion of its founder Dawson Trotman. The motto of The Navigators is "Life-To-Life Discipleship."[45] The vision and passion for evangelism and discipleship from 1933 until now is truly alive and growing.

CONCLUSION

Near the end of his life, Dawson Trotman delivered a message to his staff that titled "The Need of the Hour."[46] Trotman asked a question to his entire team: In Christian work, what is the need of the hour? A larger staff? More missionaries? A building or a bigger facility? Open doors to new places? More time? More materials? More books or cars? Peace in our land? In his message he answered the question ,and his answer was a summary of his life and passions:

> Let me tell you what I believe the need of the hour is. Maybe I should call it the *answer* to the need of the hour. I believe it is an army of soldiers, dedicated to Jesus Christ, who believes not only that He is God but that He can fulfill every promise He has ever made and that there isn't anything too hard for him. It is the only way we can accomplish the thing that is on His heart—getting the Gospel to every creature.[47]

45   The Navigators, "Navigators Annual Report 2019."
46   Dawson Trotman, *The Need of the Hour* (Colorado Springs: NavPress, 2008).
47   Trotman, *The Need of the Hour,* 12.

Trotman concluded the message by saying:

> The need of the hour, as far as I am concerned, is to believe
> that God is God and that He is a lot more interested in
> getting this job done than you and I are. Therefore, if He
> is more interested in getting the job done, has all the power
> to do it, and has commissioned us to do it, our business is
> to obey Him—reaching the world for Him and trusting
> Him to help us do it.[48]

From the first day the Jesus was Lord in Trotman's life, he had a passion
to share the gospel and make disciples. It was a command he tried
to obey every day and it was his lifestyle. It motivated every decision
of his life, and was the reason he prayed so much, risked so much,
invested so much into people, and modeled the life of a disciple where
Jesus was truly Lord. One church leader described him in these terms:
"Dawson appealed to that adventuresome quality within each one of
us, daring us to be more than mediocre, ordinary Christians. He had
the quality to bring out the best that is within us."[49]

> What, then, will endure to become a permanent page in
> church history and in fulfillment of the Great Commission?
> What would prompt a Christian leader to call him the
> prophet of the twentieth century? Or evoke such super-
> latives, as "one of the truly great men of our generation,"
> "a Christian hero," "few men of this or any generation
> influenced more lives for God," "his outreach shall endure
> through all eternity," "a truly great leader . . . what he start-
> ed will never die"? Or lead a mission executive to call The
> Navigators the great movement of the century?[50]

---

48 Trotman, *The Need of the Hour*, 21.
49 Foster, *The Navigator*, 31.
50 Skinner, *Daws*, 387–388.

This summary of Dawson Trotman, The Navigators, and the movement to make disciples will end where it began. Dawson Trotman and his ministry left God's fingerprints on many people's lives, including this author.

> Dawson did not do much writing. He was too busy making disciples. His monument was left not in marble, but in men; not in books, but in methods for living scriptural truth; not in institutions, but in principles for multiplying Christian disciples around the world.[51]

Fueled by a life transformed by the Holy Spirit, an eternal optimism, and an American entrepreneurial spirit, Dawson Trotman, and The Navigators changed the narrative of evangelism and discipleship in a truly historic sense—first in America, and then changing the landscape of evangelicals globally.

---

51 Foster, *The Navigator,* 14.

CHAPTER 14

SHADRACH MESHACH (S. M.) LOCKRIDGE: PASTOR *and* EVANGELIST

Carl J. Bradford

S hadrach Meshach (S. M.) Lockridge, a prominent African American preacher, exemplified the passionate heart of a pastor-evangelist. Born March 7, 1913, in Robertson, Texas, Lockridge, the oldest of eight children to a Baptist preacher, went on to gain worldwide notoriety as a sought-after evangelist and pastor of the Calvary Baptist Church in San Diego, California.[1] Although reared in the church, Lockridge initially did not aspire to become a pastor. The young S. M. Lockridge's outlook primarily resulted from observing both the financial burden and the personal struggles his father endured: "I looked at the ministry from a material angle. I saw him suffer from small churches. People at the time were mean, contrary, and difficult. I thought I could do anything but be a pastor."[2] Furthermore, Lockridge did not recollect from his adolescence years any of the church's members elucidating the person of Jesus

---

1 "The Rev. S. M. Lockridge: Prominent San Diego Pastor," *Los Angeles Times*, April 8, 2000, https://www.latimes.com/archives/la-xpm-2000-apr-08-me-17324-story.html.
2 "S. M. Lockridge," *Fundamentalist Journal*, vol. 8, no. 6, June 1989, 36–37.

Christ or the forgiveness found in him. Surprisingly, not until his senior year of high school did Lockridge come to experience the salvific power of Christ Jesus, which he so frequently and passionately spoke about in his sermons. He recalls, gazing at the heavens, reflecting upon God's glory and holiness, and asking Jesus to come into his soul. Unquestionably, God honored his request.[3]

When Lockridge graduated from high school at eighteen, he sensed a call from the Lord to the gospel ministry, but became convinced he could escape. However, Lockridge would soon find he could not escape. More and more, S. M. noticed that he possessed an uncontrollable urge to declare God's word. After graduating from Bishop College in Marshall, Texas, Lockridge worked for two years as a high school English teacher. Once, while teaching a high school science class, Lockridge broke out in exclamation, "In the beginning God created the heavens and the earth." Consequently, he no longer could deny the call on his life to preach God's word. Thus, in 1940 in Dallas, S. M. surrendered to the call to preach.[4]

Lockridge, over the next decade, kept himself busy. First, in 1941, he married Virgil Mae Thompson, his wife of fifty-eight years until his death. The following year he accepted a pastorate at Fourth Ward Baptist Church in Ennis, Texas. The Fourth Ward Baptist Church would be his first of multiple pastorates until 1952. Lockridge continued to pastor as he attended Southwestern Baptist Theological Seminary in Fort Worth. Eventually, he would find his permanent home at Calvary Baptist Church in San Diego, over the next four decades from 1953 to 1993.

In addition to serving as pastor of Calvary Baptist, Lockridge held many other prominent positions. He served in the academy as a professor of homiletics at the California Graduate School of Theology in Glendale. Lockridge became faculty of the Billy Graham School of Evangelism and the Greater Los Angles Sunday School Convention. He held key regional, state, and national positions

---

3   "S. M. Lockridge," 36.
4   "S. M. Lockridge," 36–37.

in Baptist church life such as Moderator of the Progressive Baptist District Association, President of the California Missionary Baptist State Convention, and was elected as the first president of the National Missionary Baptist Convention of America, where he served until retirement in 1994.[5]

However, despite all the notoriety and prominent positions, more than anything, Lockridge saw himself as, simply, a gospel preacher. Thus, he committed his life to the work of an evangelist. From humble roots to "Christian Giant," Lockridge tirelessly labored to preach the gospel, everywhere, inside and outside the church, to everyone.

HIS CONCEPTUALIZATION OF BIBLICAL EVANGELISM

Some pastors declare a commitment to discipleship, yet neglect to instruct Christ's followers in the spiritual discipline of evangelism. Not so with Lockridge. In his published work *The Challenge of the Church*, Lockridge encourages believers to fulfill the evangelistic mission rooted in the biblical commission of the Lord. He recalls the Lord's words, which charged the earliest Christians with the task of evangelizing the lost people of the world: "Go, into all the world, and preach the gospel." To appreciate Lockridge's faithfulness to the gospel ministry, it's important to understand his conceptualization of evangelism. Thus, the following explanations present the underpinning to Lockridge's methodology of evangelism, which derives from three factors: the means, territorial expanse, and message of the Lord's commission.

The Means ("Going...")

Lockridge suggests that the modern church must recognize at least five essential ideas regarding the verb "Go," to fulfill the Lord's divine charge. These elements of the verb motivated Lockridge's commitment

---

5   Janine Ungvarsky, "National Missionary Baptist Convention of America," Salem Press Encyclopedia, 2019, http://aaron.swbts.edu/login?url=http://search.ebscohost.com/login.aspx?direct=true&site=eds-live&db=ers&AN=137502311, accessed July 24, 2020; and "The Rev. S. M. Lockridge."

to apprehending a lost world with the gospel rather than passively attract unbelievers with contrived human tactics.

Identifies Christ's unerring wisdom in going

He understood that the words of the command are the divine words from God. According to Lockridge, these words which inform from eternity past to eternity future of man's capacity, inclinations, and his response given any situation or circumstance, to inform his need to be sought out. Thus, Lockridge saw that any attempt to lure man rather than going communicates that believers can save sinners by attractional methods, as opposed to divine personal contact. Furthermore, Jesus embraced the methodology of going. For He, Jesus, is the One "who came to seek and to save that which was lost."[6]

Denotes obligation in going

Secondly, Lockridge believed the verb "go" underscored the primary responsibility of the church. He did not foresee organizations, programs, or the attaining of large numerical church membership precluding God's church from her obligation. Rather, the aforementioned items are secondary tasks to "going." Additionally, he chronicled, it is the church's obligation to "know nothing save Christ and him crucified," to which Jesus declares, "upon this rock I build my church."[7]

Lends itself to the modern mode of transportation in going

Lockridge understood that by going, Jesus speaks to men and women everywhere through God's people. He observed that with the advancement of transportation every rail station, seaport, airport, and today's mobile transportation app await today's Christian who stands ready to be commissioned with the gospel. Thus, Lockridge recognized in his day and would echo today that "going" is a part of the challenge of the church and has the potential to be fulfilled,

---

6 S. M. Lockridge, *The Challenge of the Church: Provocative Discussions of Vital Modern Issues* (Grand Rapids: Zondervan Publishing House, 1969), 23.

7 Lockridge. *The Challenge of the Church*, 23–24.

presently more than ever, with the advancement of mobile apps and social media platforms.[8]

Demonstrates God's expectation of the church to go regardless of difficulties in going

Lockridge believed that the opposition to believers going was inevitable, yet incapable of hindering the missionary assignment of the Lord. He explained that no one has or will ever be more acquainted with difficulties that lie ahead for the gospel-bearer than the Lord Jesus. He recounted that the Lord and Savior of the world had to be born in a stable (Luke 2); had no home to lay his head (Matt. 8:20); was rejected by the Jews, his own people (Matt. 13:54–58); endured the mocking of religious leaders (Matt. 27:27–31); agonized in the garden (Luke 22:39–46); was judged by Pilate (Luke 23:13–25); and carried his cross and died on Calvary (John 19:17). Still, he voluntarily came to pitch his tent here on earth (John 1:14). Comparatively, Lockridge called for believers carrying the gospel to have the same mind as Jesus ,who redeemed the world even while experiencing difficulty, rejection, agony, and death. Thus, the apostle Paul declared, "Let this mind be in you, which was also in Christ Jesus" (Phil. 2:5). Jesus says, "Go" despite the difficulty.[9]

Geographical extent (into all the world)

Lockridge observed that the geographical extent of the command extends to the whole world. He stated, "Christianity is more inclusive than the local church." Thus, S. M. understood the program of God's mission to be universal, to every nation.

Lockridge devoted himself to gospel preaching in the pastorate of local churches for many years. However, just as important, he believed the gospel should be preached to the ends of the earth. His passion for evangelism consequently found an outlet in addition to the pastorate. Despite the members' voices of Calvary's congregation

---

8   Lockridge. *The Challenge of the Church*, 24.
9   Lockridge. *The Challenge of the Church*, 24.

calling for him to give more of a presence in the church, he traveled extensively for several years. Eventually, Lockridge would see his greatest outlet for evangelism transpire outside the walls of the local church. He divulged his cherished evangelistic endeavor outside of the church with the following words:

> My greatest opportunity was a few years ago when I was used in 44 countries to spread the Good News. I was sent by the Southern Baptist Foreign Mission Board to several mission fields. I preached in Southeast Asia just as the war was winding down. One of the greatest opportunities for service I've had was preaching at 21 Air Force bases around the world, beginning at the Air Force Academy in Colorado Springs.[10]

Lockridge fully understood that while the Calvary pastorate represented his Jerusalem ministry, the other gospel opportunities served as Judea, and that the uttermost parts of the world were just as much a part of his call from God. Furthermore, he observed the inclusivity of Christianity from the Great Commission passage to the church. However, he was not referring to election or justification of a person's soul but rather, territorial expanse to be invaded. He perceived local churches as command posts and refueling stations for the believer, having been engaged in the unbelieving world.[11]

Regarding any notion of selected seed spreading evangelism, Lockridge opined that any brand of Christianity that would not transcend geographical lines, racial lines, and endure persecution had not received its commission from the Lord. Thus, believers need to cross geographical lines because men in every nation stand ready to be accepted by God. On one occasion, Lockridge expressed a personal frustration toward such behavior: "I see many fellow preachers who view the ministry like a 'chosen professor,' and they try to pastor a church on

---

10 "S. M. Lockridge," 36.
11 Lockridge. *The Challenge of the Church*, 24–25.

a social and secular basis."[12] By this, Lockridge referred to other black pastors who overemphasized social issues regarding the gospel instead of the preaching of salvation. Again he opined, "I don't witness to just black folk. I take every person as I come to him, regardless of his race, economic status, or how he looks. I had to convince many people that, yes, I'm called to pastor this church, but I'm also called to go into all the world and preach the gospel to every creature."[13] Thus, Lockridge genuinely cared and labored tirelessly to see all people everywhere hear the gospel and to see the nations come to Christ.

PREACH THE GOSPEL (MESSAGE)

Despite much confusion regarding the meaning of the gospel today, Lockridge's insight into the meaning of the message returns us to the aim and purpose of evangelism. For Lockridge, to preach the gospel meant to provide the solution to a sin-sick fallen world and exaltation of King Jesus and His kingdom.

Lockridge observed in his day the effects of sin on humanity; eroding educational systems, the impoverishment of municipal efforts, and judicial measures were the results of a fallen world crying out for salvation. He believed that in order for the decay of a spoiling civilization to stop, first men would have to establish relations one with another; but even before this could transpire, Christ must be preached so that men would be saved and their hearts would change. In other words, man's condition personally and societally necessitates a changed man from a new heart. Lockridge explained the condition of a man's heart in a sermon titled "A New Heart." He propounded that the Bible speaks of myriad types of hearts: deceitful, broken, contrite, failing, fainting, foolish, hard, and so on. Lockridge wholeheartedly believed that only men with a new heart would change. Thus, David declared, "Create in me a clean heart."[14]

---

12 "S. M. Lockridge," 36.
13 "S. M. Lockridge," 37.
14 Lockridge, *The Challenge of the Church*, 30.

Motivated by the approval of Christ, Lockridge established his evangelism philosophy and conceptualization on God's missionary program. Clearly and resolutely, S. M. fully submitted himself to the Lordship of Christ. Thus, when asked at age 60 about one day retiring, he responded, "I going to go as far as I can go."[15] Obviously, Lockridge's conceptualization was nothing new that the Scriptures could not bear out. However, the uniqueness of his contribution is that he embodied the evangelistic commitment of a first-century disciple. Lockridge once said that four types of men exist. The first are men who do not call on nor do the things Jesus commands. The second are those who call on the Lord but, however, fail to obey His commandments. The third are men who do not acknowledge Jesus as Lord but morally commit to some of the things He requires. The last category is men who both call Jesus Lord and obey Him as Lord. It is the fourth category that Lockridge found himself faithfully committing to. Thus, his contemporaries stated, "He is all that you would expect a Christian to be in one package. He never changes, never wavers."[16]

HIS METHODOLOGY FOR EVANGELISTIC PREACHING

Witnesses of Lockridge's sermons readily admit their astonishment toward his preaching. At least two observable features of Lockridge's preaching are responsible for such astonishment. First, he possessed a talent to breathe life into old routine stories. Councilman and Baptist preacher George Stevens reminisced of Lockridge's impact through his humorous preaching: "He was a giant among preachers."[17]

A lucid example of Lockridge's skill was his utilization of sensory language as he elaborated on the existence of God. He stated, "offbeat theologians walked around in their subsurface playpens and emerged and announced God is dead. . . . Well if God is dead, then who assassinated him? What coroner examined him? Who signed his death

---

15   "S. M. Lockridge," 37.
16   "S. M. Lockridge," 36.
17   "The Rev. S. M. Lockridge."

certificate? Who was so well acquainted with the one pronounced dead that he could identify the deceased? What paper carried his obituary? And why wasn't I notified, because I'm the next of kin? God is spirit. He does not die by pronouncement. He does not die by assassination. He does not die by denial. He just does not die. He just as real today."[18] From the previous words, Lockridge masterfully cross-examines a dead theologian, while compelling his hearers to ponder an ill-informed claim about the living God.

While Lockridge had a great sense of humor and animated imagination, he approached the task of evangelistic preaching with reverence for the Lord Jesus Christ. Thus Lockridge's second and greatest contribution, his commitment to Christocentric exaltation, provides a model for evangelistic preaching today. He epitomized evangelistic passion and commitment when preaching about the Lord Jesus. Without fail, Lockridge celebrated Christ and His divine claims from Scripture that draw men to him. Two excerpts of Lockridge's sermons demonstrate this claim most vividly.

SERMON EXCERPT: THE LORDSHIP OF CHRIST

He came down the stairway of heaven, was born in Bethlehem, was brought up in Nazareth, was baptized in Jordan, was tempted in the wilderness: He performs miracles by the roadside; healed multitudes without medicine; made no charges for His services. He conquered everything that came up against Him. He died on the cross, went down into the grave and cleansed out the grave and made it a pleasant place to wait for the resurrection. On schedule, He rose up out of the grave with every form of power in the orbit of His omnipotence.

Men have tried to rid Him of His power; men have tried to destroy Him. If you were to try to destroy Him

---

18   S. M. Lockridge, "Jesus Is Lord," YouTube video, 35:52, uploaded May 19, 2016, https://www.youtube.com/watch?v=JBl8l9b0Yik, accessed January 3, 2020.

what would you use for power? If you try to destroy Him by fire, He will refuse to burn; if you try to destroy Him with water, He will walk on the water. If you try to destroy Him with a strong wind, tempest will lick His hand and lie down at His feet; if you try to destroy Him with the law, you will find no fault in Him; if you try to destroy Him with the seal of an empire, He will break it; if you try to destroy Him by putting Him in a grave, He will rise; if you try to destroy Him by ignoring Him or rejecting Him, you will hear a still, small voice saying, "Behold I stand at the door and knock."

Jesus is the pearl from paradise and a gem from the glory-land. He is truth's fairest Jewel. He is time's choicest Theme. He is purity's whitest Peak. He is joy's deepest Tide. He is glory's stateliest Summit. His name stands as a synonym for free healing, friendly help, and full salvation. His blessed Name is like honey to the taste, harmony to the ear, health to the soul, and hope for the heart. He is higher than the heaven of heavens and holier than the holy of holies. In His birth is our significance. In His life is our example. In His cross is our redemption. In His resurrection is our hope. At His birth men came from the east. At His death men came from the west. And the east and the west met in Him. Jesus is Lord....

The Lord is Love. The Lord is my light. The Lord is my strength. The Lord is my salvation. The Lord is my rock. The Lord is my fortress. The Lord is my deliverer. The Lord is my high tower. The Lord is my shield and buckler. The Lord is my shade upon my right hand. The lord is my keeper. The Lord is my refuge and my fortress: My God in Him will I trust. The Lord is my rock and there is no unrighteousness in Him.[19]

---

19   S. M. Lockridge, "The Lordship of Christ," YouTube video, 32:27, uploaded May 19, 2018, https://www.youtube.com/watch?v=98yWOVvvc3A, accessed January 3, 2020.

The second excerpt is undoubtedly Lockridge's most notable sermon. His sermon "That's My King" demonstrates the same Christ exaltation through a six-and-a-half-minute description of the Savior.

SERMON EXCERPT: THAT'S MY KING

He's the King of the Jews. He's the King of Israel. He's the King of Righteousness. He's the King of the Ages. He's the King of Heaven. He's the King of Glory. He's the King of Kings and He's the Lord of Lords. That's my King. I wonder; do you know Him? He's the greatest phenomenon that has ever crossed the horizon of this world. He's God's Son. He's a sinner's Savior. He's the centerpiece of civilization. He's unparalleled. He's unprecedented. I wonder if you know Him. He sympathizes and He saves. He strengthens and sustains. He guards and He guides. He forgives sinners. He discharges debtors. He serves the unfortunate. He regards the aged. And He rewards the diligent. I wonder if you know Him. His light is matchless. His goodness is limitless. His mercy is everlasting. His love never changes. His Word is enough. His grace is sufficient. His reign is righteous. And His yoke is easy, And his burden is light. I wish I could describe Him to you. But He's indescribable. He's incomprehensible. You can't get Him out of your mind. You can't get Him off of your hand. You can't outlive Him and you can't live without Him. The Pharisees couldn't stand Him, but they found out they couldn't stop Him. Pilate couldn't find any fault in Him. Herod couldn't kill Him. Death couldn't handle Him and the grave couldn't hold Him. That's my King![20]

Lockridge's impact upon North American evangelism may never be fully assessed due to the lack of documented material. However, his

---

20 S. M. Lockridge, "That's My King," YouTube video, 1:06:27, uploaded January 31, 2012, https://www.youtube.com/watch?v=4BhI4JKACUs, accessed January 3, 2020.

faithfulness to evangelism has garnered him the name of Giant Preacher. Through the years, preachers from various ages, backgrounds, and educational levels have sought to emulate Lockridge's manner of preaching. Undoubtedly, not all preachers will practice the same methodological approach to preaching Christ. However, he does leave examples for all preachers to rejoice in the divine richness of our Lord and Savior as they proclaim God's Word. Additionally, Lockridge divulges the key to a faithful evangelistic ministry for any preacher: (1) God's Word, (2) prayer, (3) God's call upon the preacher's life, and (4) reliance upon God. The late Shadrach Meshach Lockridge leaves us with these words: "Stay in the study chamber of faith and on the of prayer watchtower Study the Word, and proclaim it as the Holy Spirit leads you."[21]

---

21   "S. M. Lockridge," 37.

CHAPTER 15

BILLY GRAHAM: YOUTH *for* CHRIST *and* CRUSADE EVANGELISM

Thomas P. Johnston

More Than One Million Souls Hit the Sawdust Trail" was the advertisement for Billy Sunday in a 1917 flyer advertising one of his crusades.[1] After a successful baseball career with the Chicago White Sox, Billy Sunday worked as "advance agent" for Presbyterian evangelist J. Wilbur Chapman.[2] Chapman was known for preaching in local churches and using the "simultaneous crusade" methodology. When Chapman returned to pastoral ministry, Sunday began a career as an evangelist. Sunday preferred tents to church buildings. From 1898–1908, Sunday preached tent

---

1 Billy Sunday did not keep statistics of his meetings: "He himself did not keep records of his work. His motto seems to have been 'Forgetting those things which are behind'" (William T. Ellis, *Billy Sunday: The Man and His Message* [Philadelphia: John C. Winston, 1936], 331). On a flyer titled "More Than a Million Souls Hit the Sawdust Trail," thirteen Billy Sunday evangelistic crusades from Rockford 1904 to New York 1917 account for 280,559 professions of faith ("More Than a Million Souls Hit the Sawdust Trail," in *Basic Church Evangelism*, Jack Stanton, ed. [Kansas City, MO: Midwestern Baptist Theological Seminary, n.d.]).

2 Paulus Scharpff, *History of Evangelism: Three Hundred Years of Evangelism in Germany, Great Britain, and the United States of America* (Grand Rapids: Eerdmans, 1966), 181–82.

meetings. He began by preaching in the county seat towns of Iowa. By 1906, his fame grew and he began preaching in larger cities. The size of his meetings made it logistically necessary to move from tents to "tabernacles"—temporary wooden structures erected for the evangelistic meetings.[3] Sunday's last most prominent meeting was in New York in 1917. However, he continued preaching until he died a heart attack while preaching in Mishawaka, Indiana in 1936.

Sunday used sermons from J. Wilbur Chapman and benefited from excellent administration of his crusades. He organized his meetings much as took place in organizing sporting events. Sunday used up-to-date publicity, secured necessary logistics, and communicated with local church pastors. Toward the end of Billy Sunday's life a satirical novel titled "Elmer Gantry" was written by Sinclair Lewis in 1926. This novel depicted a scandalous evangelist whose life was characterized by booze, women, and easy money. This book dropped a cultural wet blanket on cooperative multichurch evangelism meetings for a time. It would not be until twenty years later that mass evangelism would gain significant cultural attention again.

Billy Graham changed that perception. He was a man of integrity. He became a beacon of hope to fundamentalists (soon to become evangelicals) who were decried and marginalized by the mainline denominations of that time. Following are some statistics depicting the impact of Graham's ministry on several generations:

- An estimated 2.2 billion heard him preach.
- An estimated 215 million heard him preach the gospel at live events.[4]

---

3   "Tabernacles"—or large temporary wooden structures—were used by evangelists D. L. Moody, Sam Jones, R. A. Torrey, Billy Sunday, Mordecai Ham, and Billy Graham. From 1889–1892, Thomas Ryman built the first "permanent tabernacle" for Evangelist Sam Jones in Nashville. It became Ryman Auditorium and for a long time served as the Grand Ole Opry House (Earle E. Cairns, *An Endless Line of Splendor: Revivals and Their Leaders from the Great Awakening to the Present* [Wheaton, IL: Tyndale House, 1986], 165).

4   "Billy Graham's Life & Ministry by the Numbers," https://factsandtrends. net/2018/02/21/billy-grahams-life-ministry-by-the-numbers, accessed July 22, 2020.

- He preached in more than 185 countries and territories—through various meetings, including Mission World and Global Mission.[5]
- The "Billy Graham statistics" through the end of 1998 accounted for 3,082,686 inquirers from 1947 to 1998.[6]

These statistics are truly overwhelming. They portray Graham as an innovative evangelist who made intentional use of modern communication technologies as they developed. Historian Earle Cairns explained, "Billy Graham has carried revivalistic evangelism to every major country in the world in his crusades."[7]

This chapter will highlight and summarize key components of the ministry of Billy Graham. It will begin with a brief biography of Graham's early life. We will highlight two pivotal years: 1948 and 1949. It will discuss Graham's organizational genius, and finally, Graham's cooperative strategy. We begin with the early years.

THE EARLY YEARS

While Europe was literally ending its most devastating war up to that time—the "War to End All Wars"—a baby boy was born on a farm in North Carolina who would preach the gospel to more people from

---

5   "Profile, William (Billy) F. Graham," Billy Graham Evangelistic Association, http:// billygraham.org/about/biographies/billy-graham/#biography, accessed March 11, 2021. The website "Graham's Life & Ministry by the Numbers" includes only 2.2 million inquirers.

6   "Billy Graham Crusade Statistics," Billy Graham Evangelistic Association, http:// www.billygraham.org/assets/media/pdfs/festivals/BGCrusadeChronology.pdf,   15, accessed March 11, 2021. Speaking of his 1957 crusade in New York, Graham stated, "An estimated 96 million people had seen at least one of the meetings from Madison Square Garden" (Billy Graham, *Just As I Am: The Autobiography of Billy Graham* [Grand Rapids: Zondervan, 1997], 323). John Pollock's 1979 biography of Billy Graham contained a picture with this caption: "Billy Graham closed his five-day Seoul, Korea, crusade at Yoi-do Plaza on the banks of the Han River before a crowd of more than 1,000,000. This group was the largest single crowd in the history of his ministry (1973)" (John Pollock, *Billy Graham: Evangelist to the World* [San Francisco: Harper and Row, 1979], 212b).

7   Cairns, *An Endless Line of Splendor,* 209.

more places in the world than anyone before him. On Sunday, November 3, 1918, the Austro-Hungarian Empire requested an armistice of the Allied authorities in Paris. William Franklin Graham Jr. was born on Thursday, November 7; and armistice was signed on Monday, November 11. On a dairy farm not far from Charlotte, North Carolina, Frank and Morrow Graham were holding their firstborn son.

Billy Sunday had plowed the earth in Charlotte with a revival in 1924. A group formed from that revival, the Charlotte Christian Men's Club, began praying for revival in May of 1934. They were meeting at the Graham farm! This men's club officially invited Kentucky pastor and Southern Baptist evangelist Mordecai Ham to preach a revival in Charlotte in 1934 in a five-thousand-seat tabernacle.[8] It was Ham's common practice in those days was to preach for six weeks:

- Two weeks on sin—with no invitation
- Two weeks on salvation—with an invitation
- Two weeks on separation from the world—as follow-up

Graham began attending the nightly revival meetings sometime midway through them. The meetings lasted from August 30 to November 25.[9] Sometime near his sixteenth birthday, Billy Graham went forward for the invitation as William J. Ramsay, Ham's song leader, led the group in "Just as I Am." During the invitation, a tailor named J. D. Prevatt came up to Billy and urged him to make his decision for Jesus—he prayed for him and guided him to pray. Graham checked "Recommitment" on the decision card.[10]

After high school, Graham attended Bob Jones College for one semester, and then transferred to Florida Bible Institute. It was in the Spring of 1937 that Billy preached his first sermon at a Baptist church in Bostwick, Florida. A weeklong series of meeting was prepared for

---

8   Billy Graham, *Just as I Am*, 21.
9   "Select Chronology Listing of Events in the History of the Billy Graham Evangelistic Association," Wheaton College, http://www.wheaton.edu/bgc/archives/bgeachro/bgeachron01.htm, accessed October 12, 2000.
10 Billy Graham, *Just as I Am*, 29–30.

Graham at Peniel Baptist Church in East Patalka, Florida. Eighty people professed faith in Christ that week. Graham was baptized a Southern Baptist at the conclusion of those meetings, along with some of those who made decisions for Christ. He was ordained a Southern Baptist minister several weeks later.

In 1941, while attending Wheaton College, Graham began preaching on Sundays at "The Tab"—short for Tabernacle. In 1943 he began pastoring Western Springs Baptist Church. It was from Western Springs that Graham created the "Songs in the Night" radio program, at the request of Torrey Johnson, founder of Youth for Christ. Graham reached out to WMBI soloist George Beverly Shea to provide musical segments for this radio program. On Saturday night, May 27, 1944, Graham preached to a full house of about three thousand persons at Orchestra Hall in Chicago. Later that same year, Johnson asked Graham to become the first full-time employee of Youth for Christ as their first full-time evangelist and national organizer.

In 1944 Graham had Youth for Christ (YFC) rallies in Indianapolis, Chicago, Miami, and Orlando. In the next year, he spoke at YFC rallies in Atlanta, Peoria, Minneapolis, Elgin, Asheville, and Memphis. But it was 1946 that his international ministry took off. Torrey Johnson planned YFC rallies for Graham and Chuck Templeton in Europe at the end of World War II. Graham spoke in England, Scotland, Ireland, Sweden, Denmark, Belgium, and Wales, along with engagements in the U.S. and Canada.[11] The year 1947 presented rigors equal to his 1946 schedule. But it was 1948 and 1949 when some pivotal organizational developments would shape Billy Graham's ministry far into the future.

THE PIVOTAL YEARS: 1948 AND 1949

Five formative events in took place in 1948—events that helped shape the long-term ministry of Billy Graham. First was the

---

11   Once under the auspices of his own organization, Graham planned about half of his meetings overseas, and the other half in the U.S. and Canada.

Minneapolis connection. Graham was advised of a deathbed wish of the fundamentalist Baptist statesman W. B. Riley, that he become the next president of Northwestern Bible School—the second largest Bible school of its time "with some 1,200 students enrolled."[12] Graham accepted the challenge. But he soon found that being a college president was not what God had called him to do; he resigned that position in June of 1950. It was at Northwestern that Graham reconnected with his childhood friend Grady Wilson. Wilson was vice president of the Northwestern schools at the time. Wilson later organized and led the work of the Billy Graham headquarters in Minneapolis for almost four decades.

Second was what became known as the "Modesto Manifesto." Along with some needed rest, Billy Graham was scheduled to preach in Modesto, California. In 1948, the early Graham team met at the Barrow's family peach farm in Modesto. Graham, George Beverly Shea, Cliff Barrows, and Grady Wilson rested and dreamed together. One afternoon Graham challenged them to write down all the ways that evangelists in the past had fallen, and to pray for God's mercy to deliver them from these pitfalls. The results of their responses became the Modesto Manifesto. The early Graham team identified these four concerns as main problems that had plagued evangelists in the past:

- Money
- Sexual immorality
- Inflated publicity and criticizing pastors
- Exaggerating numbers[13]

Through identifying these pitfalls, the early Graham team verbalized and codified unacceptable behaviors that they would seek to avoid. To this day the Graham team has left a sterling example in each of these areas.

---

12   "William Bell Riley," Wikipedia, https://en.wikipedia.org/wiki/William_Bell_Riley, accessed August 3, 2020.
13   William Martin, *A Prophet with Honor: The Billy Graham Story* (New York: William Morrow, 1991), 107–08.

Pivotal events three and four for the nascent Graham ministry related to meetings in Europe. The first was the YFC World Congress in Beatenburg, Switzerland, August 10–22. Torrey gathered many promising young evangelical leaders at the time, including Bob Evans, founder of Greater European Mission; Dawson Trotman, founder of the Navigators; and Billy Graham. These men gathered to discuss how to better reach the world for Christ and, along with Wheaton College graduates, provided Graham with a worldwide network of evangelicals with whom to work. Then Graham attended the organizational meeting for the World Council of Churches in Amsterdam as an official observer.[14] That meeting was held from August 21–31, 1948. Graham would vacillate between these two poles of Christianity for the rest of his ministry. The formative event pushing him toward the latter was still to come in 1949.

The fifth shaping event in Graham's ministry was his Augusta Crusade in October 1948 Augusta, Georgia. It was his second ministry apart from YFC, where his strategy was to reach the entire city, not just the youth. In Augusta, Graham received the all-out support of "virtually the entire Christian community." Later Graham wrote, "As it turned out, we followed several principles in Augusta that would become the establishment pattern for our work for years."[15]

With these five formative events in his rise to worldwide fame in 1948, Graham preached two diametrically opposed meetings in 1949. The Altoona Crusade, held for two weeks of June in Altoona, Pennsylvania, was fraught with a foment of fundamentalist fury. Graham described Altoona as the nadir of his public career. The Altoona meetings featured two rival fundamentalist [separatistic] church associations. Graham misunderstood that the repeated requests he had received were from one group. But as it turned out, they were from two rival groups, both of whom had written requests for Graham to speak. As Martin explained, the "rival ministerial associations . . . were

---

14   Martin, *A Prophet with Honor,* 103.
15   Graham, *Just As I Am,* 125.

at each other's throats and not about to cooperate in a joint venture."[16] Later Graham remarked, "But if ever I felt I conducted a campaign that was a flop, *humanly* speaking, Altoona was it!"[17]

Then came Los Angeles 1949, Graham's "watershed moment." A group calling themselves "Christ for Greater Los Angeles," who represented about two hundred churches, originally invited Graham. Graham, however, made four additional requests to that group:

- First, broaden church support to include as many churches and denominations as possible.
- Second, they were to raise their budget from $7,000 to $25,000, in order to invest more in advertising and promotion.
- Third, they were to erect a much larger tent than they had planned.
- I set another seemingly impossible condition: the committee had to put the public leadership and the platform duties of the campaign entirely in the hands of local clergy. The committee, I felt, represented too limited an evangelical constituency to make an impact.[18]

Graham wrote, "The city of Los Angeles will not be touched unless the majority of the churches are actively backing the campaign." He had learned his lesson from Altoona, and he did not want that debacle to be repeated in Los Angeles. As it turned out, he was invited to the Hollywood house of Henrietta Mears, director of Christian education at First Presbyterian Church of Hollywood. There Graham met radio personality Stuart Hamblen, who had the top radio show on the West Coast of that time. Close to the end of the three-week campaign, Graham and his team were praying if they should extend the meeting. That night, Stuart and his wife came to

---

16   Martin, *A Prophet with Honor,* 108.
17   Graham, *Just As I Am,* 134.
18   Graham, *Just As I Am,* 144.

Graham's room. Stuart repented and believed on Jesus Christ for his salvation—and they extended the meetings another week. Then Hamblen shared his testimony on his radio shows—they extended the campaign another week. That week, as Graham arrived at the tent, dozens of reporters were waiting for him. When Graham asked what was going on, one reporter answered, "You've just been kissed by William Randolph Hearst." Billy Graham became the headline story of two Los Angeles papers, and in papers in New York, Chicago, Detroit, and San Francisco. From that time on Graham was in the public eye. While Graham had already published *Calling Youth to Christ*,[19] in 1950 Chicago fundamentalist publisher Robert Van Kampen published *Revival in Our Time: The Story of the Billy Graham Evangelistic Campaigns.*[20] This surge of fame was possibly rivaled by his London 1954 meetings when the Archbishop of Canterbury, Geoffrey Fischer, pronounced the benediction to a packed house at Wembley Stadium.[21] This blessing opened up the entire British Commonwealth to Graham's future ministry.

The touchstone question which Graham addressed before his Los Angeles Campaign was determining boundaries for Christian cooperation. All churches and denominations have some kind of boundaries—largely dictated by their statements of faith. Cooperative evangelism usually challenges these boundaries. At play is the insurmountable doctrinal distinction between "love and truth" or "grace and the law." Only Jesus bridged this impassible divide. Whereas church meetings leave doctrinal definitions for future heredity, each generation must wrestle with the application of these seemingly opposing doctrinal constructs. In 1949, Graham favored greater cooperation over doctrinal conformity. Los Angeles 1949 thrust Graham to nationwide prominence, and it was his administrative genius coupled with his preaching ability that carried his ministry forward.

---

19 Billy Graham, *Calling Youth to Christ* (Grand Rapids: Zondervan, 1947).

20 *Revival in Our Time: The Story of the Billy Graham Evangelistic Campaigns including Six of His Sermons*, special edition for Northwestern Schools (Wheaton, IL: Van Kampen, 1950).

21 Graham, *Just As I Am*, 233–34.

GRAHAM'S ORGANIZATIONAL GENIUS

As his ministry was growing, Graham had the administrative savvy to glean from others who were strong in their ministry. Graham patterned much of his early crusade preaching after what he saw in evangelist Mordecai Ham. First of all, Graham worked with the local Christian Businessmen's Association in his early days. Second, Graham began to use tents for his meetings, as well as tabernacles. Third, Graham wrote impassioned sermons with emotive titles, just as did Ham. Fourth, just as Mordecai Ham worked with music evangelist William Ramsay, so Graham recruited George Beverly Shea to be his soloist and Cliff Barrows as his song leader. Fifth, Graham used a "come forward" invitation, as did Ham. While Graham's method adapted with the developments in communication technology, it is clear that in his early years he emulated Ham's revival methodology.

Then, as Graham's ministry grew in notoriety, he benefited from the thirty years of experience of Willis Haymaker. Haymaker came on as crusade director after Los Angeles 1949. He brought phenomenal experience to this task, since he had been organizing evangelistic campaigns for evangelists like Billy Sunday, Gipsy Smith, Bob Jones Sr., and Jimmy Johnson since 1918.[22] Although it was tweaked and adapted, Haymaker's organizational methodology became the standard for the Graham association throughout its history.

Graham also received invaluable assistance in the follow-up of inquirers. In the early days of his meetings, Graham and his team would pray with inquirers one after another well into the night. Dawson Trotman, founder of the Navigators, leveraged the advice of Jethro and told Graham that he needed to train counselors to do that work. So in 1949, Trotman assisted in the training of counselors for the Los Angeles 1949 crusade. "We've got to help Billy Graham"

---

22 Stanley High, *Billy Graham: The Personal Story of the Man, His Message, and His Mission* (New York: McGraw-Hill, 1956), 234; "Willis Haymaker's *Suggested Plan of Organization of a Billy Graham Crusade*, c. 1950," Billy Graham Center Archives, https://www2.wheaton.edu/bgc/archives/docs/hay1.html, accessed August 4, 2020.

he wrote his Navigators staff. [23] In 1951 Trotman spent six months assisting Graham in developing a systematic follow-up program for those who came forward at his meetings. He then sent two Navigators staff members to oversee the Graham follow-up ministry, Lorne Sanny and Charlie Riggs. In this way, Graham greatly benefited from the combined experiences of Willis Haymaker and Dawson Trotman as he organized two essential aspects of evangelistic meetings.

In a similar fashion, Graham combined the vision of Torrey Johnson with the citywide strategy of J. Wilbur Chapman to conquer the world for Christ. Johnson had enthused Graham through his worldwide strategy in the YFC World Congress in Beatenburg. Chapman had influenced Graham through Billy Sunday's well-organized citywide crusades methodology—by way of Sunday's advance man, Willis Haymaker.

Following is a geographic overview of Graham's intentional efforts to conquer the world for the gospel of Christ.

- North America, 1949–1962
- Europe, 1954–1955
- India and the Far East, 1956
- North America, New York, 1957
- Central America, 1958 (simultaneous crusades)
- Australia, 1959 (simultaneous crusades)
- Africa, 1960 (simultaneous crusades)
- North America, Florida, 1961 (simultaneous crusades)
- South America, 1962[24]

Archbishop Fischer's 1954 benediction at Wembley opened up Graham's ministry to the British Commonwealth—and he took the opportunity provided to him. Graham preached before the Queen in 1955 during an All-Scotland Crusade. In 1956 he preached in

---

23   Betty Lee Skinner, *Daws: The Story of Dawson Trotman, Founder of the Navigators* (Grand Rapids: Zondervan, 1974), 322.

24   Thomas P. Johnston, *Examining Billy Graham's Theology of Evangelism* (Eugene, OR: Wipf & Stock, 2003), 24.

Bombay, Madras, New Delhi, Calcutta, and numerous other cities of India. He preached in Hong Kong. The year 1957 was consumed by the New York Crusade, with Saturday evening meetings televised on ABC. In 1959, Graham preached the Southern Cross Crusade in Australia and New Zealand. And in 1960, Graham preached throughout English-speaking Africa, most of them former English colonies. Thirteen years after Los Angeles—that is, by 1962—Graham had literally achieved his goal of preaching across the globe.[25] His ministry kept its foundational emphasis, as Graham reached to take on new endeavors.

The other influencers and parallels are too many to examine. Evangelist Charles Fuller had his weekly radio program, the "Old-Fashioned Revival Hour." Evangelist Reuben A. Torrey wrote thirty-one books. Evangelist R. E. Neighbour wrote ninety-two books. Graham had the administrative savvy to incorporate that which was useful to him in his giftset and apply that to the furthering of the gospel.

Graham was also in the forefront of technological innovations for most of his ministry. He utilized roving microphones before it was common practice. He used television and radio to diffuse his message. He started World-Wide Pictures in 1950, along with a movie theater evangelism ministry. Also, in 1950 the Billy Graham Evangelistic Association (BGEA) was incorporated, with an office in Minneapolis. Under the leadership of George Wilson, the Minneapolis office made great strides in direct mail solutions; a phone bank with 125 phones was also housed at that office to answer the telephones while crusades were being broadcast all across the U.S.

The BGEA introduced use of simulcast crusade, satellite crusades, and went live on the internet in 1996. Graham delivered his final message in 2013 through the My Hope project, which was televised on 480 stations with a participation of 26,000 churches across North America.[26] At Amsterdam 2000, there were more nations and territories

---

25   John Corts concurred that this was probably accurate (John Corts, personal interview by author, January 29, 2001, Minneapolis; handwritten notes in author's possession).
26   "Billy Graham, Evangelist to the World, Dead at Age 99," Billy Graham Evangelistic Association, February 21, 2018, https://billygraham.org/story/billy-graham-evangelist-to-the-world-dead-at-age-99, accessed August 4, 2020.

represented than had ever been together in one place for one purpose at the International Conference for Itinerant Evangelists. The headline in Christianity Today read: "Amsterdam 2000 Called the Most Multinational Event Ever: 10,287 evangelists and other participants represent 209 nations and territories."[27] It must be stated that this was the last in a significant series of Graham-sponsored meetings on evangelism: Berlin (1966), Lausanne (1974), Amsterdam (1983, 1986), North American Conference for Itinerant Evangelists (Louisville, 1994).

Originally developed from a dream in 1953, Graham laid the plans for *Christianity Today*. The first edition was published from Washington, D.C. in October 1956. Graham's father-in-law, veteran Presbyterian missionary, L. Nelson Bell, served as its first editor. Graham later initiated *Decision Magazine* in 1960. The BGEA cofounded the Evangelical Council for Financial Accountability with World Vision in 1979. It is clear that Billy Graham was a gifted administrator. He used these gifts to advance gospel ministry, and in so doing impacted worldwide evangelicalism.

AN ANALYSIS OF GRAHAM'S MINISTRY

Graham's ministry exemplifies the issues that beguile a multichurch evangelist. He was attacked by some mainstream clergy and theologians for being conversionistic and literalistic in his reading of the Bible. He was attacked by some fundamentalists for working with mainstream church groups. Some Calvinists shunned him because he used the invitation system. Some Jews accused him of antisemitism. It appears that he was attacked from all sides.

Five of Graham's first ten "Hour of Decision" sermons were addressed against separating fundamentalists. His experience in the Altoona Crusade marked him for the rest of his life. Some of his harshest criticism came from U.S. fundamentalists and Irish Protestants.

---

27   Ted Olsen, "Amsterdam 2000 Called the Most Multinational Event Ever," *Christianity Today*, August 2, 2000, https://www.christianitytoday.com/ct/2000/julyweb-only/32.0d.html, accessed August 4, 2020.

Graham worked hard to gain the blessing of Archbishop of Canterbury, Geoffrey Fischer. He did get it in 1954. Graham courted the Lutheran World Federation. He never received their full blessing. Graham visited Pope John Paul II in Rome and carried correspondence for him. These efforts and interchanges may prove uncomfortable for some evangelicals.

Graham's doctrinal shifts have been chronicled in my doctoral dissertation.[28] There is no doubt that he adjusted his doctrinal and methodological positions over time. This movement was particularly noteworthy in his communication of the sin nature of man, in his ecumenical efforts, and in his drift toward a type of universalism. Yes, the onset of his Parkinson's in the middle 1990s must be taken into account. Yes, those who advised him must be taken into account. The Billy Graham of 1949 was different that the Graham of 1999.

It would be good for evangelists and pastors to learn from Graham. He was a powerful and articulate man of God. He was definitely a master communicator and gifted administrator. He truly called millions of persons to consider their lost condition and to receive Christ alone as their hope of salvation. And yet this chapter is not hagiography. Lessons can also be learned from his life. Everyone casts a shadow, with the exception of Jesus Christ. Our shadows are removed by the light from the cross. The admonition of Hebrews 13:7 rings true: "whose faith follow, considering the outcome of their conversation."

Billy Sunday experienced one million "hitting the sawdust trail." Billy Graham beheld three million inquirers responding at live events. It was estimated that Billy Sunday preached to 100 million people during his lifetime, always preaching to audiences in the continental United States.[29] Billy Graham, however, was calculated to have preached to 215 million during live events in 285 countries and territories of the world. Rarely is such passionate gospel preaching and personal magnetism combined with such unwavering integrity and administrative adroitness.

---

28 Johnston, *Examining Billy Graham's Theology of Evangelism*, 218–307.
29 "Billy Sunday: American Evangelist," *Encyclopedia Brittanica,* https://www.britannica.com/biography/Billy-Sunday, accessed March 3, 2021.

CHAPTER 16

BILL BRIGHT: CAMPUS CRUSADE *and* UNIVERSITY EVANGELISM

....
....

Greg Mathias

Exiting the side door of Colorado State University's Moby Arena, I turned the corner and was face-to-face with Bill Bright, the founder and president of Campus Crusade for Christ. Campus Crusade's National Staff Conference takes place every other year. These conferences are full of motivational sermons, ministry updates, and opportunities for staff to reenergize and regroup before heading back to their respective campuses and ministry assignments.

It was 1999 and I was one person in a sea of thousands of staff members. In that moment, Bill Bright had every right to walk past me, but he stopped and took an interest in the young man in front of him. He peppered me with personal and ministry questions, then asked if he could pray for me. After praying, he continued on his way.

That brief interaction was insignificant by most accounts, but it left an indelible impact on this surprised Campus Crusade staff member. The man who built a multimillion-dollar ministry with more than 25,000 staff in more than 190 countries cared about individual people. Bill Bright was still the ordinary Oklahoman who fell in love with Jesus and his mission to rescue people from sin.

BILL BRIGHT

William Rohl Bright was born on October 19, 1921 just outside of Coweta, Oklahoma. He was one of seven children. The influence of his parents along with his modest upbringing are key influences in who Bright would later become.

With a five-thousand-acre ranch to run it is not surprising that Bill's father, Forrest Dale Bright, prioritized working hard and self-sufficiency above religious matters. Bill's mother, Mary Lee Rohl, on the other hand modeled faithfulness in Bible study and prayer. She prayed consistently for her children and was determined to provide spiritual nurturing for them. She was convinced that Bill would have an impact for the Lord. Before Bill was born, Mary was confronted with a high-risk pregnancy after losing her previous child during birth. In that moment, Mary prayed for a healthy birth and committed her child's life to the service of the Lord.[1]

Bill Bright grew up with a strong work ethic in a modest household. Although his mother was faithful in taking her children to the Methodist Church, Bright, like his father, did not consider religion an essential aspect in his life. His preference was to work hard and make money. His drive took him to Northeastern State College after graduating high school. While his work ethic did not translate wholly to the academic side of college, he blossomed in his social and leadership skills. After graduating from college, the allure of opportunity and the potential for success took Bright to Los Angeles. When plans to join the military fell through due to a ruptured eardrum, he was now free to exercise his entrepreneurial spirit.

THE LOS ANGELES YEARS

The move to Los Angeles in 1944 was a defining moment in Bill Bright's life. While there, he was invited to attend Hollywood

---

1   John G. Turner, *Bill Bright & Campus Crusade for Christ: The Renewal of Evangelicalism in Postwar America* (Chapel Hill: The University of North Carolina Press, 2008), 15.

Presbyterian Church, where he was introduced to a different kind of Christianity than what he had grown up with in Oklahoma. The wealth and glamour of Hollywood Presbyterian appealed to Bright. He was introduced to businessmen and women, movie stars, and others who were all came together at church. However, it was a Sunday school teacher that would have a lasting impact on young Bill Bright.

Dr. Henrietta Mears was the director of Christian education and the teacher of the college department. Mears was a strong, wealthy, and influential church leader in the life of Hollywood Presbyterian. Through her teaching ministry, she wielded influence in the lives of young, goal-oriented men and women like Bill Bright. Mears was not afraid to engage the intellectual side of Christianity and expose her students to current scholarship. She was theologically conservative and doggedly committed to the infallibility of Scripture.

She was also dedicated to evangelism. She consistently sent out her students to the surrounding area, including the college campuses of UCLA and USC to share the gospel. In her teaching, she believed that each lesson was an opportunity to explain the way of salvation. Henrietta's primary concern in all she did was winning people to Christ.[2]

The exposure to the bold teaching of Henrietta Mears gave Bright a new appreciation for Christianity. He was confronted with a vibrant faith prepared to boldly engage the world around it. This captivating faith peaked Bright's interest and revealed his own need for salvation. In the spring of 1945, while listening to Dr. Mears teach on Acts 9, Bill Bright went home to his apartment and gave his life to Christ.[3]

As Bright grew in his faith and involvement in ministry, it began to shape his entire life including his business and love interests. Bright's increasing involvement in the Hollywood Presbyterian college department led to a deepening dissatisfaction with his work growing his specialty-foods business, Bright's California Confections. During this time, he also rekindled an old friendship from his hometown of

---

2 Turner, *Bill Bright & Campus Crusade for Christ*, 22.
3 Michael Richardson, *Amazing Faith: The Authorized Biography of Bill Bright* (Colorado Springs: Waterbrook Press, 2000), 22–23.

Coweta, Oklahoma, with Vonette Zachary. Their relationship was a whirlwind that eventually led to marriage on December 30, 1948.

CAMPUS CRUSADE FOR CHRIST

The Los Angeles years provided many momentous and memorable moments, but there were also seasons of frustration. As Bright grew in his faith he determined to get better equipped for ministry, first going to Princeton Theological Seminary and later transferring to a new seminary start-up closer to home, Fuller Theological Seminary. While he was not averse to the classroom and he deeply admired many of his professors, Bright was torn because he wanted to spend his time focused on evangelism. Each time Bright was involved in leading someone to Christ, the idea of spending his time "to see human spirits transformed" captivated more and more of his attention.[4]

In the spring of 1951, the vision for Campus Crusade for Christ came to full fruition. For Bright it was truly a vision from God. He described this moment as "rich, meaningful, and yet indescribable" and confessed, "without apology all I can say is I met with God."[5] It was this vision from God that solidified Bright's plans to reach the world for Christ and work toward fulfilling the Great Commission in his lifetime.

The name for this new ministry, Campus Crusade for Christ, was given to Bright by one of his Fuller professors and mentors, Dr. Wilbur Smith. At that time, Bright sold his business and withdrew from seminary to focus on this new ministry from God. Bright envisioned the college campus as the hub of need and opportunity. There was a need to combat the growing secularization on college campuses, and there was an opportunity to reach and influence tomorrow's leaders for Christ. The slogan for this new ministry was: "Reach the campus for Christ today—reach the world for Christ tomorrow."[6]

---

4   Richardson, *Amazing Faith*, 50.
5   Richardson, *Amazing Faith*, 61.
6   Richardson, *Amazing Faith*, 61.

WIN, BUILD, SEND

The strategy Bright would employ in reaching college campuses was directly influenced by his time under the ministry of Dr. Mears. Her principles were: "canvas your neighborhood, teach the Word, win people to Christ, enlist for service."[7] These principles provide the framework for the mission of Campus Crusade for Christ—win, build, and send. Campus Crusade's ministry philosophy revolves around these three principles: win people to Christ, build them up in the faith, and then send them out to fulfill the Great Commission.

Winning people to Christ was the heartbeat of the Campus Crusade vision. Bright was passionate about sharing the gospel with anyone he met and wanted evangelism to be the driving force in his new ministry. From that starting point, Bright developed and implemented the use of evangelistic tracts for Campus Crusade. Wanting to have a simple and clear gospel message for his staff to share on campuses, Bright developed the The Four Spiritual Laws:

1. God loves you and offers a wonderful plan for your life (John 3:16; 10:10).
2. Man is sinful and separated from God. Therefore, he cannot know and experience God's love and plan for his life (Rom. 3:23; 6:23).
3. Jesus Christ is God's only provision for man's sin. Through him you can know and experience God's love and plan for your life (Rom. 5:8; 1 Cor. 15:3–6; John 14:6).
4. We must individually receive Jesus Christ as Savior and Lord; then we can know and experience God's love and plan for our lives (John 1:12; 3:1–8; Eph. 2:8–9; Rev. 3:20).[8]

What was striking for many was the beginning point of the Four Laws. Against the tide of other evangelistic presentations that began

---

7   Richardson, *Amazing Faith*, 26.
8   Adapted from https://crustore.org/four-laws-english.

with man's sinful condition and the judgment of God, Bright was convicted that God's love was a better starting point. For Bright, starting with God's love represented all that his ministry represented. For he had been "captivated by the vastness of God's love and compelled to share that great love with all who would listen." So the Four Laws began on a positive note. This small innovation changed evangelism on college campuses.

While the Four Laws shocked many due to its insistence that God loves sinners, for Bright they represented the essence of the gospel and gave his staff an evangelistic tool they could take to college campuses. In a few short minutes, a staff member could recite these four laws and lead someone to Christ.[9] Remember, Bright was a businessman and he was now in the "business" of reaching the lost and fulfilling the Great Commission. He wanted his staff to have a compelling and memorable gospel presentation to give to lost college students.

Bright's vision was for his staff to infiltrate the campuses with the gospel message. Campus Crusade promoted what Bright characterized as aggressive evangelism. "By aggressive evangelism," Bright meant "going to men with the good news of our living Christ and His love and forgiveness, not in argumentative tones nor with high pressure techniques, but taking the initiative to tell (as the Apostle Paul wrote) all men everywhere about Christ."[10] Use of the Four Laws gospel tract freed staff up to more aggressively engage the campus and share their faith. While they could not control a person's response to the gospel message, they could control how many times they initiated a gospel conversation. Bright defined successful witnessing as "simply taking the initiative to share Christ in the power of the Holy Spirit and leaving the results to God."[11] One finds success in sharing the gospel,

---

9   Originally staff members memorized the Four Spiritual Laws. The gospel tract initially began printing in 1965.
10   Bill Bright, *Come Help Change the World* (Old Tappan, NJ: Fleming H. Revell, 1970), 95.
11   Bill Bright, *Witnessing without Fear: How to Share Your Faith with Confidence* (San Bernardino, CA: Here's Life, 1987), 69.

not in the results. This definition, along with the Four Spiritual Laws became the centerpiece for Campus Crusade's evangelistic efforts.[12]

VICTORY AND REPRODUCIBILITY

Keswick theological influences are common in Bright's methodology. Keswick theology, also known as the Higher Life Movement, is a school of thought emphasizing Christian holiness that was promoted in Keswick, England, and was widely influential in evangelical circles. It encourages living a "victorious life" and promotes living a higher level of Christianity as one encounters the Holy Spirit and matures in the Christian life. In introducing his *10 Basic Steps toward Christian Maturity*, Bright wrote, "The Christian who has been living in spiritual defeat, powerless and fruitless, wondering if there is any validity to the Christian life, will find hope in these pages."[13] He continued by encouraging his audience to read *The Four Spiritual Laws* and *Have You Made the Wonderful Discovery of the Spirit-Filled Life?* In these booklets one finds the "basic principles you need to live that victorious Christian life and be an effective leader of your group."[14] Bright wanted all believers to experience the abundant life promised in John 10:10 and not settle for being an "average Christian."[15] The message of a Spirit-filled and victorious Christian life resonated with college students.

In the same way Bright equipped his staff with a simple and clear gospel presentation, he also wanted to furnish them with discipleship and training materials. The emphasis on clear and easy materials led to writings like the Transferrable Concepts series. Based upon the Great Commission mandate to make disciples and Paul's admonition

---

12   The Four Spiritual Laws are now more popularly contained in the tract, *Would You Like to Know God Personally?* The Four Spiritual Laws has been translated into all the major languages around the world. See http://www.4laws.com/laws/languages.html.

13   Bill Bright, *10 Basic Steps toward Christian Maturity: Leader's Guide* (Orlando, FL: NewLife Publications, 1994), 10.

14   Bright, *10 Basic Steps toward Christian Maturity*, 12.

15   "The thief comes only to steal and kill and destroy. I came that they may have life and have it abundantly" (John 10:10 ESV).

to Timothy about spiritual multiplication,[16] the Concepts are a series of ten booklets designed to help a disciplemaker pass along the essentials of the Christian faith to a new or immature believer in a step-by-step approach. A believer can "master each of these concepts by reading it thoughtfully at least six times until you are personally prepared to communicate it to others 'who will also be qualified to teach others.'"[17] These booklets, along with other writings and materials, are designed to be reproducible and are an essential aspect of Campus Crusade's methodology.

CCC AND UNIVERSITY EVANGELISM

Estimating the impact of Bill Bright and Campus Crusade on university evangelism proves difficult. Campus Crusade has ministry hubs on or near thousands of campuses across the United States and around the world. Each of these campuses represents a vast number of evangelistic conversations and decisions for Christ.

With the college campus as the focus, Bill Bright and Campus Crusade helped influence university evangelism in at least these four ways:

1. **Evangelism as priority.** Reaching the lost is the heartbeat of Campus Crusade. The substantial emphasis from the beginning on reaching the lost led to the creation of the Four Spiritual Laws, which changed evangelism everywhere, especially on the university campus. Even today, when given the opportunity to share the gospel many people still appeal to a version of the Four Laws. Campus Crusade continues to make initiative evangelism the focus of their ministries on college campuses.

---

16   "And what you have heard from me in the presence of many witnesses entrust to faithful men, who will be able to teach others also" (2 Tim. 2:2 ESV).

17   From "What Is a Transferable Concept" in the frontmatter of each of the Transferable Concepts booklets.

2. **Evangelistic pragmatism.** Truly, this could be a continuation of the previous point as it flows from the evangelistic priority of Bill Bright and Campus Crusade. In efforts to reach people for Christ, Campus Crusade is often quick to adapt its evangelistic methods but not the gospel message to attract students, and are often critiqued as, at times, remaining too "close to the center of mainstream American culture."[18]

3. **Marketing the message.** From gospel tracts to Transferable Concepts to many other varied training materials, Bill Bright focused on simplicity, clarity, and reproducibility. Birthed out of his business background, packaging the Christian message helped equip his staff to have a wide impact on the college campus. Today, whether you are Campus Crusade staff in the United States or somewhere around the world, you are expected to use the same materials. This model of packaging and reproducibility has influenced other campus ministries in their own efforts to equip students and staff to reach the university campus.

4. **The Holy Spirit.** Bill Bright wanted nothing more than for believers to live their lives in surrender to the Holy Spirit. He was convinced that a life yielded to the Spirit would produce joy and gospel fruit: "According to the Lord Jesus, the only way we can demonstrate that we are truly following Him is to produce fruit, which includes introducing others to our Savior as well as living holy lives. And the only way we can produce fruit is through the power of the Holy Spirit."[19] This emphasis on the Holy Spirit exposed Campus Crusade to criticism, but for Bright the Spirit was central to a Christian life committed to winning, building, and sending.

---

18 Turner, *Bill Bright & Campus Crusade*, 232.
19 Richardson, *Amazing Faith*, 256–257.

CONCLUSION

He is perhaps God's supersalesman who has utilized the technology of his day to "go and make disciples of all nations." The number of people that Bill Bright and his coworkers in Campus Crusade have reached with the gospel would be the envy of any advertising agency's report to a client. Yet, Bill Bright is not fully satisfied: hence he strives to share the gospel with every person on earth by the end of the year 2000. And if his past and current achievements are anything to go by, who is to doubt his intention and desire to fulfill his stated aim in five short years?

A detailed strategy marshaled from a lifetime of experience in marketing, coupled with a strong commitment entrenched in the Christian faith, sets Bill Bright aside from many others. He is a convinced layman whose abundant energy for the cause of the faith has been richly rewarded. A preacher who has no pulpit of his own but who, to paraphrase John Wesley, has the world as his parish.

Some may be critical of Bill Bright, but no one can surely doubt the genuine nature of this man who has denied himself the luxuries of life for the gospel of Jesus: who did forsake corporate success for the relentless task of telling the "ever new" story of the babe from Bethlehem.[20]

The words above are an excerpt from the official statement publicizing Bill Bright as the twenty-sixth recipient of the Templeton Prize for the Progress in Religion in 1996. Other notable previous recipients of this prestigious prize at the time of Bright's award included Mother Teresa, Billy Graham, and Charles Colson.[21] This statement, in part, serves to reflect the humility, complexity, and faithfulness of Bill Bright. On July

---

20 Richardson, *Amazing Faith*, 214.
21 For a complete list of Templeton Prize recipients, see https://www.templetonprize. org/templeton-prize-winners-2/?utm_source=google&utm_medium=paid%20 &utm_campaign=templetonprizegooglead.

19, 2003, after a prolonged battle with pulmonary fibrosis, Bill Bright passed away, but not before encouraging his staff to continue doing all they could to reach the lost and fulfill the Great Commission:

> Rejoice with me because I am no longer in this earthly tent. I am in the presence of the living God, satisfied at the deepest core of my being. And rejoice with me because I have finished all He called me to do. . . . God has laid a message on my heart for you all. For you not yet believers: Seriously look at the magnificent offer of love and forgiveness that God extends you. Before this day is over, receive Jesus as your Savior and Lord. Consider that God loves you and offers a wonderful plan for your life. Take seriously that because each of us is sinful and separated from God, we cannot know and experience God's love and plan. Know that Jesus Christ is God's only provision for man's sin. Through Him you can know and experience God's love and plan for you. Finally, you must individually receive Jesus Christ as Savior and Lord; then you can know and experience God's love and plan. Those four points are the heart of God's good news to humanity. If you do not yet know Jesus Christ personally, please consider those points.
>
> For you who know Jesus Christ personally I have a word for you: Do not settle for mediocrity. You are a child of the God of the universe. Surrender to Him. Become His slave. I can assure you, after more than 50 years of experience, there is no greater adventure than following Him.[22]

From his conversion in 1945 until his dying breath, Bill Bright dedicated his entire life to reaching the world for Christ and working toward fulfilling the Great Commission.

---

22 These are words from a video to Campus Crusade staff from Bill Bright recorded just before his death, found at https://www.cru.org/content/dam/cru/about/bill-bright-memorial/life_lived_well.pdf.

Campus Crusade for Christ International, known as Cru in the United States, is the umbrella for more than seventy other ministries across the United States and around the world. Besides the campus ministry, one of the most successful ministries is the *Jesus* film. Since 1979, the *Jesus* film has been viewed by more than 8.1 billion people in more than 1,800 languages in 225 countries.[23] There is little doubt that Campus Crusade is unparalleled in its evangelistic impact around the world.

While the leadership of Campus Crusade has changed,[24] and continues to confront many changes and challenges in the world, the original vision of Bill Bright remains unchanged. Campus Crusade for Christ remains committed to winning, building, and sending. Bill Bright has passed the baton of sharing the good news of Jesus Christ in order to fulfill the Great Commission to a whole new generation of Campus Crusade staff and university students.

---

23   Statistics from https://www.jesusfilm.org/about/learn-more/statistics.html.
24   Bill Bright as president of Campus Crusade International and Cru. He was followed by Steve Douglass, who was succeeded in 2020 by Steve Sellers.

CHAPTER 17

D. JAMES KENNEDY: TRAINING *the* LAITY *in* PERSONAL EVANGELISM

Eddie Pate

Suppose you were to die today and stand before God and He were to ask you, 'What right do you have to enter my Heaven?'—What would you say?" That's the question that a young Arthur Murray dance instructor, D. James Kennedy, heard one Sunday morning on the radio, spoken by Donald Gray Barnhouse. That question would change his life completely and become one of two diagnostic questions used to introduce the Evangelism Explosion gospel presentation that Kennedy would develop later. Evangelism Explosion is "perhaps the best known and most widely used evangelistic training curriculum in church history. EE officials say millions have come to Christ using this program, which has spread to every nation on earth."[1]

---

1   Stan Guthrie, "A Passion for Souls: Remembering D. James Kennedy," *Christianity Today*, September 6, 2007, https://www.christianitytoday.com/news/2007/september/136-43.0.html.

CHILDHOOD TO COLLEGE

D. James (Jimmy) Kennedy, was born November 3, 1930, during his parents' two-week stopover in Augusta, Georgia, on a trip from Jacksonville, Florida to Chicago.[2] His father George was a traveling salesman and his mother Ermine was an alcoholic. George and Ermine Kennedy were nominal Methodists; in practice, they had no spiritual roots.[3]

The "D" in the name comes from his grandfather, Dennis James Kennedy. Just two months before his maternal grandmother died, she summoned her grandson and made an unusual request: first, that he lead her in a prayer to profess Christ; and secondly, that his official name be D. James Kennedy. Though his friends called him Jim and his parents Jimmy, D. James Kennedy has been his official name ever since.[4]

Jim Kennedy spent most of his young life in the Chicago suburb of Evanston, Illinois. He was a shy child for the most part. He was in the Boy Scouts of America and commented that Boy Scouts camps "gave me my only true relief from a really difficult life at home."[5] At about age 15, because of his father's asthma, the family relocated from the Chicago area to Tampa, Florida. Though he had played some high school football and even done some boxing while in Chicago, in Florida he "traded his football helmet for a two-foot-tall hat covered in white fur."[6] Jim was the drum major for the band and excelled at the clarinet. He would often lose himself in the music to escape the realities of his alcoholic mother who had publicly embarrassed him on more than one occasion. At the annual band concert at Plant High School during his senior year, Jim played Gershwin's "Rhapsody in Blue." A talent scout in attendance from the University of Tampa

---

2   Thomas H. Stebbins, *D. James Kennedy's Explosion of Evangelism* (Fort Lauderdale, FL: Evangelism Explosion Publishing 2002), 1.

3   Stebbins, *D. James Kennedy's Explosion of Evangelism,* 1.

4   Herbert Lee Williams, *D. James Kennedy, The Man and His Ministry* (Fort Lauderdale, FL: Coral Ridge Ministries, 1990), 27.

5   Williams, *D. James Kennedy,* 29.

6   Mary Lou Davis, *The Truth That Transformed Me: The Life of D. James Kennedy* (Ross-Shire, UK: Christian Focus, 2006), 21.

heard him and offered him a full music scholarship that night.[7] Jim was off to college at the University of Tampa.

During his first two years of college, Jim "ran himself ragged between school and work, leading the marching band as drum major, playing in the Latin band, running a ski school, rowing on the crew team; weightlifting and boxing. Whatever he did, Jim strove for excellence."[8] After his first two years of college, at twenty years of age, Jim saw an ad for a dance instructor job at the Arthur Murray Dance studio. He applied and got the job. He was good at it and the job paid well. Jim saw the opportunity for advancement and dropped out of college to work full time for Arthur Murray. Jim was a good dancer, entering and winning dance contests, and by age 22 was chosen to "serve as a member of the National Dance Board, a group of mentors responsible for creating and formulating steps for the instructional programs."[9]

LIFE CHANGE

When Anne Lewis showed up at the Arthur Murray Dance Studio in Tampa with her date to watch him in a dance lesson, Jim Kennedy took notice. While teaching a dance lesson to an older woman, Kennedy noticed Anne right away and told a fellow instructor, "No doubt about it, that's the girl I'm going to marry." [10] Anne "tried out" or did an evaluative dance with Jim to see what level she might be, he invited her back for ten individual lessons at $100. Anne was a good dancer and also had worked as a water skier. She and her family were part of the Presbyterian Church in Lakeland, Florida. After the ten dance lessons ended, Jim and Anne continued to correspond and date from her home in Lakeland and his in Tampa. One evening, Anne invited him to drive over on a Sunday to Lakeland to attend church with her and her family. Anne asked what church Jim attended. He said that he

---

7   Davis, *The Truth That Transformed Me*, 25.
8   Davis, *The Truth That Transformed Me*, 40.
9   Williams, *D. James Kennedy*, 38.
10 Williams, *D. James Kennedy*, 40.

didn't go to church, didn't think it mattered much, and in fact didn't know anyone who went to church besides Anne. He told Anne (as if from a recitation), "You can be just as good a Christian without going to church." Anne pushed back. "Oh no you can't, Jim Kennedy."[11] The two parted that evening, Jim stumbled into this apartment and went to sleep late, as usual, and set the alarm for later Sunday morning as well.

The next morning the voice of the radio preacher startled him and woke him up. As he twisted in bed to turn the knob of the radio to a musical selection, he heard the preacher say, "Young man, if you were to die tonight and stand before Almighty God and He asked you; 'What right do you have to come into my Heaven?' What would you say?"[12] Jim thought he'd tried to live a good life but as he listened he heard the gospel and salvation by faith alone. As Jim contemplated the message that he was hearing, "something undeniably miraculous had happened to him."[13] Whether at that moment, or a week later when after reading about Christ's death on the cross for our sin, Jim slipped from his chair to his knees and said, "Oh God, I'm so sorry. I didn't know. I didn't know what you had done for me. Forgive me. Forgive me. Come into my heart and never let me forget what you have done for me."[14] Jim was saved.

He began to think differently from that point on and see a radical change in his own actions, habits and desires. He found an old Bible in his closet and bought the only religious book available at a nearby bookstand, *The Greatest Story Ever Told*. He couldn't get enough. He started attending a Presbyterian church where his high school band teacher was going. He also began going to a Bible Study of his age group on Sunday evenings and devoured it. After a few weeks, the group leader left and ask Jim to take the lead. Anne Lewis had noticed the change in Jim's life and soon realized that she had "churchianity" but never had "Christianity." The first person Jim led to the Lord after his salvation was the woman who would soon be his wife.

11   Davis, *The Truth That Transformed Me*, 55.
12   Davis, *The Truth That Transformed Me*, 57.
13   Williams, *D. James Kennedy*, 56.
14   Davis, *The Truth That Transformed Me*, 60.

Jim's career at the Arthur Murray Dance Studio was going well. In fact, unbeknownst to him they were about to offer him a job in Sarasota, Florida as a part-owner of the studio there. One day, locked in his office at the studio, he came to believe God had a special call and purpose for his life. He prayed, stretched out, full length, face to the floor, "Lord, do you really want me to quit this job? Are you sure you want to use someone like me?" He didn't hear any voices, or see any visions, but he picked up the phone and called to resign.[15] With only $13 in his checking account, Jim left his job and went immediately to see his pastor. Jim explained that he felt like God might be calling him to be a pastor. Dr. Campbell was also the chairman of the Presbyterian Home Mission Committee for that area of Florida. Knowing Jim's zeal and gifts, he gave him an opportunity to preach the next weekend at a small Presbyterian church in Clearwater, Florida that would soon need a pastor.

With that in motion and an unexpected Christmas bonus of $300, Jim hurried by the jewelry store and drove to Lakeland with a proposal for Anne. Anne was excited to see him and after driving her to scenic Lake Hollingsworth, parked the car, grabbed the ring, and offered a three-part marriage proposal:

1. I have quit my job at the studio which means I am almost flat broke.
2. I am going into the ministry, and I know you always said you didn't want to be a preacher's wife.
3. Will you marry me?[16]

Anne said yes.

The Kennedys were married some nine months later, then headed to Columbia Theological Seminary near Atlanta to continue training for the ministry. For two summers, Jim would travel back to Tampa to finish his undergraduate degree in English at the University of Tampa.

---

15   Stebbins, *D. James Kennedy's Explosion of Evangelism*, 6.
16   Stebbins, *D. James Kennedy's Explosion of Evangelism*, 7.

As graduation neared, he applied to the Presbyterian World Mission Committee as a missionary candidate for the Belgian Congo. As he waited to hear their response to his application, one of his professors advised him to send out resumes to five presbyteries in Florida and inquire about pulpits that needed to be filled.[17] With no word from the World Missions Committee, Jim accepted an offer from the Home Missions Committee of the Everglades Presbytery to start what would become Coral Ridge Presbyterian Church, a new church start in the northern sector of Fort Lauderdale. In June of 1959, Jim accepted the pastorate on an interim basis while he awaited word on the Congo from the World Missions Committee. The new church met in a schoolhouse cafeteria and required setup and teardown each week. Three months into the pastorate, he received word that an asthmatic condition had shown up in the course of physical evaluation and that he was disqualified from international missions.[18] He would continue on with the church plant as their permanent pastor, and stay for forty-seven years until his death in 2007.

The Kennedys expected the new church plant to immediately grow and prosper. It didn't. In fact, ten months into the work, the original attendance of about forty-five had dwindled to seventeen. Kennedy was humbled and humiliated. He did the math and figured that unless something changed in a few weeks, he'd be preaching to his wife, and she had even threatened to go down the street to the Baptist church![19] His attempts to share the gospel seemed to yield no fruit; he didn't enjoy it and felt lost when it came to sharing Christ one-on-one.

With a church that seemed to be sinking and knowing something needed to change but unsure what, a letter arrived from Kennedy Smartt, pastor of the Ingleside Presbyterian Church in Scottsdale, Georgia. The Kennedys knew Smartt from their time at Columbia Seminary; they had attended the church some and Jim had preached in Kennedy Smartt's pulpit. Smartt had written to invite Jim to conduct

---

17   Stebbins, *D. James Kennedy's Explosion of Evangelism*, 118.
18   Stebbins, *D. James Kennedy's Explosion of Evangelism*, 11.
19   Williams, *D. James Kennedy*, 96.

a ten-day evangelistic meeting. Anne thought it was a good idea, but Jim said, "I've just about decimated Coral Ridge Presbyterian. What if I bring the plague across state lines and wipe out Ingleside Presbyterian?"[20] Regardless, Jim took Smartt up on his invitation and travelled up to Georgia.

When Jim arrived at Ingleside Presbyterian Church, Smartt let him know that not only would he be preaching each evening but that he would be sharing the gospel every day, morning, and afternoon, in homes and door-to-door in the community. He was fully aware of his lack of knowledge as to how to witness to anyone. That night in the hotel he prayed for Jesus to return! He knew Kennedy Smartt would be watching "Kennedy Dumbs'" feeble attempts to witness.[21] Smartt arrived the next morning, excited and ready to go share Christ.

Kennedy and Smartt's first visit was to a man named Hank. Smartt introduced Jim Kennedy to Hank and then allowed Jim to take the lead in sharing the gospel. Jim began a sales pitch that sounded like something from his life as a dance instructor. He told Hank that he needed to turn from his wicked ways and repent, pointing his finger at Hank's chest. As the conversation continued, Hank was getting agitated. Jim continued, "We are all sinners in the hands of an angry God." Hank's irritation manifested with him lunging toward Jim Kennedy, with Kennedy Smart stepping in and calming the situation down.[22] Smartt then said, "Hank, let me ask you a question, if you died tonight are you sure you'd go to Heaven? What if I could tell you how to know for sure that when you die you'd go to Heaven, would you be interested? Suppose you were to stand before God and He were to say to you, 'Hank, why should I let you into my Heaven?' What do you think you would say?"[23] Hank was interested, Kennedy Smartt clearly shared the gospel with him and clarified what it meant to accept Jesus and receive eternal life. Smartt then led Hank in a prayer, repeating after him and repenting of his sin and asking Jesus to take control of his life.

---

20   Davis, *The Truth That Transformed Me*, 139.
21   Davis, *The Truth That Transformed Me*, 143.
22   Davis, *The Truth That Transformed Me*, 145.
23   Davis, *The Truth That Transformed Me*, 145–146.

I asked Kennedy Smartt the same question Jim Kennedy asked him, "Where did you learn to do that?" He said that Bill Iverson, a friend who'd led a revival a year earlier, had done that. Bill (who still lives and pastors in New Jersey) had been a three-letter athlete in football, basketball, and track at Davidson. He stood at six foot six and Smartt said he would talk to anyone.[24] Smartt recalls that his church was in a mill town; there was a cotton mill and a textile mill. People in the community were either working at the mill or at home, depending on their shift. The owner of the mill had given permission and even asked for them to share the gospel in the mill.

Meanwhile, over the next several days, Jim Kennedy watched Smartt and eventually helped lead more than fifty people to Christ.[25] Kennedy Smartt is still active in evangelism and serves as "chaplain to the community" at Chestnut Mountain Presbyterian Church in Georgia.

D. James Kennedy returned to Florida after the evangelistic campaign with Kennedy Smartt and began to practice that same method in his church. He realized after several months, that he alone, or sometimes with his wife Anne, would only be able to reach a limited number of people. He began to take others with him and train them in evangelism. Jim had discovered "the secret of witnessing, of effective, productive, personal witnessing. He had learned how to deactivate the paralyzing fear that had thwarted all of his previous feeble evangelizing efforts. He had discovered the sure way to lead a person to Christ in a one on one situation."[26] The church started to grow, from seventeen to sixty-six, just eleven months after it began in May 1960. By 1967, Coral Ridge was singled out as the fastest growing church in the denomination. As pastors around the country began to ask how he had done it, Jim began to hold Evangelism Explosion workshops, the first in February of 1967.[27]

Throughout the rest of his life, Kennedy continued to have a passion for souls. Further, Kennedy was active in the "religious right"

---

24   Conversation with Kennedy Smartt, October 9, 2019.
25   Conversation with Kennedy Smartt.
26   Williams, *D. James Kennedy,* 111.
27   Williams, *D. James Kennedy,* 121.

movement of the 1980s along with Jerry Falwell, Pat Robertson, and James Dobson. Kennedy's Coral Ridge Ministries included radio and television and claimed an audience of 3.5 million people. The "Coral Ridge Hour," Kennedy's weekly message, was broadcast in more than 145 countries and on more than six hundred stations. Kennedy also founded a seminary and a school and wrote more than sixty-five books.[28]

Stan Guthrie sums up the impact and focus of D. James Kennedy's life well: "I believe Dr. Kennedy, for all his passion for 'reclaiming America,' would agree that claiming souls for the Savior is his best and most lasting work. You may not agree with all of Dr. Kennedy's priorities. But it's hard to argue with his passionate commitment to see people come to Christ. It was a commitment this pastor lived—and died—by."[29]

UNIQUE FEATURES OF EVANGELISM EXPLOSION

Dedicated Commitment

It was in the late 1980s that I was first exposed to Evangelism Explosion (EE) and the Southern Baptist Home Mission Board's similar evangelism tool Continuing Witnessing Training (CWT). Compared to evangelism methods that would follow, Evangelism Explosion requires a dedicated commitment to on-the-job witnessing training, memorization of the gospel outline, and direct evangelism in teams of three with a commitment to reproduce soul-winning disciplers. The commitment required for EE almost seems almost unrealistic in today's Twitter and Instagram world of evangelism. The "course" is designed to take place over four "semesters" of training in a local church. A semester is defined as four and a half months; thus the commitment involved in the training is two to three years.[30]

---

28 Neela Banerjeesept, "Rev. D. James Kennedy, Broadcaster, Dies at 76," *The New York Times*, September 6, 2007, https://www.nytimes.com/2007/09/06/us/06kennedy. html.

29 Guthrie, "A Passion for Souls."

30 D. James Kennedy, *Evangelism Explosion*, revised edition (Wheaton, IL: Tyndale House Publishers, 1977), xiv.

On-the-Job Training

Evangelism Explosion has three kinds of training: class instruction, homework, and on-the-job training. In my evangelism classes I spend a session talking about evangelism and fishing. No one learns to fish from a textbook on fishing. I've never seen a manual with a new rod and reel or a cane pole with "how to" instructions on how to catch fish! People, kids, and adults all learn to fish by fishing and by being with people who know how to fish. On-the-job training is a missing ingredient to most of our evangelism "programs" today. Few of our young seminary students here in the West have grown up to be able "fishers of men." They want to be good witnesses, but they don't know how. It's rare that they have watched their pastor or another trainer in evangelism. There have been thousands of sermons preached on evangelism, and our responsibility is to go and witness. Evangelism is more caught than taught. Try taking people with you as you share Christ and see what happens!

Gateway Seminary once had a campus in Brea, California, across the street from the Brea Mall. I loved taking students to the mall and just leading them in talking to people. For many students this was the first time they had talked with someone about Christ outside of a Sunday Bible study group or in church. They were immediately surprised at how simple and normal it was. Their fears began to dissipate. D. James Kennedy said, "the average person can no more learn to evangelize in a classroom than he can learn to fly a plane in the living room. The missing link in modern evangelistic training, which was so thoroughly provided by Christ is 'on the job' training."[31]

Multiplication of Witnesses

Returning from his week with Kennedy Smartt, D. James Kennedy began to lead people to Christ. Soon however, Kennedy recognized that he could never reach the numbers of lost people in his community by doing evangelism by himself. Evangelism by

---

31   Kennedy, *Evangelism Explosion*, 5.

addition would never reach the world. The church needed multiplication, training evangelists who trained evangelists who trained evangelists. "What he needed to do, he realized, was not just to win people to Christ; he needed to train people to win people to Christ. The Bible calls it 'equipping the saints' by transferring to them techniques that work."[32] Convinced also that the church must "evangelize or fossilize," he made evangelism training a foundational part of his ministry throughout his life. A pillar of the EE program is that it is more important to train a soul-winner than to win a soul.

Every year I ask students at Gateway Seminary to do a survey of their churches related to their overall evangelism strategy. I've learned to expect that very few the churches surveyed train people in evangelism. How can we expect to see our communities changed and people come to Christ if we are not witnessing and multiplying witnesses? Kennedy found that about 96 percent of converts never win anyone to Christ because they are not equipped to do so.[33] Multiplying witnesses is both biblical and essential if we are to reach our communities and the world. During the EE program, witness trainees not only learn to share Christ, but begin to pray and seek out others who they can train next to share Christ.

FINDING, DEVELOPING, AND SHARING CHRIST WITH PROSPECTS

Our students at Gateway are required to "report" on eight evangelistic conversations over the course of an eight- to fifteen-week semester. Many find these "verbatims" a difficult assignment because they cannot identify eight lost people who might need to hear the gospel. They live and work in a Christian bubble and have no intentional plan to meet and develop new friendships with a thought of sharing Christ with them. The majority of their reports describe a conversation

---

32 Stebbins, *D. James Kennedy's Explosion of Evangelism*, 15.
33 Kennedy, *Evangelism Explosion*, 5.

that struggles to get to the gospel with people that Oscar Thompson referred to in *Concentric Circles of Evangelism* as "Person X."

The Evangelism Explosion method develops a list of potential "prospects" with whom the trainer and trainees can share Christ. Just like fishing, if you're teaching someone to fish, you wouldn't first go to a challenging fishing spot that rarely produces any fish! Finding a place that often produces fish is a good idea when learning to share Christ and teach others to do the same. The Evangelism Explosion plan develops a prospect list from people who have visited church worship services, people who are friends and relatives of church folks, attenders to the weekly Sunday school, and new residents to name a few.[34] Developing a solid prospect list, praying for those people, and intentionally sharing Christ with them can yield good results.

A PLANNED GOSPEL PRESENTATION

The idea of sharing the gospel with a planned, memorized, intentional presentation could sound to some like a slick sales pitch, maybe even inauthentic. In a generation where everything needs to be organic and relational, could something like a memorized gospel presentation outline with a detailed introduction and conclusion not only work, but be genuine and right? While clearly stating that salvation is from God,[35] D. James Kennedy says, "The essential things which we are trying to teach our people are: how to get into the gospel and find out where the person is spiritually, how to present the gospel itself, how to bring the person to a commitment to Jesus Christ at the conclusion, and how to vitally relate the new convert to the family of God."[36] Trainees start by memorizing a gospel outline, make it their own, and then begin to add details and "meat" to their gospel presentation.

The gospel outline itself is below:

---

34 Kennedy, *Evangelism Explosion*, 10.
35 Kennedy, *Evangelism Explosion*, 45.
36 Kennedy, *Evangelism Explosion*, 12.

I. Grace
    A. Heaven is a free gift. It is not earned or deserved. (According to the Scriptures heaven, eternal life, is absolutely a free gift.)
    B. It is not earned or deserved (Rom. 6:23).

II. Man
    A. Is a sinner (Matt. 5:48; Rom. 3:23)
    B. Cannot save himself (Eph. 2:8–9)

III. God
    A. Is merciful—therefore, God doesn't wish to punish us
    B. Is just—therefore, must punish sin

IV. Christ
    A. Who he is—the infinite God-man
    B. What he did—Christ paid for our sin (John 1:1, 14; Isa. 53:6) and purchased a place in heaven for us, which he offers as a gift (Isa. 53:10; John 14:2; Rom. 6:23).

At this point, EE has a wonderful, clear, and simple illustration that often helps to clarify an understanding of what Christ did. Using Isaiah 53:6, the one sharing the gospel speaks about our sin. He holds the Bible in one hand and allows it for a moment to represent our sin. Then the witness quotes Isaiah 53:6 and "the Lord has laid on Him the iniquity of us all," shifting the Bible from one hand to other to show how our sin was transferred to Jesus.[37]

V. Faith
    A. What it is not—mere intellectual assent or temporal faith (Eph. 2:8).
    B. What it is—"trusting for Jesus Christ alone for our salvation."[38]

---

37 Kennedy, *Evangelism Explosion*, 21, 40.
38 Kennedy, *Evangelism Explosion*, 16–44.

To illustrate "trusting" EE has another illustration that clarifies what it means to trust. While pointing to a chair the witness asks, "Do you believe this chair exists? Do you believe it will hold you? It is not holding you now. How could you prove that you believe it exists and can hold you? Answer? By sitting in it. This simple illustration often helps to clarify what it means to trust in Jesus. It's more than believing Jesus existed."[39]

Even with an effective outline, EE understands that the outline does not save anyone; the Holy Spirit does. In Evangelism Explosion, Kennedy describes witnessing like shipbuilding. A riveter places a rivet into the side of a steel ship with one hand and holds a pneumatic gun to the rivet with the other hand. There are four elements involved: the riveter, the steel ship, the rivet, and the pneumatic gun. The steel ship represents the hard heart of the hearer, the riveter is the witness, and the rivet is the gospel. The pneumatic gun is the Holy Spirit. We can't push the rivet through on our own. The Holy Spirit must do that.[40]

PURPOSEFUL INTRODUCTION AND CONCLUSION

There are usually two "speed bumps" or hurdles that witnesses have when facing a gospel conversation: getting into and getting out of the conversation! Once the conversation actually gets to the gospel, many believers (students) can remember the life (sinless), death (for our sin), burial, and resurrection (that shows Jesus is who he said he was and could do what he said he could do! (I like the way Jimmy Scroggins states the importance of the resurrection in his illustration of the Three Circles). An outline, as stated above, can help to organize and present the gospel clearly and back it with significant Scripture.

But how do you get from talking about baseball, the kids' program at school, or the changes at work to the gospel? A good introduction helps to determine where a person is spiritually and if there is a hunger to hear what you have to say, and makes a smooth transition to the

---

39 Kennedy, *Evangelism Explosion*, 22–23.
40 Kennedy, *Evangelism Explosion*, 46.

gospel. Evangelism Explosion has both a planned, clear introduction and a simple conclusion that works.

The introduction follows a simple outline and leads to two diagnostic questions, beginning with a conversation about the person, who they are and what they do—their "secular life." The introduction then moves to their "church background," a short testimony, and then the two questions, a variation on the questions Kennedy heard on the radio and with Kennedy Smartt. First, "Have you come to a place in your spiritual life where you know for certain that if you were to die today you would go to Heaven?" and second, "Suppose you were to die today and stand before God and he were to say to you, 'Why should I let you into my Heaven?' What would you say?"[41] Between the two questions, another simple statement is inserted that gains permission to continue (one of the things that makes Evangelism Explosion a direct but also relational method) toward sharing the gospel: "Would you like for me to share with you how I made that discovery and how you can know it too?"

When the gospel has been presented, how do you end? How do you land the plane? Is it enough to just encourage the listener to "think about things" or tell them that you'll be praying for them? The transitional statement in the conclusion or commitment section of the Evangelism Explosion gospel presentation is one that I use all the time; it fits, it's not awkward, and it works. Once the gospel has been shared, simply ask first, "Does this make sense to you?"[42] The answer to this question will allow you to proceed or to review what area(s) might not make sense. This initial qualifying question is followed by a commitment question: "Would you like to receive the gift of eternal life which Christ is offering you?" This is followed by some clarification to make sure that the person is aware that repentance of sin and submitting to the Lordship of Christ is part of this commitment. The witness might now suggest they simply pray to God and express this commitment. EE has a model prayer that can be used, but also adapts

---

41 Kennedy, *Evangelism Explosion*, 26.
42 Kennedy, *Evangelism Explosion*, 67

to the individual emphasizing prayer for the individual and prayer with the individual. This is further followed up with an emphasis to get the new believer connected to other believers and the church.

FINAL THOUGHTS

The D. James Kennedy story is one of God's providence and plan. A young boy from a dysfunctional home becomes a dance instructor, gets saved through a radio broadcast, and develops a method to share the gospel that might well have led more people to faith in Christ than another other method in history! His life and ministry have made an eternal impact in a number of ways.

All who knew him, however, talked mostly not about his views on abortion or school prayer, but about his integrity and warm pastor's heart. To me, that heart is most exemplified not in the imposing Coral Ridge Presbyterian Church (with a thirty-story steeple, and thereby known as "the rocket-ship-to-God church"), in the school and seminary he founded, in his media empire, nor in his now-defunct Center for Reclaiming America for Christ. Rather, his heart is exemplified in two simple questions:

1. Do you know for sure that you are going to be with God in heaven?
2. If God were to ask you, "Why should I let you into my heaven?" what would you say?[43]

---

43   Guthrie, "A Passion for Souls."

CHAPTER 18

THE JESUS MOVEMENT
and CHUCK SMITH'S
CALVARY CHAPEL

Preston L. Nix

A most unlikely event at a most unlikely time, initially among a most unlikely group of people, started in the late 1960s and continued through the early 1970s. This event profoundly affected the youth culture of this country and the spiritual climate of the church, as well as the nation itself with some effects that still persist today. The event became known as the Jesus Movement or the Jesus Revolution—a spiritual awakening that exploded onto the national scene at a time of conflict and unrest in the United States that started among an antiestablishment, countercultural group of rebellious young people known as hippies. The Jesus Movement was "primarily a youth movement" that touched the lives of thousands of baby boomers, resulting in more people coming to faith in Christ and being baptized than at any other time in the nation's history.[1] Further, a most unlikely

---

1   Greg Laurie and Ellen Vaughn, *Jesus Revolution: How God Transformed an Unlikely Generation and How He Can Do It Again Today* (Grand Rapids: Baker Books, 2018), 191, 214.

church became "the Mother Church of the Jesus Movement"[2] and
a most unlikely pastor became the "father figure"[3] to multitudes of
young people who were reached with the gospel and baptized in
the Pacific Ocean. The very traditional church that experienced a
radical transformation as a result of the Jesus Movement was Calvary Chapel in Costa Mesa, California. The somewhat convention-
al pastor who initially despised hippies but whose heart underwent
a radical change toward them resulting in literally thousands of
them being converted to Christ was Chuck Smith.[4] In this chapter,
the story of the national spiritual awakening known as the Jesus
Movement which touched the youth culture of the day in a profound way and the critical role that Calvary Chapel and its pastor
Chuck Smith played in the Jesus Movement will be explored.

THE UNEXPECTED EMERGENCE
OF THE JESUS MOVEMENT

The decade of the 1960s was a period of unprecedented societal change
and serious internal conflict in the United States of America. The times
were revolutionary. The call for revolution throughout the nation was
evidenced by the Vietnam War protests, anti-government protests,
the civil rights movement, the women's liberation movement, the gay
rights movement, the modern environmental movement, race riots
in major cities, student protests on college and university campuses,
and the rejection of traditional moral values as well as the rejection
of the traditional church. The various countercultural movements of
the era were unapologetically anti-authority, reflecting the rejection
of and even rage against what the younger generation called "the

---

2   Malcolm McDow and Alvin L. Reid, *Firefall 2.0: How God Has Shaped History Through Revivals* (Wake Forest, NC: Gospel Advance Books, 2014), 279. See also Laurie, 245, 249.
3   Larry Eskridge, *God's Forever Family: The Jesus People Movement in America* (New York: Oxford University Press, 2013), 72. In fact, the pastor was called "Papa Chuck" or "Daddy Chuck" by the younger generation in the church.
4   Eskridge, *God's Forever Family*, 68–69. See also Laurie and Vaughn, *Jesus Revolution*, 245, 249.

establishment"—that is, the mainstream of society's "reigning values of conformity and the rat race of material success and achievement."[5] Rejecting the values of conformity and the pursuit of materialism of their parents, the Boomer generation sought to find meaning and purpose in life through sex, drugs, and rock and roll. "They were more interested in achieving higher levels of consciousness through drugs, grooving on the music of the day, and enjoying sexual adventures free from the convention of marriage."[6] They "sought peace, love, and community in the utopian visions of the day." They "thought that drugs would bring spiritual enlightenment, or that sex would bring love, or that music would bring community, or that all these things would bring freedom."[7] In their cry for revolution in society and their adoption of a defiant, revolutionary lifestyle free from the restraints of "the establishment," instead of the freedom and fulfillment they so desperately sought, they found bondage and emptiness.

Having tried everything the world had to offer but finding nothing to fulfill the longings of their hearts, they became desperate in their search to fill the void in their lives. At that juncture in time, the Spirit of God began moving in a supernatural way, touching the lives of this desperate generation of youth. In the midst of the "political, social, moral, scientific, [and] violent," revolutions of the day,[8] first, the hippies and then the general youth population discovered the ultimate Revolutionary, the Lord Jesus Christ, who radically revolutionized their lives.[9] Some of the initial appeal of Jesus was that he was viewed by them as a long-haired, antiestablishment revolutionary with something to say to their generation. In fact, one of the prominent religious posters during the Jesus Movement, illustrating this appeal of Jesus, was printed as an Old Wild West "Outlaw Wanted" poster with a prominent picture of Jesus which read in part:

5   Laurie and Vaughn, *Jesus Revolution,* 14.
6   Laurie and Vaughn, *Jesus Revolution,* 14.
7   Laurie and Vaughn, *Jesus Revolution,* 231.
8   Billy Graham, *The Jesus Generation* (Grand Rapids: Zondervan Publishing House, 1971), 9.
9   Bill Bright, *Revolution Now!* (San Bernardino, CA: Campus Crusade for Christ, Inc., 1969), 25–50.

WANTED: JESUS CHRIST. Alias: The Messiah, The Son
of God, King of Kings Lord of Lords, Prince of Peace, Etc.
Notorious leader of an underground liberation movement.
Wanted for the following charges: Interfering with busi-
nessmen in the temple. Associating with known criminals,
radicals, subversives, prostitutes and street people. AP-
PEARANCE: Typical Hippie type, long hair, beard, robe,
sandals. . . . BEWARE: This man is extremely dangerous.
His insidiously inflammatory message is particularly dan-
gerous to young people who haven't been taught to ignore
Him yet. He changes men and claims to set them free.
WARNING: HE IS STILL AT LARGE![10]

Jesus the first-century revolutionary "fit the times" in the experience
of the baby boomers in the second half of the twentieth century and
while the multitude of revolutionary movements unfolded in their
generation, the Lord Jesus Christ began to move and work in the
hearts and lives of the youth population of the nation and the Jesus
Movement was born.

The Jesus Movement actually began to emerge among the hippie
population in the late 1960s on the west coast of the United States.
"Virtually simultaneous outbreaks" of the religious revival occurred
primarily in several California cities starting in 1967 and 1968, which
make pinpointing a specific place of origin or a particular person responsible for the launch of the movement impossible to determine.[11]
In fact, one who was heavily involved in the movement from its
inception expressed the view of many at the time when he declared
simply that God was responsible for starting the Jesus Movement. He
went on to say, "It was spontaneous, clearly led by the Holy Spirit."[12]
However, through the leadership of various individuals, the Lord set
the movement in motion.

---

10   See Figure 4.1 in Eskridge, *God's Forever Family,* 97.
11   Alvin Lee Reid, "The Impact of the Jesus Movement on Evangelism among Southern
     Baptists" (PhD diss., Southwestern Baptist Theological Seminary, 1991), 11.
12   Duane Pederson with Bob Owen, *Jesus People* (Pasadena, CA: Compass Press, 1971), 34.

Ted Wise was a converted drug addict who along with his wife began to witness to the hippies in San Francisco's Haight-Ashbury district, considered the "mecca of the counter-culture."[13] They began a coffeehouse ministry called The Living Room, which touched the lives of an estimated thirty to fifty thousand young people with the gospel during a two-year period. Their work was used to spark a movement that saw massive numbers of "flower children" turn from drugs to Jesus.[14] They also began a Christian commune called The House of Acts.

Simultaneously a movement began in Southern California under the ministry of Pastor Chuck Smith at Calvary Chapel in Costa Mesa, and Lonnie Frisbee who moved there from Haight and was instrumental in helping the church reach out to the hippie population in the surrounding area. Frisbee and his wife also opened a coffeehouse called The House of Miracles under Calvary Chapel's sponsorship.[15] Because of the critical role that Chuck Smith and Calvary Chapel played in the Jesus Movement, a more detailed account of their part in the story will be included later in the chapter.

Don Williams, who was the college minister at the First Presbyterian Church in Hollywood, led the church to sponsor a coffeehouse ministry known as The Salt Company. From its beginning in 1967, The Salt Company not only touched the lives of thousands of young people with the gospel, but also affected many who became leaders in the Jesus Movement, including Larry Norman and Duane Pederson. Norman, who often performed at the coffeehouse, became a leader in the music scene of the Jesus Movement and was called "The Father of Christian Rock." Pederson, who coined the terms "Jesus People" and "Jesus People Movement,"[16] was highly influential in the Jesus Movement through the publication of the underground *Hollywood Free Paper*. The publication became the "national" Jesus People paper

---

13   McDow and Reid, *Firefall 2.0*, 279.

14   McDow and Reid, *Firefall 2.0*.

15   Alvin Reid, "The Effect of the Jesus Movement on Evangelism in the Southern Baptist Convention," *Baptist History and Heritage* 30, no. 1 (January 1995): 41.

16   Pederson, *Jesus People*, 34–35.

and along with other underground Jesus papers served as evangelistic tracts and "foldable, portable bulletin board[s] for various Jesus People hangouts and events."[17] Pederson received assistance in the printing and distribution of his paper from both The Salt Company and First Presbyterian Church. A young artist named Lance Bowen helped with the layouts and cartoons for the paper. Bowen is credited with originating the "key Christian symbol of the Jesus Movement," the One-Way sign consisting of an upheld fist with the index finger pointing toward heaven with a small cross above it.[18]

Linda Meissner, who had worked with David Wilkerson in New York, traveled to Seattle in 1968 to set up the Teen Center. She also opened The Ark which was a place for teens to hangout and "rap," and The Eleventh Hour coffeehouse which later was moved to a larger building and renamed the Catacombs. By 1971, the Catacombs became likely the largest coffeehouse in the Jesus Movement.[19] Meissner also published an underground paper *Agape* and formed the evangelistic outreach group the Jesus People's Army.

In 1969, Jack Sparks, who had a PhD and was a former professor of statistics at Penn State, started the Christian World Liberation Front (CWLF) on the campus of the University of California at Berkeley. The organization was modeled after the radical left of the day and was designed to provide an "edgy" Christian witness in its context. The CWLF published a widely distributed underground Jesus paper as well, *Right On*. Sparks began CWLF with a commune in his own home, and by 1971, thirty-two communes consisting of at least six hundred Jesus People had spread across the San Francisco Bay area.[20]

As the Jesus Movement continued to spread other individuals and their ministries impacted the youth population in different parts of the country. Southern Baptist Arthur Blessitt opened a Christian nightclub named His Place on Sunset Strip in West Hollywood, California, and ministered primarily to drug users, runaways, and street people,

---

17   Eskridge, *God's Forever Family*, 161, 3.
18   McDow and Reid, *Firefall 2.0*, 279.
19   Reid, "Impact of Jesus Movement," 17.
20   Reid, "Impact of Jesus Movement," 16.

leading many to faith in Christ.[21] Later, he became famous for carrying a large wooden cross throughout the United States and around the world. Another Southern Baptist evangelist, Sammy Tippit, became a leader of the Jesus Movement in Chicago with the founding of a street witnessing ministry known as God's Love in Action.[22] Also in Chicago, Jim and Sue Palosaari, Linda Meissner, Glenn Kaiser, and others founded Jesus People USA, which continues to minister in the city through social ministries and beyond through its *Cornerstone* magazine and the Rez (Resurrection) Band.[23] Danny Flanders began Maranatha, a ministry that targeted the underground youth culture of Washington, D.C.[24]

THE CRITICAL ROLE OF CHUCK SMITH AND CALVARY CHAPEL IN THE JESUS MOVEMENT

Although various personalities and their respective ministries played significant roles in the emergence and spread of the Jesus Movement, none were as critical as the role that Pastor Chuck Smith and Calvary Chapel played in the movement. Calvary Chapel in Costa Mesa became the "largest single embodiment of the developing Jesus movement in Southern California."[25] This traditional, conservative church was "literally deluged in the earliest storms of the Jesus Movement."[26] As indicated previously, Calvary Chapel was an unlikely church to become "the Mother Church of the Jesus Movement" and Chuck Smith was an unlikely pastor to become the "father figure" to multitudes of the young people who were touched through his ministry. Chuck Smith, a balding, middle-aged pastor who had grown tired of the denominational politics and bureaucracy, left the International Church of the Foursquare Gospel, the denomination

---

21 Reid, "Effect of Jesus Movement," 43.
22 McDow and Reid, *Firefall 2.0*, 280.
23 McDow and Reid, *Firefall 2.0*.
24 Reid, "Impact of Jesus Movement," 19.
25 Eskridge, *God's Forever Family*, 68.
26 McDow and Reid, *Firefall 2.0*, 279.

founded by Aimee Semple McPherson.[27] After successfully growing a home Bible study into the 150-member Corona Christian Center, his wife Kay was shocked when Chuck told her that he felt led of the Lord to become the pastor of the struggling Costa Mesa congregation. When Smith began his ministry at Calvary Chapel in December of 1965, twenty-five people were in attendance in the run-down church building.[28] Within six months, the entire church building was painted and remodeled, but more importantly the congregation doubled in size. In the next six months, the membership doubled again and after eighteen months the original twenty-five had grown to 150.[29]

As Smith ministered to his growing suburban church, Kay began to have a burden for the hippies who were gathering at nearby Huntington Beach. She made her husband drive over to the beach, where they observed the long-haired kids "staggering down the street or zoned out on the beach" due to drugs and alcohol.[30] Upon seeing their appearance and watching their behavior, Smith said, "My original thought was 'Why don't they cut their hair and get a job and live a decent life?' I saw them as parasites upon society."[31] He wanted nothing to do with those rebellious young people. In great contrast, Kay had tears in her eyes and blurted out, "They're so lost. We've got to reach them! They've got to know a different life! They've got to know Jesus!"[32] The Lord used "his wife's concern for the hippies' temporal and eternal needs" to change Chuck's heart toward them and they began to think about how they could make contact with these troubled youth.[33]

The Smiths were aware that hippies were not going to show up spontaneously at their middle-class, conservative, suburban church. As a result, Kay asked the boyfriend of their college-age daughter who

---

27   Eskridge, *God's Forever Family,* 68.
28   Chuck Smith with Hugh Steven, *The Reproducers: New Life for Thousands* (Glendale, CA: Regal Books, 1972), 13, 19–22.
29   Smith, *The Reproducers,* 25.
30   Laurie and Vaughn, *Jesus Revolution,* 87.
31   Eskridge, *God's Forever Family,* 69.
32   Laurie and Vaughn, *Jesus Revolution,* 87.
33   Eskridge, *God's Forever Family,* 69–70.

had come to Christ out of the Haight-Ashbury movement in San Francisco if he could bring a "real-live hippie" over to their house. She said to him, "We just want to understand their world. We want to know how they think, what they believe, and how we can help."[34] Soon thereafter, the daughter's boyfriend arrived at their home with a long-haired, bearded, flower child hippie wearing a linen tunic named Lonnie Frisbee. He was visiting back home in Costa Mesa from the San Francisco Bay area and not only did he look like Jesus but also, he was a dynamic witness for Jesus to fellow hippies and anyone who would listen to him share his faith. Lonnie Frisbee and Chuck Smith "had nothing in common in terms of personality, life experience, background, or appearance," but when they met "something big and volatile was about to happen that only God could orchestrate."[35]

Smith thought, "This might be the very person to help us begin reaching the great numbers of hippies who are migrating to the beach areas."[36] Smith shared the burden that his wife and he had for the mass numbers of hippies who had moved into their area and their desire to minister to them and lead them to faith in Jesus Christ. Believing that Lonnie could relate to the hippies and teach him how to reach out to them, Smith asked Lonnie if he would come and help them with that kind of ministry. Lonnie was excited about the proposal, and two weeks later he and his wife Connie left San Francisco and moved in with the Smiths. The relationship between Chuck Smith and Lonnie Frisbee and what they began to do together to reach the lost and hopeless youth around them was what God used to place Calvary Chapel at "ground zero" of the Jesus Movement.

Knowing that many of the new hippie converts would need a place to stay, food to eat, and "an atmosphere where Bible-reading and prayer could replace drugs and sex as their main pastimes,"[37] Calvary Chapel established a communal house—the House of Miracles—overseen by Lonnie and Connie Frisbee along with another

---

34 Laurie and Vaughn, *Jesus Revolution*, 88.
35 Laurie and Vaughn, *Jesus Revolution*, 88–89.
36 Smith, *The Reproducers*, 38.
37 Eskridge, *God's Forever Family*, 70.

young convert named John Higgins. By the end of the first week, twenty-one young men received Christ and moved into the House of Miracles.[38] Lonnie and John spent each day witnessing on the beach, winning hippies to Christ, and then bringing them to the house. By the end of the second week, almost fifty young people were living in the house. Because of the overflow at the House of Miracles with kids sleeping in the backyard, a run-down hotel was renovated as a second commune. The witnessing efforts from those in the hotel yielded sixty-five converts the first week, and by summer's end more than five hundred had been saved, including members of the Diablos motorcycle gang. Calvary Chapel opened many more communal houses and The Risen Sun coffeehouse to continue to minister to the great numbers of young people coming to faith in Christ.

Simultaneously at the Calvary Chapel campus, worship services shifted from traditional to more informal to accommodate the influx of the hippies and other young people. The Lord used the Bible teaching of the father figure Pastor Chuck Smith and the novelty of the passionate hippie preacher Lonnie Frisbee to bring in the throngs of young people who began flocking to the church.[39] A new auditorium was built to accommodate the growing attendance, but on opening day, ushers scrambled to find extra chairs for the overflow crowds. The second Sunday some people had to sit on the floor. The third Sunday, not even standing room was available in the foyer. After five Sundays, Smith decided to move to two services, both of which overflowed in two months. A year later, the church doubled its seating capacity by pushing out the side walls and using folding chairs. By mid-1971, the church began holding three morning worship services, setting up five hundred extra chairs on the outside patio so everyone could have a place to sit.[40]

---

38 Smith, *The Reproducers*, 44.
39 Eskridge believed that the hippie preacher Lonnie Frisbee, "clad in bell bottoms and speaking in the vernacular of the street," was "key in pulling in the crowds of young people during Calvary Chapel's early expansion." See Eskridge, *God's Forever Family*, 72–73.
40 Smith, *The Reproducers*, 62–63.

Although the church experienced phenomenal growth under the different preaching styles of these two men, not all the members were happy with the new hippie preacher as well as the new direction of Calvary Chapel. Several had concerns that the barefoot hippies' dirty feet and dirty jeans would soil the new shag carpet and padded pews in the new auditorium. Arriving early one Sunday morning, Pastor Chuck was both shocked and saddened when he saw a sign put up by some church members which read, "No Bare Feet Allowed in the Church." Incensed, he took down the sign and called a meeting of the church board and membership after the morning worship service to address the situation. One writer concluded that what happened in that meeting was "a pivotal turning point in the history of Calvary Chapel and probably for the entire Jesus movement."[41] After reminding the group of the great work God had been doing "among the drug and hippie culture" through their church and that in reality the church members were "on trial before the young people," Pastor Chuck declared,

> If because of our plush carpeting we have to close the door to one young person who has bare feet, then I'm personally in favor of ripping out all the carpeting and having bare concrete floors. If because of dirty jeans we have to say to one young person I am sorry you can't come into the church tonight, your jeans are too dirty, then I am in favor of getting rid of the upholstered pews. Let's get benches or steel chairs or something we can wash off. But let's not ever, ever, close the door to anyone because of dress or the way he looks.[42]

During the following months, an overwhelming majority of the older established membership experienced a change of attitude toward the hippies and embraced the vision of their pastor and as a result, the already impressive growth of the church continued to an even greater degree.[43]

---

41   Eskridge, *God's Forever Family,* 75.
42   Smith, *The Reproducers,* 60–61.
43   Smith, *The Reproducers.* See also Laurie and Vaughn, *Jesus Revolution,* 239.

While adding the multiple Sunday morning worship services to Calvary Chapel's schedule, the church began holding three weekly youth night services with upward of two thousand in attendance every night. These youth gatherings sometimes lasted up to three or four hours and included rock music, prayer, and a Bible study.[44] So many were being saved in the worship services and through the various outreach ministries of the church that monthly baptisms were held along a rocky beach called Pirate's Cove in Corona del Mar State Park. Sometimes more than five hundred young people would be baptized at one time. In 1970 alone, Pastor Chuck Smith baptized more than two thousand youth in the Pacific Ocean.[45] These public ocean baptisms became recognized images of the Jesus Movement throughout the country in secular press coverage.[46] Sometimes crowds of over more than three thousand spectators would come to watch these outdoor baptismal services. Pastor Chuck Smith seized upon the opportunity to preach the gospel to the crowds gathered on the beach and won many more to Christ.[47]

In addition to the communal and coffee houses and special services targeting the younger generation, other ministries developed as the church continued to grow which contributed to the spread of the Jesus Movement. Cassette tapes of the verse-by-verse Bible teaching of Pastor Chuck Smith were recorded and were sent out literally around the world.[48] A new genre of music known as Christian Rock music or Jesus music began to arise during the Jesus Movement, as formerly pagan musicians got saved and began to write songs out of their new life experience in Christ.[49] Several Jesus music groups came

---

44   McDow and Reid, *Firefall 2.0*, 279.
45   McDow and Reid, *Firefall 2.0*.
46   Chuck Smith and Tal Brooke, *Harvest* (Old Tappan, NJ: Chosen Books, 1987), 21, 13. The baptisms were covered by *Time, Look, Newsweek, Life,* and *Reader's Digest*, all major popular national magazines at that time. For a firsthand description of the special baptismal services, see the chapter "Hold Me Down a Long Time" in Smith, *The Reproducers*, 90–99.
47   Elmer Towns and Douglas Porter, *The Ten Greatest Revivals Ever: From Pentecost to the Present* (Ann Arbor, MI: Servant Publications, 2000), 158.
48   Smith, *The Reproducers*, 67–69.
49   Donald E. Miller, *Reinventing American Protestantism: Christianity in the New Millennium* (Berkeley: University of California Press, 1997), 37.

out of Calvary Chapel. The best known of these original groups was Love Song, called "the Beatles of the Christian music world."[50] Pastor Chuck indicated that Love Song "opened up a whole new dimension at Calvary . . . kids started coming in tremendous numbers just to hear the music."[51] Not only did Love Song attract large groups of young people, but also they inspired other groups to form and use their musical talents for Jesus. Love Song, Children of the Day, Country Faith, Blessed Hope, and other groups began to hold concerts in high schools, local auditoriums, as well as at Calvary Chapel and some went on national and international tours. Love Song originally had signed with United Artists in order to get their music and message out to a national audience. Love Song and other Christian artists began to combine their talents to produce more Jesus music albums. In order to handle skyrocketing record sales and concert bookings as well as the massive follow-up mailings and Bible correspondence courses sent to the thousands of new converts, Calvary Chapel formed a subsidiary organization called Maranatha Music/Publishing.[52] Maranatha became a major influence in the music industry, promoting quality Christian praise and worship music for decades following their founding, in response to the ministry needs at Calvary Chapel during the Jesus Movement.

As membership at the church continued to grow, Chuck Smith began to mentor young converts to start Calvary Chapels in neighboring cities.[53] People then could experience the type of worship experience that Calvary Chapel offered without having to commute to Costa Mesa. Converts who felt a call to ministry and had spent time at Calvary Chapel under the teaching and leadership of Pastor Chuck Smith, were sent out to start other similar churches and the Calvary Chapel movement was born.[54] The multiplication of Calvary

---

50   McDow and Reid, *Firefall,* 285.
51   Smith, *The Reproducers,* 80.
52   Smith, *The Reproducers,* 80–81.
53   Miller, *Reinventing American Protestantism,* 34.
54   Miller, *Reinventing American Protestantism,* 34–35. For accounts of the dramatic life stories of eight of the "spiritual sons" of Pastor Chuck Smith who founded some of the most influential of the Calvary Chapels, see Chuck Smith and Tal Brooke, *Harvest*

Chapel churches elsewhere contributed to the continuing growth of the Jesus Movement in Southern California and across the country. At one point during a two-year period in the mid-1970s, Calvary Chapel performed more than eight thousand baptisms. During that same time frame, the church saw at least twenty thousand converts to Christ through their outreach efforts.[55] By the mid-1980s Calvary Chapel had become a megachurch, listed as number 18 among the twenty largest churches in the world.[56] The explosive growth of Calvary Chapel started, from the human standpoint, as a result of the burden of a pastor and his wife for the hippies who had congregated on the beaches near their church. However, the Spirit of God who burdened them for those hippies already had begun to move in various places in various ways to touch the lives of the rebellious, antiestablishment youth culture with the saving message of Jesus Christ, who revolutionized their lives. Pastor Chuck Smith's Calvary Chapel was a chosen instrument in the hands of God that played a critical role during the Jesus Movement.

THE PARTICULAR FEATURES OF THE JESUS MOVEMENT

Although Calvary Chapel played a critical role in the Jesus Movement initially reaching hippies for Christ, the antiestablishment societal "dropouts" were not the only group of people impacted by the spiritual awakening among the younger generation. The hippies who came to Christ mostly out of the drug culture and from the streets originally were called "Jesus Freaks" by the press.[57] They were also known as "Jesus People," "Street Christians," or even "Evangelical Hippies." They

---

(Old Tappan, NJ: Chosen Books, 1987). The most well-known of these converts is Greg Laurie, who at the age of twenty went to Riverside, California and started Harvest Christian Fellowship which became one of the largest churches in America, with an average weekly attendance of fifteen thousand. Laurie also conducts Harvest Evangelistic Crusades around the country, winning thousands to Christ each year.

55   Miller, *Reinventing American Protestantism*, 21.

56   See John N. Vaughn, *The World's Twenty Largest Churches* (Grand Rapids: Baker Book House, 1984), 8.

57   Pederson, *Jesus People*, 35. See also Jess Moody, *The Jesus Freaks* (Waco, TX: Word Books, 1971).

became the most publicized group in the secular media, although they only comprised one segment of the movement.[58] The second group impacted by the Jesus Movement were the young people in more traditional churches and parachurch youth organizations and schools.[59] Duane Pederson, who began his ministry among the hippies, reported that "Though the Movement started as a ministry to the street people, it is much wider than that now. It is reaching the campuses—both high school and college. And it's definitely ministering to the youth of the establishment churches."[60] In reality, the Jesus Movement had a wider influence on the "straight" youth culture of the nation as the movement continued to spread from coast to coast.

As the Jesus Movement grew, unique ministries developed to reach the younger generation with the gospel as well as to minister to their needs. Two of those ministries that targeted the hippie population, identified previously in the discussion on the emergence of the Jesus Movement, were coffeehouses and communes. Hundreds of Christian coffeehouses sprang up throughout the country and became "evangelistic centers where refreshments were served, music was played, and youth off the street could take refuge."[61] In addition to music and singing, Bible studies with group discussion were held, the gospel was shared, and those present were given opportunities to trust Christ for salvation. Because so many of the young people who came to Christ were off the streets and needed a place to live, individual believers, churches, and other parachurch organizations began to provide housing for the Jesus People. The new converts lived together in communes, also called communities or Christian houses, where they shared household chores and were expected to live moral and disciplined lives. They held Bible studies together, worshipped together, and encouraged one another in their newfound faith in Jesus.

---

58 Reid, "Effect of Jesus Movement," 42.
59 "The Jesus Movement: 40 Years Later," panel discussion of professors, New Orleans Baptist Theological Seminary, YouTube video, 40:38, published January 16, 2013, https://www.youtube.com/watch?v= rEhsyDtlqlg.
60 Pederson, *Jesus People*, 34, 120.
61 McDow and Reid, *Firefall*, 280.

Jesus marches, festivals, and rallies featuring Christian folk-rock groups along with Christian entertainers and popular youth speakers began occurring around the country as the movement spread. The marches for Jesus were similar to marches for civil rights and other causes of the day, at which hundreds and sometimes thousands of youth took to the streets to declare their faith in Jesus Christ. The first major Faith Festival was held in Evansville, Indiana in March of 1970. Pat Boone and several Christian folk-rock singing groups were featured at the festival.[62] The first in a series of Jesus Rallies in Chicago in March of 1971 drew nine thousand, while that same year one Faith Festival had fifteen thousand in attendance.[63] In addition to Jesus Music festivals, many youth musicals were written and performed by large youth choirs touring throughout the United States in the late 1960s and early 1970s. Some of the best known of these musicals were *Good News*, *Tell It Like It Is*, *Celebrate Life*, and *Natural High*. The youth musical became "a powerful medium for reaching young people with the gospel" and as used on the youth choir tours was "perhaps the most organized witnessing approach from the local church involving youth."[64]

One of the major events of the Jesus Movement was Explo '72, sponsored by Campus Crusade for Christ.[65] In June of that year, eighty thousand participants traveled from all fifty states and sixty-eight nations to Dallas, Texas for a weeklong training conference focused on world evangelization. At that time, Explo '72 was the largest gathering of students and Christian laymen ever to descend on one city.[66] To close out the conference on Saturday, a Jesus Music festival was held that lasted eight hours, attended by a crowd estimated at 150,000.[67]

During the Jesus Movement, revival broke out among students on several school campuses. Probably the best known among evangelicals

---

62   Reid, "Effect of Jesus Movement," 43.
63   Reid, "Effect of Jesus Movement," 43.
64   Reid, "Impact of Jesus Movement," 100, 110.
65   Billy Graham gave credit to Campus Crusade for Christ for playing "a major role in sparking the new 'Jesus Revolution.'" Graham, *The Jesus Generation*, 141.
66   McDow and Reid, *Firefall*, 282.
67   McDow and Reid, *Firefall*.

was the powerful revival that occurred at Asbury College in 1970.[68] The revival began during a regular chapel service that turned into a protracted time of prayer and confession that lasted 185 hours.[69] Students from Asbury who were touched by the revival scattered across the country to share testimonies of their experience at other schools and churches as well. Through the influence of those students many other campuses and churches experienced spiritual renewal. Southwestern Baptist Theological Seminary was one of the schools that saw a similar revival break out on its campus after Asbury students shared in a chapel service there.[70]

The Jesus Movement "featured a deep conviction about evangelism."[71] Personal witnessing became a major focus of the movement as the young people who became followers of Jesus wanted to share the freedom and joy they had found in Christ with others. The twin slogans that became prominent during the Jesus Movement — "One Way through Jesus" and "Jesus Is Coming Soon"—added a sense of urgency to their evangelistic efforts.[72] Other creative methods were employed to share the gospel including tracts, stickers, posters, bumper stickers, underground newspapers, and T-shirts. And as discussed previously in the chapter, the outdoor mass baptismal services that resulted from the many young people won to Christ performed in the Pacific Ocean, swimming pools, and other bodies of water provided a dramatic public witness for Christ as well.

A BRIEF ASSESSMENT OF THE JESUS MOVEMENT

The Jesus Movement that swept across the country in the late 1960s and early 1970s can be classified as a specialized revival in that the

---

68   Alvin L. Reid, "The Zeal of Youth: The Role of Students in the History of Spiritual Awakening," in *Evangelism for a Changing World: Essays in Honor of Roy J. Fish*, eds. Timothy K. Beougher and Alvin L. Reid (Wheaton, IL: Harold Shaw Publishers, 1995), 243.

69   For a firsthand account of the revival at Asbury, see Robert E. Coleman, ed., *One Divine Moment* (Old Tappan, NJ: Fleming H. Revell, 1970).

70   Reid, "Zeal of Youth," 243.

71   McDow and Reid, *Firefall*, 281.

72   McDow and Reid, *Firefall*, 281.

movement primarily affected the youth population of the nation. Because the revival spread mainly through the youth culture, some aspects of the movement were somewhat "idealistic and superficial."[73] Controversial aspects included emotional experiences, the charismatic element, and the unfortunate development of a few aberrant groups, including the Children of God, The Way International, and the Tony Alamo Foundation.[74] However, the Jesus Movement was a true spiritual awakening that touched an entire generation of desperate young people at a revolutionary time in the nation and as a result, "changed American and church history."[75]

In addition to the record numbers of conversions and baptisms, the impact of the Jesus Movement still can be seen in the revolution in church music and worship styles it caused, the rise of the contemporary megachurch it fostered, the emphasis on prayer and spiritual awakening it encouraged, the focus on the work of the Holy Spirit it renewed, and the record number of leaders in the church it produced.[76] The Jesus Movement was the last spiritual awakening and religious revival to touch this nation. Considering the turmoil of the present day, reflected in the loss of civility and morality, the serious political divide, racial unrest, mass shootings, lawlessness, terrorism, and the drug epidemic, a spiritual awakening is desperately needed in America. Fifty years have passed since the Jesus Movement began to sweep across this nation. May the Spirit of God move once again among this present generation of youth as well as the rest of society and bring this country back to the only One who has the power to change the eternity destiny of a soul and the future direction of a nation, the Lord Jesus Christ!

---

73   McDow and Reid, *Firefall,* 278.
74   Reid, "Zeal of Youth," 243. See also Reid, "Effect of Jesus Movement," 42.
75   Laurie and Vaughn, *Jesus Revolution,* 252.
76   McDow and Reid, *Firefall,* 284–286. See also Laurie and Vaughn, *Jesus Revolution,* 252 and Reid, "Zeal of Youth," 243–244.

CHAPTER 19

DONALD MCGAVRAN, C. PETER WAGNER, *and* CHURCH GROWTH EVANGELISM

Chuck Lawless

I do not remember the first time I heard the phrase "church growth" as a movement. I know I wanted my church to grow when I was a pastor, but I did not use the term then in any intentional way. It likely was not until I began to consider a PhD concentration in the early 1990s that I seriously began to look at "church growth" as a movement. What I quickly learned is that many church leaders had a strong opinion about "church growth"—they were either in favor of it as a valid missiological strategy or opposed to it as nothing more than man-centered pragmatism. Seldom did I find anyone knowledgeable about the movement who did not have an opinion.

The "movement" itself has waned since then, but its influence on American evangelism has been strong enough that it warrants this chapter. In particular, this chapter focuses on the work of Donald A. McGavran and C. Peter Wagner. Out of their own international missions experience and via their classroom leadership at Fuller Theological Seminary, both men called for the primacy of evangelism in church growth.

BACKGROUND OF THE MOVEMENT

To understand church growth evangelism, one must first understand the background of the movement. Thom Rainer has described the history of the movement in terms of four eras, beginning with the "McGavran Era" (1955–1970).[1] McGavran, a missionary to India, is rightly known as the father of this movement. He was born in India into a missionary family in 1897, with grandparents and parents serving on the mission field. He served in various roles himself, including educator, administrator, evangelist, and researcher within the Christian Church (Disciples of Christ).

In these various roles, he carried the responsibility of evaluating growth of the mission stations associated with his denomination. He became burdened that only eleven of 145 mission stations were experiencing growth, even while other mass movements of conversions to Christ were occurring in India.[2] A primary question of McGavran's life thus became, "Why do some churches grow, but others do not?" Research became his focus, and his 1955 book titled *Bridges of God* marked the beginning of what would become the Church Growth Movement.[3] Compelled by the Great Commission call to make disciples of the nations/peoples of the world (Matt. 28:18–20), McGavran devoted his life to that task.

The Bridges of God quickly produced debate. C. Peter Wagner, in his preface to McGavran's magnum opus, *Understanding Church Growth*, pointed out four issues of debate in *Bridges*:

---

1 Thom S. Rainer, "Church Growth at the End of the Twentieth Century: Recovering Our Purpose," *Journal of the American Society for Church Growth* 6 (1995): 59–71. The remaining eras are the "Identity Crisis Era, part 1 (1970–1981)," the "Wagner Era (1981–1988)," and the "Identity Crisis Era, part 2 (1988 to the Present [the time of Rainer's article])."

2 Gary L. McIntosh, *Donald A. McGavran* (Boca Raton, FL: Church Leader Insights, 2015), 91. In this chapter, I have chosen to capitalize "Church Growth" when referring to the movement itself.

3 Donald A. McGavran, *The Bridges of God* (London: World Dominion Press, 1955; Eugene, OR: Wipf & Stock, 2005).

1. The *theological* issue suggests that the central purpose of missions was to be seen as God's will that lost men and women be found, reconciled to himself, and brought into responsible membership in Christian churches. Evangelism was seen not just as proclaiming the gospel whether or not something happened, but as making disciples for the Master.

2. The *ethical* issue is one of pragmatism. McGavran became alarmed when he saw all too many of God's resources—personnel and finances—being used without asking whether the kingdom of God was being advanced by the programs they were supporting. McGavran demanded more accountability in Christian stewardship. He wanted efforts evaluated by their results.

3. The *missiological* issue is McGavran's people movement theory. Before the days of the conscious application of cultural anthropology to evangelistic strategy, McGavran intuitively recognized the fact that decision-making processes are frequently quite different from one culture to the next. Whereas most Western missionaries and their converts were preaching an individualistic gospel and expecting people to come to Christ one by one against the social tide, McGavran . . . concluded that this was not the way multitudes could or would come to Christ. Important decisions, according to their worldview, were community decisions. Therefore, the way to approach many of the world's peoples with the gospel had to be through the encouragement of a multi-individual, mutually interdependent conversion process whereby members of families, extended families, clans, villages, and tribes would become Christian at the same time. This process was labeled a people movement.

4. The *procedural* issue is the distinction between discipling and perfecting as two discreet stages of Christianization. Discipling brings an unbelieving individual or group to commitment to

Christ and to the body of Christ. Perfecting is the lifelong process of spiritual and ethical development in the lives of believers.[4]

McGavran later became the founding dean of the School of World Missions at Fuller Theological Seminary in Pasadena, California, in 1965. From that platform, he had opportunity to influence missiological thinking through the projects of his graduate students and his own numerous articles and books on church growth around the world. In 1970 McGavran published *Understanding Church Growth*, the book which "established [him] as a premier foreign mission strategist."[5] It was in this book that he expanded his thoughts on the principle of people movements, the principle of receptivity (that is, missionaries should prioritize resources where peoples are most responsive to the gospel), and the homogeneous unit principle (stated most simply for this chapter as "people like to become Christians without crossing racial, linguistic, or class barriers"[6]). Throughout the work, though, winning the lost among the people groups of the world remained the priority.

Thom Rainer, on the other hand, suggests that the Church Growth Movement in America experienced an identity crisis beginning in 1970, when McGavran began to return to his roots: studying church growth around the world.[7] That identity crisis continued until 1981, when McGavran's Fuller Seminary colleague and former missionary to Bolivia, C. Peter Wagner, published his book *Church Growth and the Whole Gospel.*[8] In this book, Wagner recognized and responded to criticisms of the Church Growth Movement while also prioritizing evangelism.

---

4   C. Peter Wagner, "Preface," in *Understanding Church Growth*, rev. and ed. by C. Peter Wagner (Grand Rapids: Eerdmans, 1990), ix–xi.

5   George G. Hunter III, "The Legacy of Donald A. McGavran," *International Bulletin of Missionary Research* (October 1992): 158.

6   Donald A. McGavran, *Understanding Church Growth*, rev. and ed. by C. Peter Wagner (Grand Rapids: Eerdmans, 1990), 163. McGavran defines a homogeneous unit as "simply a section of society in which all the members have some characteristics in common"; *Understanding Church Growth*, 69.

7   Rainer, "Church Growth at the End of the Twentieth Century," 64–65.

8   C. Peter Wagner, *Church Growth and the Whole Gospel: A Biblical Mandate* (San Francisco: Harper and Row, 1981).

In 1984, Wagner became the first holder of the Donald A. Mc-Gavran Chair of Church Growth at Fuller Seminary.[9] He, along with George Hunter, was instrumental in the formation of the North American Society for Church Growth in 1984—a forum that marked the growth of the movement in North America and provided professors and practitioners opportunity to present their ongoing research in the discipline.[10] Wagner's leadership of this movement continued into the late 1980s and early 1990s, when he ventured more into the study of prayer and spiritual warfare. For both McGavran and early Wagner, however, evangelism remained a priority—as the next section of this chapter will show.

THE PRIMACY OF EVANGELISM

As noted above, McGavran used the term "discipling" to describe the process of "helping a people (a segment of *non-Christian* society) turn from non-Christian faith to Christ";[11] in other words, we might best equate McGavran's "discipling" with what we call "evangelism." "Perfecting," in contrast, was for McGavran the "whole complex of process of growth in grace"[12]—or, in the more commonly held term today, "discipleship." Despite the confusion of McGavran's definitions with current usages today, we must hear his position to best understand his evangelistic focus: "Discipling is one thing, perfecting is another. . . . The second stage overlaps the first, but it cannot precede it without destroying it."[13]

Indeed, central to McGavran's thinking was the primacy of evangelism over against other important ministry responsibilities:

> The chief and irreplaceable purpose of mission is church growth. Social service pleases God, but it must never be

---

9   C. Peter Wagner, ed., *Church Growth: State of the Art* (Carol Stream, IL: Tyndale, 1986; Kindle edition, Shippensburg, PA: Destiny Image, 2014), location 110.

10   McIntosh, *Donald A. McGavran*, 329.

11   McGavran, *Understanding Church Growth*, 123.

12   McGavran, *Understanding Church Growth,* 123.

13   McGavran, *Bridges of God* (Eugene, OR: Wipf & Stock, 2005), 16.

296   Chapter 19—Chuck Lawless

substituted for finding the lost. Our Lord did not rest content with feeding the hungry and healing the sick. He pressed on to give his life a ransom for many and to send out his followers to disciple all nations. Service must not be so disproportionately emphasized at the expense of evangelism that findable persons are continually lost.[14]

Wagner likewise affirmed the priority of the evangelistic mandate over the cultural mandate, which he summarized as "social responsibility."[15] Indeed, he argued that the evangelistic priority acted like a magnet: "when placed above the cultural mandate, it tends to pull them both up. When placed below the cultural mandate, it tends to pull them both down."[16] While Wagner's journey took him to a differing conclusion later in life, his focus on the evangelistic mandate was clear in his years of leading the Church Growth Movement.[17]

1-P, 2-P, AND 3-P EVANGELISM

McGavran was a missionary researcher who regularly used numbers and phrases to summarize and concretize his findings, and he left his mark on other Church Growth leaders who described evangelism. For example, Wagner delineated evangelism as presence, proclamation, and persuasion evangelism (or 1-P, 2-P, and 3-P evangelism).[18]

"Presence evangelism" is simply doing good works as a means to minister to others; in fact, Wagner went so far to say that some who do presence evangelism do not do so with the goal of converting nonbelievers—a fact that would certainly question the use of "evangelism" in this phrase.[19] Elmer Towns is more charitable when

---

14 McGavran, *Understanding Church Growth*, 22. For McGavran, one could not legitimately separate biblical church growth from the evangelistic task.
15 C. Peter Wagner, *Strategies for Church Growth* (Ventura, CA: Regal Books, 1989), 99.
16 Wagner, *Strategies,* 110.
17 See C. Peter Wagner, *On Earth as It Is in Heaven: Answer God's Call to Transform the World* (Ventura, CA: Regal, 2012).
18 Wagner, *Strategies,* 118–123.
19 Wagner, *Strategies,* 118.

he summarizes presence evangelism as "living the gospel before the lost."[20]

"Proclamation evangelism" assumes the necessity of believers providing a Christian presence among nonbelievers, but it further affirms that evangelism is nothing less than telling the gospel "in such a way that people will hear and understand it."[21] Hence, doing good deeds before others is not itself evangelism. At best, it is pre-evangelism "soil work," to gain a hearing from nonbelievers.

"Persuasion evangelism," then, is a step beyond simply proclaiming the good news. According to Towns, persuasion evangelism involves compelling the nonbelieving to turn to Christ; it includes "persuading or motivating the unsaved to respond" to the gospel and then leading them into responsible church membership.[22] With this understanding, one is thus not fully evangelized until he or she has become a Christ-follower and part of a local church. Wagner instead concludes, "the final goal of evangelism is measured in how many people validate their decisions for Christ by continuing steadfastly in the apostles' doctrine and fellowship and in breaking of bread and prayers."[23]

McGavran likewise taught that the Great Commission task was not complete with evangelism. His words were, in fact, quite clear:

> A decision is often the first step. However, we deceive ourselves if we believe that a person who has made a decision for Christ, who has prayed, "I accept Jesus Christ into my life," has truly become a disciple. We must make sure that he or she really follows Christ, really lives as a disciple. The goal is that day by day, hour by hour, minute by minute, one lives yielded to Christ as a responsible part of the Body. This is what it means to be a disciple.[24]

---

20 Elmer Towns, "Evangelism: The Why and How," in *Church Growth: State of the Art*, ed. C. Peter Wagner, Kindle location 397.

21 Wagner, *Strategies*, 120.

22 Towns, "Evangelism," 413.

23 Wagner, *Strategies*, 123.

24 Donald A. McGavran and Winfield C. Arn, *Ten Steps for Church Growth* (San Francisco: Harper and Row, 1977), 52–53. Italics in original.

McGavran then continues with even more explicit words: "Believers must become part of the church; *otherwise the reality of their belief is in question.* This high view of the church must be maintained. A low view of the church, held by secular relativists, is that belonging to the church is more or less a matter of choice. If you like it, you belong; if you don't, you don't. Church Growth Christians reject any such low view."[25]

E-0, E-1, E-2, E-3 EVANGELISM

One of McGavran's early faculty hires at Fuller Seminary was Ralph Winter, a Presbyterian missionary in Guatemala. Given McGavran's commitment to the local church, it is not surprising he attributes his interest in Winter to a single sentence he recalled from Winter's writing: "Much more important than all the gimmicks and gadgets of missionary life is bringing men and women into accountable fellowship in the local church."[26]

It was Winter who first proposed the E-scale of evangelism that recognizes cultural differences when doing evangelism. The scale views the evangelistic task in terms of increasing cultural distances between the evangelist and the evangelized.[27] E-0 evangelism is evangelizing church members, which assumes that some persons on church membership rolls do not give evidence of Christian conversion. E-1 evangelism, which Winter calls "the most effective type of evangelism,"[28] is "near-neighbor" evangelism within the same culture.[29] E-2 and E-3 are cross-cultural evangelistic efforts, with increasing differences between cultures. E-2 is evangelism within a similar yet distinct culture, and E-3 is evangelism within a quite different culture from

25   McGavran and Arn, *Ten Steps,* 31. Emphasis added.
26   Donald A. McGavran, *Effective Evangelism: A Theological Mandate* (Phillipsburg, NJ: P & R, 1988), 85. While McGavran did not provide a source, he did quote a similar statement in *Understanding Church Growth,* 34. The source there is Ralph Winter, "Gimmickitis," *Church Growth Bulletin,* January 1966.
27   Ralph D. Winter and Bruce A. Koch, "The Unreached Peoples Challenge," in *Perspectives on the World Christian Movement,* eds. Ralph D. Winter and Steven C. Hawthorne (Pasadena, CA: William Carey, 2009), Kindle locations 16499–16531.
28   Winter and Koch, "The Unreached Peoples Challenge," Kindle location 16526.
29   McGavran, *Understanding Church Growth,* 48, uses the "near-neighbor" language.

the evangelist. As the world becomes increasingly global *and* local, these latter differences of culture may, in fact, be found within the same neighborhood.

Understanding these cultural gaps guides the evangelist in determining best approaches to evangelism. Winter pointed out that "the gospel often expands within a community but does not normally 'jump' across cultural boundaries between peoples, especially those created by hate or prejudice";[30] hence, the task of evangelism and missions requires the believer to connect with other cultures and cross boundaries to reach much of the world. In fact, McGavran in 1970 asserted that 70 percent of the unreached non-Christians would require E-2 or E-3 evangelism.[31] Wagner, in a statement that seems equally relevant now more than thirty years after its writing, argued that evangelism in the United States required similar consideration: "All this says that planning evangelistic strategies must now take seriously the challenge for E2/3 evangelism as well as the more traditional E-1."[32]

A brief summary is in order here. For the early leaders of the Church Growth Movement, evangelism was primary. The local church was central. Obeying the call to disciple the people groups of the world was nonnegotiable. One can certainly debate the influence of this movement in North America today, but its roots directed church leaders to the evangelistic task.

REFLECTIONS ON MCGAVRAN, CHURCH GROWTH, AND THEOLOGICAL EDUCATION

Donald McGavran stepped down as dean at Fuller in 1971, but he continued his research and writing until his death in 1990, just over three months after the passing of his beloved wife, Mary.[33] His friend and colleague, Peter Wagner, died in 2016.[34]

---

30 Winter and Koch, "The Unreached Peoples Challenge," Kindle location 16522.

31 McGavran, *Understanding Church Growth*, 49.

32 Wagner, *Strategies*, 177–178.

33 McIntosh, *Donald A. McGavran*, 342–343.

34 Ed Stetzer, "C. Peter Wagner (1930–2016), Some Thoughts on His Life and Passing," https://www.christianitytoday.com/edstetzer/2016/october/in-memory-of-c-peter-wagner.html.

One of McGavran's final books was titled *Effective Evangelism: A Theological Mandate.*[35] This book is a series of lectures McGavran first presented at Westminister Theological Seminary in Philadelphia. Gary McIntosh points out that McGavran used the term "effective evangelism" synonymously with "church growth."[36] Rainer, who also recognizes McGavran's overlapping use of these phrases, wonders whether his use of "effective evangelism" later in his life was a reaction to a church growth philosophy and movement that had lost its evangelistic primacy:

> When he was a missionary in India in the 1930s to the 1950s, McGavran was wary of using the word "evangelism" since almost every deed and ministry was being done in the name of evangelism. Church growth, a results-oriented term, came to replace evangelism, a process-oriented term. Is it likely then, that by 1988, he returned to the nomenclature of evangelism, because he saw much in church growth that was not truly evangelistic? Had perceptions of church growth broadened to the point that the term was no longer understood to be "effective evangelism," but everything else under the sun?[37]

This question remains relevant today. Where churches *are* growing, they are often growing more by transfer growth (gaining members from other churches) than by conversion growth (reaching nonbelievers).[38] It seems fair to argue that some churches equate church growth more with *decisions* made than with *disciples* made. Personal evangelism is hardly a priority for most believers.[39] Few churches

---

35 McGavran, *Effective Evangelism.*
36 McIntosh, *Donald A. McGavran*, 327.
37 Rainer, "Church Growth at the End of the Twentieth Century," 63. Rainer (p. 67) defines church growth as "evangelism that results in fruit-bearing church members."
38 See Lifeway Research, "Rapid Church Growth through Conversions Uncommon," https://www.baptiststandard.com/news/faith-culture/rapid-church-growth-through-conversions-uncommon.
39 Barna Research, "Sharing Faith Is Increasingly Optional to Christians," https://www.barna.com/research/sharing-faith-increasingly-optional-christians; Lifeway Research, "Evangelism More Prayed for Than Practiced by Churchgoers," https://lifewayresearch.com/2019/04/23/evangelism-more-prayed-for-than-practiced-by-churchgoers.

or their leaders seem to share the evangelistic burden of McGavran and Wagner.

In *Effective Evangelism*, McGavran focused on seminaries as a primary resource for reviving this passion. While maintaining the primary role of the local church, he nevertheless challenged Christian training institutions to renew their focus on evangelistic training. His assessment is of course dated now, but he concluded in 1988, "I believe I am correct when I state that most theological training schools do not count evangelism or church growth an essential part of their curricula."[40] Rather, he argued that a "*maintenance mentality* [that is, a focus on 'maintaining and improving existing churches' rather than evangelizing people and planting new churches] *still dominates most seminary faculties*."[41]

I suspect that the writers of this volume would argue that many seminaries today are more committed to training students to do evangelism. I equally suspect, though, that many of us might contend that more attention to effective evangelism resulting in disciples in the local church is still warranted. McGavran, in fact, suggested in 1988 that seminaries should include at least five such courses in their Master of Divinity program:[42]

1. *The first would teach the theology of evangelism—finding and folding the lost and multiplying congregations of the redeemed.* . . . This is an essential part of all true theology.

2. *The second course would teach how to train laymen and laywomen for evangelism.* Lay people, if trained in evangelism, are most effective communicators. They reach their fellow workers, fellow faculty members, fellow employers and employees.

3. *The third course would teach how to multiply congregations in North American Anglo and minority populations.* Each of

---

40   McGavran, *Effective Evangelism*, 1.
41   McGavran, *Effective Evangelism*, 3 (emphasis in the original).
42   McGavran, *Effective Evangelism*, 6–7. The courses are listed using McGavran's precise words, including the italics.

the multitudinous segments of American society is a distinct population, in which Christian congregations must be multiplied.

4. *A fourth course would accurately describe the state of the churches and denominations in other continents.* Do they comprise 1 percent or 90 percent of the population? Are they growing or declining?

5. *The fifth course would deal with the ways of evangelism that God was most greatly blessing to the redemption of women and men.* The ways of evangelism differ for various populations. . . . Because the ways of effective evangelism are so numerous and vary from population to population and from age to age, this fifth course may run for two semesters.

Few of us serve in institutions where curricular space easily allows for this many courses in effective evangelism, particularly in a time when degree-shortening is often taking place. Nevertheless, one must wonder whether our attention to evangelistic training, in coordination with local church equipping, is sufficient to train the next generation to reach North America and the nations.

CONCLUSION

If Donald McGavran were still present among us today, I think he would be pleased that evangelism professors are writing a book on the history of North American evangelism. If, however, we ourselves are not doing evangelism, McGavran would hardly welcome our words without our actions. Our own passion for and obedience to God "*who finds persons*"—that is, a God who "wants them *found*"[43]—could result in a new positive chapter in North American evangelism.

---

43   McGavran, *Understanding Church Growth*, 21.

CHAPTER 20

JOHN PIPER, DESIRING GOD, *and the* YOUNG-RESTLESS-*and*-REFORMED

....

....

Bo Rice

The task set before me in this chapter is to trace the impact that John Piper, Desiring God, and the Young-Restless-and-Reformed movement all have had on evangelism in recent years. Some have said that the popular resurgence of Calvinism (referred to as New Calvinism by some) will be the death of evangelism in the modern church. However, I don't believe this can be any further from the truth. There is little doubt that some Calvinists today are not very evangelistic. This is not due to a faulty view of evangelism or misunderstood doctrine, though. One might argue that the real problem is a cold and indifferent heart to the commands of God. Interestingly, you can argue that there are Arminians who do not share the gospel. Again, this is not due to their faulty view of evangelism or their Arminian views. Like the Calvinist, a cold and indifferent heart is to blame.

There are some Calvinists who argue that their doctrinal beliefs will kill certain kinds of evangelism but never real biblical evangelism. Many Calvinists adamantly oppose what they consider to be unbiblical, man-centered evangelism. They also argue that Calvinism strengthens evangelism where biblical methods are employed in the carrying out of the Lord's clear command in the Great Commission.

So why do some people argue that Calvinism will be the death of evangelism in the local church? I believe it stems from a misunderstanding of the doctrinal foundation upon which Calvinism rests. There are those who think that Calvinism is primarily rooted in the doctrinal foundations of predestination and election. Those who misunderstand believe that Calvinists don't emphasize evangelism because their views of predestination and election allow them to do so. Some have asked, "If God decides who is saved, then why bother in sharing the gospel? If the elect always come to Jesus somehow, can't they do it without me evangelizing? If they aren't elect, why should we bother in the first place?" Questions like these might make some logical sense. However, this certainly is not what the Bible teaches, nor what Calvinists believe. The doctrinal foundation where most Calvinists begin is the absolute sovereignty of God. And those same Calvinists have no issue with joining the sovereignty of God with a zeal for evangelism. In fact, they argue that faithful evangelism is necessary from those who trust in the complete sovereignty of God. Realizing that a sovereign God ordained evangelism and proclamation to accomplish his desired purposes is all the motivation a Calvinists needs in order to be faithful. Faithful Calvinists share the gospel out of joyful obedience to all people and trust the Holy Spirit to do the work saving the elect.

One of the best-known members of the New Calvinism movement is John Piper. He served as Pastor for Preaching and Vision of Bethlehem Baptist Church in Minneapolis, Minnesota, for thirty-three years. His influence on the resurgence of Calvinism among evangelical Christianity in the younger generations is unquestionable. He is a prolific author, who has impacted a generation of conservative evangelicals by championing the fundamentals of sixteenth-century Calvinism. In his magnum opus *Desiring God*, Piper argues that pursuing maximum joy in the life of a believer is essential to glorifying God. He discusses the implications of this paradigm for conversion, worship, love, Scripture, prayer, money, marriage, missions, and suffering. Piper's view of conversion, as summarized in *Desiring God*, is an excellent explanation of God's role and man's responsibility in evangelism and salvation from a Calvinistic perspective.

Piper begins by summarizing the first question of the Westminster Shorter Catechism: "The chief end of man is to glorify God and enjoy Him forever." Piper states, "Not that I care too much about the intention of seventeenth-century theologians. But I care tremendously about the intention of God in Scripture. What does God have to say about the chief end of man? How does God teach us to give Him glory? Does He command us to enjoy Him? If so, how does this quest for joy in God relate to everything else? Yes, everything!"[1] In everything that we do, including evangelism, the chief end is to glorify God by enjoying him forever. This biblical principle is summarized by Paul in 1 Corinthians 10:31: "So, whether you eat or drink, or whatever you do, do everything for the glory of God."[2]

Piper's understanding of man's chief end flows from his view of God: "The chief end of God is to glorify God and enjoy Himself forever." Piper summarizes,

> His happiness is the delight He has in Himself. Before creation, He rejoiced in the image of His glory in the person of His Son. Then the joy of God "went public" in the works of creation and redemption. These works delight in the heart of God because they reflect His glory. He does everything He does to preserve and display that glory, for in this His soul rejoices. . . . All the works of God culminate in the praises of His redeemed people. The climax of His happiness is the delight He takes in the echoes of His excellence in the praises of the saints. This praise is the consummation of our own joy in God. Therefore, God's pursuit of praise from us and our pursuit of pleasure in Him are the same pursuit. This is at the heart of the great gospel![3]

---

1   John Piper, *Desiring God: Meditations of a Christian Hedonist* (Colorado Springs: Multnomah Books, 2011), 17–18.
2   Scripture references in this chapter come from the Christian Standard Bible.
3   Piper, *Desiring God,* 50.

This serves as the foundation of God's desire for his own praise as his people find their enjoyment in him.

Understanding God's desire for his own praise and man's need to find all of his joy in God alone leads Piper to stress the necessity of conversion. Piper is intentional in his emphasis of conversion beyond a simple understanding of believing in Jesus. Piper states, "The world abounds with millions of unconverted people who say they believe in Jesus. It does no good to tell these people to believe in the Lord Jesus. The phrase is empty. . . . Could it be that today the most straightforward biblical command for conversion is not 'Believe in the Lord,' but, 'Delight yourself in the Lord?'"[4] At this point, one must fully understand what is meant by conversion and why it is necessary to experience true joy in God. Piper asks, "Why is conversion so crucial? What is there about God and man that makes it necessary? And what has God done to meet our desperate need? And what must we do to enjoy the benefits of His provision?"[5] Piper then puts forth six crucial truths summarizing the need of man and God's provision.

Piper begins with the important understanding of why God created man in the first place—God created us for his glory. God created us "in His image" so that we could be his image-bearers and bring forth his glory to the world. "Why God should want to give us a share in shining with His glory is a great mystery. Call it grace or mercy or love—it is an unspeakable wonder. Once we were not. Then we existed—for the glory of God!"[6] This leads to the second truth related to conversion: it is the duty of every person to live for the glory of God. Pointing to 1 Corinthians 10:31 again, Piper argues that it is our duty to live for God's glory since that is the reason God made us. The question of what it means to glorify God is key. Glorifying God, for Piper, means acknowledging God's glory, to value it above all things, and to make it known. Glorifying God is the duty of every person, not just those who have trusted in the good news of

---

4 Piper, *Desiring God*, 55.
5 Piper, *Desiring God*, 55.
6 Piper, *Desiring God*, 56.

the gospel. Romans 1:20–21 explains how God will judge all people because everyone has access "to the knowledge that we are created by God and therefore are dependent upon Him for everything, thus owing Him gratitude and trust of our hearts. Deep within us we all know that it is our duty to glorify our Maker by thanking Him for all we have, trusting Him for all we need, and obeying all His revealed will."[7] No one is without an excuse for not glorifying God.

At this point, we realize how desperate the condition is of every individual. The third truth related to conversion is that every one of us has failed to glorify God as we ought. Romans 3:23 is clear that everyone has sinned and fallen short of the glory of God. Our sin results in us dishonoring the glory of God again and again. Piper contends that the evil of sin is not the harm it does to us or to others. The true evil of sin is the obvious disdain it reveals for God. The fourth truth is that each of us is deserving of God's eternal condemnation. Each of us deserves death because of our sin. Piper says, "Having held the glory of God in contempt through ingratitude and distrust and disobedience, we are sentenced to be excluded from the enjoyment of that glory forever and ever in the eternal misery of hell."[8] The most frightening news in the world is that we all have fallen under God's condemnation and that he preserves his glory by pouring out wrath on our sin. However, this leads to the best news in the world—the gospel! The fifth truth of conversion is that God has provided a way of salvation that upholds his glory. The good news that brings God glory is that he sent his Son to die for sinners and to conquer their death by his glorious resurrection.

The question that remains: "What must we do to be saved?" The sixth truth of conversion provides the answer to the question. Piper says that the benefits purchased by the death of Christ belong to those who repent and trust in him. He argues that not everyone is saved from the wrath of God simply because Jesus died for sinners. He contends that there is a condition that each person must meet in

---

7   Piper, *Desiring God,* 57.
8   Piper, *Desiring God,* 58.

order to be saved: "I want to try to show that the condition, summed up here as repentance and faith, is conversion and that conversion is nothing less than the creation of a Christian Hedonist."[9] Piper goes on to describe how conversion involves both repentance and faith, both of which result in a profound change of heart.

Piper defines repentance as turning from sin and unbelief. He describes faith as trusting in Christ alone for salvation. Both are equal parts to conversion. At the same time, Piper emphasizes that conversion is a gift of God: "Repentance and faith are our work. But we will not repent and believe unless God does His work to overcome our hard and rebellious hearts. This divine work is called regeneration. Our work is called conversion."[10] According to Piper, conversion involves an act of the will by which the person repents of sin and submits his/her self to the authority of Christ and places his/her hope and trust in Christ. Every person is responsible to do this and will be condemned if they do not. At the same time, the Bible teaches that, because of sinfulness, no one can do this on their own. The regenerating work of the Holy Spirit must come first. Once it comes, repentance turns us away from sin, faith embraces Christ, and a new desire for pleasing God develops in our lives.

So, how does all of this relate to evangelism and what is the motive for evangelizing for the Calvinist? For the Calvinist, two primary motives to practice evangelism emerge from Piper's understanding of conversion: the first is loving God and bringing him glory, the second is loving our fellow man and concern for his good. The first motive is most important for the Calvinist. As Piper contends, the chief end of man is to glorify God. One of the primary ways for a person to glorify God is by obeying his Word and fulfilling his revealed will. In fact, Scripture teaches us that man reveals his love for God by keeping his commandments (1 John 5:3). Evangelism is clearly one of the activities that God has commanded of every believer. Naturally, if we love God and are concerned for his glory, we should keep the

---

9   Piper, *Desiring God,* 63.
10   Piper, *Desiring God,* 65.

command of evangelizing all of the nations. As believers, we glorify God by evangelizing, not simply as an act of obedience, but also because it brings God glory when we make known his works of grace. The second motive behind evangelism for the Calvinist is love of fellow man and concern for his good. J. I. Packer states, "The wish to win the lost for Christ should be, and indeed is, the natural, spontaneous outflow of love in the heart of everyone who has been born again."[11] As believers who have experienced the grace and mercy of Christ, we know that we can do no greater good to any man than to share the truth of Christ with him. If we truly love our neighbor as commanded in Scripture, then we will certainly want him to enjoy the same salvation we have experienced in Christ. Packer summarizes this thought:

> If we ourselves have known anything of the love of Christ for us, and if our hearts have felt any measure of gratitude for the grace that has saved us from death and hell, then this attitude of compassion and care for our spiritually needy fellow-man ought to come naturally and spontaneously to us. It was in connection with aggressive evangelism that Paul declared that "the love of Christ constraineth us." It is a tragic and ugly thing when Christians lack desire, and are actually reluctant, to share the precious knowledge that they have with others whose need of it is just as great as their own.[12]

Every believer must realize the great privilege it is to evangelize. Our desire to see people saved should motivate us to share the good news of the gospel every opportunity we have. If we ever find ourselves avoiding the opportunity to share our faith, then we should realize that we are yielding to sin and not exhibiting true love for our fellow man.

---

11   J. I. Packer, *Evangelism and the Sovereignty of God* (Downers Grove, IL: IVP Academic, 1991), 75.
12   Packer, *Evangelism*, 76–77.

Tracing the renewed interest in Calvinism among the younger generations of evangelicalism was something that Collin Hansen did recently in his work *Young, Restless, Reformed*. Hansen gives special attention to the Passion movement and the role Piper has played. Hansen contends that Piper is a fixture at Passion because he "lends academic weight, moral authority, and theological precision to the conference. More than that, Piper shares Passion's overarching vision . . . two themes beloved by Calvinists—God's sovereignty and glory."[13] Hansen acknowledged Piper's view of the Passion movement and Calvinism: "Piper attributes the growing attraction of Calvinism to the way Passion pairs demanding obedience with God's grandeur. Even without an explicitly Calvinist appeal, Passion exemplifies how today's Calvinists relate theology to issues of Christian living such as worship, joy, and missions."[14] Hansen notes that one of the goals of Passion is to encourage students to devote themselves to evangelism and global missions. It's interesting to think that this movement that espouses Calvinists doctrines encourages its participants to be fully committed evangelists.

In his work, Hansen goes on to document several conversations that he had with young Calvinists who were affiliated with Piper's church in Minneapolis. He recalls a conversation he had with a student named Matt: "Calvinism is such a comfort and a means to follow Christ more passionately. . . . I feel pretty overwhelmed by my sin a lot of the time. And when I evangelize, I reach this point with people where I can't convince them. I've studied; I've tried my best. And what do I pray for? God, break their heart. Make the cross irresistibly compelling so they just see there's no other hope."[15] He reported the conversation that he had with another student named Laura:

> Lately I've been thinking about how Reformed theology
> frees me up to do ministry. . . . I have a real passion for

---

13   Colin Hansen, *Young, Restless, Reformed: A Journalist's Journey with the New Calvinists* (Wheaton, IL: Crossway Books, 2008), 17.
14   Hansen, *Young, Restless, Reformed*.
15   Hansen, *Young, Restless, Reformed*, 30.

missions, and I was over in the Middle East last summer. It was really hard to be there because I was in a town where missionaries have been active for more than a decade, but not a single person has come to faith. . . . It was the most freeing thing to realize that their salvation is not dependent on me spending enough time with them or me explaining the gospel in the best way or me being an expert in the language. . . . It freed me up to love being there even if I wasn't seeing fruit.[16]

One can't help but be struck by the commitment of these students to both their understanding of Calvinists doctrine and the work of missions and evangelism.

So, what impact has the resurgence of Calvinism in the American evangelical church had on evangelism? While some might argue it is leading to the death of personal evangelism in the local church, others might rightly point to an invigorated hope in the work of evangelism. Calvinists begin with a desire to bring glory to a sovereign God who is in control of all things. Many Calvinists argue that the doctrines of predestination and election spurs on faithful missions and evangelism. Certainly, there have been some who misused these doctrines to excuse inactivity, but that is not in keeping with what the Bible teaches nor what most Calvinists espouse. When Paul had just about reached the end of all hope in Corinth after spending countless hours sharing the truth of the gospel, the Lord encouraged him to stay the course and continue to proclaim the gospel because the Lord already had chosen people in the city (Acts 18). This led to Paul's faithful preaching in the city for another year and a half. It was Paul's strong belief in the sovereignty of God that kept him faithful to the task even when there seemed to be no evangelistic fruit. Many Calvinists would argue that the only evangelistic hope that any believer has in this sinful, hard-hearted world is that the Lord has a certain number of people who are elect and still wandering in lostness, waiting on

---

16 Hansen, *Young, Restless, Reformed,* 43–44.

someone to speak the truth of the gospel to them in order that they might respond. The obedient Calvinist sees it as his/her mission to seek them out, speak the truth of the gospel to them, and trust the Holy Spirit to do the work of drawing them unto salvation.

I was first exposed to this resurgent form of Calvinism while in college at Auburn University. I was in a "preacher boys" group with a local pastor who mentored young men called to the ministry. One semester, we read *Desiring God* together. Conversation about the book was deep and rich. We marveled at the grace and mercy of our sovereign God. I began to think deeply about the doctrines of grace. After graduation, I attended seminary at New Orleans Baptist Theological Seminary. A fellow seminarian and I read through *Desiring God* and wrestled with the implications of the book. We decided to fly to Minneapolis to attend a pastors' conference at the church of John Piper. The year was 2007 and the subject was on the holiness of God. R. C. Sproul was the keynote speaker. The worship was powerful. The conversations were thought-provoking. The glory of Christ was emphasized. The mission of the church was highlighted. The task of evangelism was reiterated. I remember coming away from the conference energized by the greatness of our God and challenged to be obedient to the commands found in Scripture. My zeal for evangelism was renewed.

I must confess that I still wrestle with the points of Calvinism. There are many places and points where I find a great deal of agreement. There are a few places and points where I do not. Regardless, I am grateful for those Calvinists who champion for the cause of Christ. I am influenced by their writings, sermons, and podcasts. I am encouraged by their desire to honor our sovereign Lord by being obedient to make disciples among all the nations. I do not believe that Calvinism will be the death of evangelism in the SBC or any other denomination. In fact, I believe just the opposite. I am encouraged to see a young generation that is passionate about proclaiming the glory of Christ. I am excited to see faithful Calvinist speak the truth of the gospel in obedience to the Great Commission while trusting God to work out whether someone is predestined or not. *Soli Deo Gloria!*

CHAPTER 21

SOUTHERN BAPTIST PERSONAL EVANGELISM METHODOLOGIES, 1970–2000

....
....

Matt Queen

From its inception, the Southern Baptist Convention, through its agencies and churches, has identified itself closely with the practice of evangelism. While its structure and name has evolved over the years, the Southern Baptist Convention's use of a domestic mission board in North America has elevated the task of evangelism and has assisted Convention churches in their practice of evangelism.[1] Through its Department of Evangelism, the Home Mission Board (HMB) historically has promoted evangelism through perennial programs of congregational evangelism that included but was not limited to church and simultaneous revivals, open enrollment Sunday schools, cultivative (or relationship-based) evangelism, personal evangelism, event evangelism, and media-based evangelism.

---

1   For histories of Southern Baptist evangelism through its domestic mission board in North America, now referred to as the North American Mission Board, see Robert L. Hamblin, "Home Mission Board Influence on Southern Baptist Evangelism, 1900–1985," *Baptist History and Heritage* 22 (January 1987): 17–26; Charles S. Kelley, "Back to the Future: An Analysis of Southern Baptist Evangelism," *The Theological Educator* 51 (Spring 1995): 149–151; and J. B. Lawrence, *History of the Home Mission Board* (Nashville: Broadman, 1958).

Since the beginning of the twenty-first century, the North American Mission Board (NAMB, formerly the Home Mission Board) also added mercy ministry and church planting to its promotion of evangelism within the Convention.

A CONCISE HISTORY OF MID-TO-LATE 20TH CENTURY SOUTHERN BAPTIST PERSONAL EVANGELISM TRAINING METHODOLOGIES[2]

During the latter part of the twentieth century and into the twenty-first century, the Southern Baptist Convention utilized both personal evangelism presentation models and their corresponding gospel tracts to assist churches and individuals in practicing personal evangelism.

These models and the gospel tracts associated with them represent a complete telling of the gospel not only as Southern Baptists have understood it, but also as the Convention has trained its laity to communicate the gospel for more than fifty years. The following survey of Southern Baptist personal evangelism presentation models represents and assesses the ways that Southern Baptists received training from 1970–2000 to communicate the gospel through the medium of personal evangelism.

Lay Evangelism School

The HMB developed and implemented Lay Evangelism School as the first Southern Baptist personal evangelism training model.[3]

---

2   The content of this chapter has been modified from Matthew Burton Queen, "A Theological Assessment of the Gospel Content in Selected Southern Baptist Sources," (PhD diss., Southeastern Baptist Theological Seminary, 2009), 140–181.

3   All references to Lay Evangelism School will be indicated as LES, unless otherwise noted. Witness Involvement Now, or WIN, takes its name after the title of the personal evangelism training model's student manual; however, WIN refers to more than just this training plan. The designation of WIN includes a number of programs that either stemmed from or were associated with it. For example, Lewis Drummond explains that emerging out of WIN came a youth version titled WOW schools (Win Our World), as well as the LES program (Lay Evangelism Schools), which he describes as "a longer-term training period without quite the intensity as the every-night schedule

Kenneth S. Chafin, Director of the HMB's Evangelism Section from 1970–1973, instituted several changes to the Southern Baptist program of evangelism.[4] Chafin's vision to make personal evangelism the primary method of evangelism for Southern Baptists began with his implementation of LES.

The HMB created LES for other reasons besides the new direction in evangelism that Chafin wanted to take. John Mark Terry asserted that the decline in both the reported baptisms and the evangelistic activities of local congregations alarmed officials at the HMB.[5] As a result, they designed LES and established partnerships with the state departments of evangelism in order to promote training within the churches of the Convention. The HMB evangelism personnel, in partnership with the state conventions, launched LES by conducting schools in Atlanta with pastors and laymen from all over the nation.[6] LES then multiplied exponentially as these newly trained facilitators returned home and trained others in their own states.

In order to present the gospel, the LES incorporated a trainee's personal testimony of faith in Christ and a gospel tract. Concerning the specifics of LES method, Chuck Kelley explained:

> The process involves ten hours of training and includes brief lectures, individual and small group activities, and at least one evening of actual evangelistic visitation. Participants

---

of WIN." Drummond, "Training for Evangelism in Southern Baptist Life," *Baptist History and Heritage* 22 (January 1987): 32. Robin Jumper affirms the synonymous nature of WIN with other program names when he writes, "The program [is] known by several different names: Lay Evangelism Witness Plan, Witness Involvement Now (WIN), WIN School, and Lay Evangelism School (LES)." George Robin Jumper, "An Investigation of the Concept of Committing to Christ as Lord in Conversion in Selected Southern Baptist Convention Gospel Presentations" (PhD diss., New Orleans Baptist Theological Seminary, 1990), 92.

4   Ronald W. Johnson, "An Evaluation of the Home Mission Board Programs of Evangelism in Local Churches" (DMin diss., The Southern Baptist Theological Seminary, 1988), 13. Probably the most noticeable of these changes comes from the fact that "[Chafin] broke from the tradition of emphasizing revivals and began placing more emphasis on personal evangelism." Jumper, "An Investigation," 91.

5   John Mark Terry, *Evangelism: A Concise History* (Nashville: B&H, 1994), 188.

6   Hamblin, "Home Mission Board Influence," 25.

are taught to share their personal testimonies and explain how to become a Christian by reading through a witnessing booklet (tract) with a prospect. The school itself is followed by a weekly visitation program lasting ten weeks and including brief witness training each week.[7]

After the HMB learned that a large number of participants did not complete the visitation component after the ten-week training, some alterations occurred. The updated LES strategy consisted of a longer term of less intense training than was previously required. It also included a weekly visitation component to address the weaknesses in the program.

LES, through WIN, utilizes four objectives in order to revitalize Southern Baptist churches through personal evangelism. The *Teacher's Manual* stressed: "Every person who participates in WIN should have four objectives: 1. To share a personal testimony of his experience with Christ with a non-Christian; 2. To clearly communicate the truth of the gospel of Christ to a non-Christian; 3. To daily experience a full and meaningful life and grow in Jesus Christ; and 4. To make witnessing part of a daily lifestyle in Jesus Christ."[8]

How to Have a Full and Meaningful Life, the gospel tract that accompanied this personal evangelism training program, specifically embodied LES's gospel presentation. In his investigation of selected Southern Baptist gospel presentations, Robin Jumper concludes, "[LES was] the major personal evangelism training methodology of the period of the 1970's. A part of this methodology was the use of the evangelism booklet and gospel presentation titled, 'How to Have a Full and Meaningful Life.' The researcher concluded that 'How to Have a Full and Meaningful Life' was the representative gospel presentation of this period."[9] The WIN training taught trainees to use this tract in order to share the gospel with unbelievers.

---

7 Charles S. Kelley, Jr., *How Did They Do It: The Story of Southern Baptist Evangelism* (New Orleans: Insight, 1993), 77.
8 *Witness Involvement Now: Teacher's Manual*, rev. ed. (Alpharetta, GA: Home Mission Board, 1996), 11.
9 Jumper, "An Investigation," 110.

The tract shared a number of similarities with Campus Crusade's *The Four Spiritual Laws*, which preceded *How to Have a Full and Meaningful Life*.[10] Five major principles contained in *How to Have a Full and Meaningful Life* form its gospel content. These principles included:

1. God loves you. He offers you a full and meaningful life.
2. This life is made possible by Christ's death and resurrection.
3. You enter this life though a "spiritual birth."
4. Failure to turn your life over to Jesus Christ is sin.
5. This life becomes yours when you turn from your sin and accept Christ as your Lord and Savior.[11]

In addition to its evangelistic presentation, the tract also included a very brief follow-up and discipleship component at the end of the booklet for new believers who responded to the gospel message it communicated.

LES expressed the gospel message through *How to Have a Full and Meaningful Life* by first explaining full and meaningful life that God offers unbelievers. The booklet described the full and meaningful life as "abundant," "everlasting," and "full of peace and joy."[12] It then asserted that Jesus has made this full and meaningful life available through his death and resurrection. Through Christ's death and resurrection, God affords unbelievers "forgiveness of sin," "fellowship in the family of God," and "strength for daily living."[13] An unbeliever receives these benefits only when he receives Jesus as Lord and Savior. Taken as a whole, these elements comprised LES's presentation of the gospel.

Overall, LES served Southern Baptists as a viable personal evangelism training model that both presented their understanding of the gospel and yielded favorable results. Concerning its strengths

---

10 Terry, *Evangelism*, 188.
11 *How to Have a Full and Meaningful Life*, (Nashville: The Sunday School Board of the SBC, 1971; reprint, Nashville: LifeWay, 1997), 2, 4, 6, 8, 10 (page citations are to the reprint edition).
12 *How to Have a Full and Meaningful Life*, 3.
13 *How to Have a Full and Meaningful Life*, 4–5.

and weaknesses, Chuck Kelley touted LES's simplicity, well-designed materials and content, and portability for different size groups or churches. He also identified LES's visitation strategy as its greatest weakness.[14] C. B. Hogue, former director of the HMB's Evangelism Section, referred to WIN/LES as a remedy for doubtful discipleship within the Convention.[15] Hogue's positive assessment, however, leads to the question as to why LES was deemphasized quickly under his administration.[16]

The gospel as presented through the LES strategy resulted in overwhelming responses in terms of those trained and those baptized. First, Robin Jumper reported that more than 103,000 laity participated in 1972 alone.[17] Because no formal Southern Baptist personal evangelism training model existed before LES, a previous comparison cannot be made; however, these results do prove noteworthy. Some within the Convention believed that the gospel presented through LES aided in the increase of reported baptisms by Southern Baptists. In its annual report to the Southern Baptist Convention, the Home Mission Board reported:

Perhaps the greatest single event in the latter half of this century has been the Lay Evangelism Witness Plan (WIN). Careful evaluations have been made both of materials and of performance and follow-through. It is note-worthy that in 1971, the first full year for the Lay Evangelism Witness Plan, our Convention baptized the third highest number

---

14   Kelley, *How Did They Do It*, 46, 77–78.
15   C. B. Hogue, "Evangelism in Our Contemporary World," in *Evangelism Today & Tomorrow*, eds. Charles L. Chaney and Granville Watson (Nashville: Broadman, 1993), 104.
16   Chuck Kelley addresses this decision when he writes, "Hogue moved the evangelism program back from a nearly exclusive emphasis on personal evangelism to a more balanced program featuring personal evangelism, mass evangelism, and the development of evangelism materials and services. . . . For some reason the WIN program (hereafter called Lay Evangelism School or LES) was put on the shelf while it was still popular and effective, and TELL was promoted in its place. . . . The mystery is why the Lay Evangelism School, which had so much momentum, was deemphasized in order to promote TELL. Consider it the Baptist version of New Coke and a lesson on the results of misreading your market." Kelley, *How Did They Do It*, 47–49.
17   Jumper, "An Investigation," 94.

in its history. This is a continuing project and pastors and leaders are unanimous in acclaiming it to be the answer for the needs of this day.[18]

Continuing Witness Training

After serving for three years, Kenneth Chafin left the board. In 1973 C. B. Hogue succeeded him as director of the Evangelism Section of the HMB. Due to the popularity and effectiveness of James Kennedy's Evangelism Explosion, particularly among Southern Baptists, many of their pastors requested a similar personal evangelism training model that was more Southern Baptist in its orientation.[19] The evangelism division of the board explored the possibilities of fulfilling that request. In addition to the numerous requests from pastors, great concern rose from within the board concerning the decline in baptisms. In order to reinvigorate the denomination's program of evangelism, the board's leadership proposed the development of a new personal evangelism training model.[20] From 1978–1980, Hogue and Howard Ramsey led a task force to develop a Southern Baptist brand of Evangelism Explosion.

At the end of Hogue's tenure, the HMB piloted Continuing Witness Training seminars that involved 165 churches of thirty state conventions.[21] A year later, in 1982, the Board released CWT publicly. A younger program than LES, CWT resulted in tremendous success and notoriety within the Convention. Lewis Drummond claimed

---

18   "Home Mission Board Report," *Annual of the Southern Baptist Convention* (Nashville: Executive Committee, SBC, 1972), 154.

19   "Home Mission Board Report" (1972), 49. Kelley reports that in response to the pastors' requests, "The evangelism division negotiated with the [Evangelism Explosion] EE organization, asking them to develop a format of EE designed for Southern Baptist churches, reflecting more closely Southern Baptist doctrine and practices. When the request was turned down, Southern Baptist leaders asked the [Home Mission Board] to develop a Southern Baptist evangelism training program incorporating the apprenticeship approach pioneered in [Evangelism Explosion]. The Continuing Witness Training (CWT) program of the Home Mission Board is the result of that request." In this same discussion, Kelley offers the similarities and differences between Evangelism Explosion and Continuing Witness Training on page 80.

20   Terry, *Evangelism*, 188.

21   "Home Mission Board Report" (1982), 122. All references to Continuing Witness Training will be indicated as CWT, unless otherwise noted.

that CWT has probably been "the most successful of the training programs in evangelism among Southern Baptists up to the present time."[22] CWT's substantially long tenure of use by Southern Baptist churches and seminaries attested to this fact.

Ronald W. Johnson, former HMB editor of the evangelism section, summarized Continuing Witness Training as "an apprenticeship approach to learning to share the gospel message."[23] Drummond described the general approach of the CWT strategy as simple in its nature: "A leader, usually the pastor, becomes 'certified' by intensive training at a regional center. He or she can then begin training the laity on a local church level. They are in turn certified, and they can thus train others that then leads to their certification—and on and on."[24] Beyond the process of the strategy, the "Model Presentation" articulated the heart of CWT.

The Model Presentation represented CWT's presentation of the gospel. As the *Pastor/Leader Manual* explained, the "Model Presentation" existed in order to "ensure the sharing of the complete gospel" and to "offer a standard presentation for equipping witnesses in local churches throughout the Southern Baptist Convention."[25]

The Model Presentation comprised two forms within the training manuals and a third in its corresponding gospel booklet. The CWT training manuals referred to the first of these forms as the basic outline. The main points of the outline included:

I. Introduction
    A. Family
    B. Interests
    C. Religious Background
    D. Exploratory Questions

---

22 Drummond, "Training for Evangelism," 32.
23 Ronald W. Johnson, "An Evaluation of the Home Mission Board," 15.
24 Drummond, "Training for Evangelism," 32. For other exhaustive explanations, see Hogue, "Evangelism in Our Contemporary World," 104–105; and Jumper, "An Investigation," 97–98.
25 *Continuing Witness Training: Pastor/Leader Manual* (Atlanta: Home Mission Board, 1982), 32.

II. Gospel
    A. God's Purpose
    B. Our Need
    C. God's Provision
    D. Our Response

III. Leading to a Commitment
    A. Commitment Questions
    B. Clarification
    C. Prayer

IV. Immediate Follow-Up.[26]

An apprentice's memorization of this basic outline fulfilled the requirement to receive certification in CWT. Chuck Kelley praised the Home Mission Board in its advanced approach through CWT, as opposed to the Board's previous methodology in WIN. He stated, "[WIN] trained participants to witness by using a tract which summarized the gospel. Participants in [CWT] were trained to witness by memorizing a presentation of the gospel. The growing sophistication of the training methodology produced a more sharply defined explanation of the gospel."[27]

The training manuals also presented a second form of the Model Presentation, known as the dialogue outline. The dialogue form of the Model Presentation consisted of mock conversations between fictional characters named Bob Meades, Jack Peck, Peggy Simmons, and Ann Bolton. These mock conversations embodied examples of ways how apprentices present and respond with the core content of the Model Presentation outline to unbelievers interested in hearing

---

26   *Continuing Witness Training: Apprentice Manual* (Atlanta: Home Mission Board, 1982; reprint, 1995), 171–174 (page citations are to the reprint edition); and *Continuing Witness Training: Equipper Manual* (Atlanta: Home Mission Board, 1982), 23–25. These manuals present a fuller explanation of this outline.

27   Kelley, *How Did They Do It*, 160.

and/or accepting the gospel.[28] The manuals included a session titled "Dealing with Objections and Questions," in order that it might offer examples through the fictional characters of ways to respond to unbelievers who responded with negativity and criticism.

The third form of the Model Presentation emerged in the *Eternal Life* tract. It explained the meaning of everlasting life and the way unbelievers could obtain it. Chuck Kelley summarized the booklet's meaning of everlasting life this way: "[*Eternal Life* encourages witnesses] to explain eternal life as the quality of God's life as well as its endless quantity. In other words, when a person comes to Christ, he begins to experience the kind of life God has. . . . The believer's life is a life of fulfillment as opposed to search, supply as opposed to need, and possibility as opposed to limitation."[29]

Eternal Life's presentation of the gospel began with two multipurpose questions (e.g., "Do you know for certain that you have Eternal Life and that you will go to heaven when you die?" and "Suppose you were standing before God right now and He asked you, 'Why should I let you into My heaven?' What do you think you would say?"), which serve as a "hook," as well as a diagnostic litmus, for its readers. It then presented four truths expressed through the Model Presentation:

1. God's purpose is that we have eternal life.
2. Our need is to understand our problem.
3. God's provision is Jesus Christ.
4. Our response is to receive Jesus.[30]

The concluding pages of the tract included discipleship components for those who made a positive response to the gospel.

Eternal Life spoke to the issue of sin much earlier in its presentation than did *How to Have a Full and Meaningful Life*. The booklet explained that because of God's holiness and justice, he must punish

---

28 The presentation of this dialogue form can be found in *Continuing Witness Training: Apprentice Manual*, 177–185 and *Continuing Witness Training: Equipper Manual*, 27–36.

29 Kelley, *How Did They Do It*, 137.

30 *Eternal Life*, NIV (Alpharetta, GA: North American Mission Board, 1997), 4, 6, 8, 10.

the sin that results from human nature and personal choice. However, God made provision for man's forgiveness by sending his Son, Jesus Christ. Jesus came to earth as fully God and fully man, died on the cross for mankind's sin, and was raised from the dead. In order to receive God's provision through Jesus, individuals must repent of their sins, surrender to Jesus as Lord, and place faith in him. The booklet then encouraged respondents to pray a scripted prayer of commitment in order to receive eternal life.

Naturally, CWT and its Model Presentation possessed noticeable strengths and weaknesses. Floyd Alan Paris believed the strengths of the Model Presentation included its clarity, as well as the ways it presents the concepts of repentance and surrender.[31] Chuck Kelley also offered a critique: "Its strengths include [its] thoroughness of training and actual witnessing experience. . . . Weaknesses include the extensive requirements of memorizing a plan of salvation and spending at least two and a half hours in training each week for thirteen weeks."[32] Unlike Evangelism Explosion, CWT dealt with the issue of believer's baptism for those who accept Christ.

FAITH: EVANGELISM THROUGH THE SUNDAY SCHOOL

After using Evangelism Explosion for three years, First Baptist Daytona, Florida, culminated its own program of evangelism twenty-five years ago. Due to its practice of evangelism through Sunday school and its preference for a Baptist brand of evangelism, the church's ministry shifted from Evangelism Explosion to a blend of Sunday school and evangelism training. They referred to this ministry endeavor as Evangelism and Sunday School, or E/S.[33] As E/S became more successful, LifeWay Christian Resources, formerly the Sunday

---

31   Floyd Alan Paris, "A Church Growth Analysis of Continuing Witness Training in Selected Southern Baptist Churches" (PhD diss., Mid-America Baptist Theological Seminary, 1997), 20.

32   Kelley, *How Did They Do It*, 80–81.

33   Bobby H. Welch, *Evangelism through the Sunday School: A Journey of FAITH* (Nashville: LifeWay, 1997), 26.

School Board, began the necessary process to adopt and develop it into an educational evangelism program.

Great alarm spread across the Convention and its entities when *Annual Church Profile* reports from 1980–1996 revealed some startling figures. Leaders of the Baptist Sunday School Board's Church Growth Group found that while the United States population and Southern Baptist church membership had increased 15 percent in those sixteen years, Southern Baptist Sunday school enrollment had grown only 11 percent, Sunday school attendance had increased only 3 percent, and that Southern Baptist baptisms had decreased 12 percent.[34] NAMB sought to address the problem of decreased baptisms by reexamining the CWT model. In its 1998 report at the annual Convention, NAMB stated that it would rebuild CWT, as well as develop "new training and equipping tools for Southern Baptists to intentionally share the good news of Jesus Christ."[35] However, this data also concerned another Southern Baptist entity.

The 1980–1996 statistical data concerned Jimmy Draper, Jr., then-president of LifeWay Christian Resources. Under Draper's leadership, LifeWay adopted and adapted First Baptist Daytona's E/S program because of its blending of Sunday school with evangelism. As a result, FAITH: Evangelism through the Sunday School was created.[36]

So as not to interfere with the Southern Baptist Convention's ministry assignment to NAMB, Draper enlisted the cooperation of then-president of NAMB Bob Reccord. Concerning the nature of this cooperative effort, Reccord explained, "Although the Southern Baptist Convention has primarily entrusted the North American Mission

---

34 Welch, *Evangelism through the Sunday School,* 22.
35 "North American Mission Board Report" (1998), 218.
36 All references to FAITH: Evangelism through the Sunday School will be indicated as FAITH, unless otherwise noted. Bobby Welch explains, "The FAITH Sunday School evangelism ministry, or just FAITH for short, refers to an entire approach, system, and process that incorporates several components as a result of combining Sunday school and evangelism in a local church. In particular, FAITH is the word upon which an acronym is based. That acronym on [sic] FAITH is the outline for the gospel presentation. Consequently, the entire ministry, with all of its components, was given the name FAITH." Welch, *Evangelism through the Sunday School,* 25–26.

Board with evangelistic strategies, the North American Mission Board is proud to partner with LifeWay Christian Resources in the development of [the] FAITH: Sunday School Evangelism Strategy."[37] As such, NAMB gave its blessing for LifeWay to produce FAITH and to make annual reports concerning FAITH to the Convention. LifeWay chose Bobby Welch, First Baptist Daytona's long-tenured pastor, as FAITH's spokesperson. In January 1998, "FAITH: Evangelism through the Sunday School [launched] at First Baptist, Daytona, Florida, where 28 originator churches were trained in FAITH. A total of 5,572 people representing 1,592 churches participated in the FAITH evangelism strategy training through September 30, 1998."[38] After its launch, the number of churches, trainees, and clinics continued to grow until 2007, when the number of churches utilizing it declined. LifeWay reported that more than 8,800 churches used FAITH, more than 422,400 trainees had been certified, and 509 FAITH clinics had been conducted through 2007.[39] During that period of time, FAITH expanded its curriculum to include Spanish and Korean versions, a student edition, and the publication of ongoing discipleship training modules.

Carson Moseley offered an assessment on the evangelistic effect of the FAITH model in a sampling of Southern Baptist Convention churches. Concerning the training structure of the FAITH program, he describes:

> [FAITH] is pastor led, the pastor teaches the learning sessions during the course of the 16-week FAITH Journey and fully participates in both learning and visitation times. The FAITH teams are comprised of three people per FAITH team from the same Sunday school class or department,

37   Bobby Welch and Doug Williams, *A Journey in FAITH: Journal* (Nashville: LifeWay, 1998), vii.

38   *Annual of the Southern Baptist Convention*, "LifeWay Christian Resources Report," (1999), 240.

39   This statistical data was compiled from "LifeWay Christian Resources Report," *Annual of the Southern Baptist Convention* (1999), 240; (2000), 209; (2001), 194; (2002), 185; (2003), 156; (2004), 172; (2005), 200; (2006), 231; and (2007), 154.

with at least one female member on each team. During
the 16 weeks of FAITH training, FAITH participants are
expected to memorizethe FAITH evangelistic presentation
in segment and be able to present what they have learned
in actual visitation. Practice times are provided during the
learning sessions to facilitate memorization and ease of
presentation.[40]

The ongoing publication of new FAITH discipleship training modules provided continued training sessions for certified trainees. These
advanced training sessions were offered to advanced trainees while
the new trainees were being trained.

Unlike LES and CWT, FAITH presented the gospel in the form
of an outline without using a corresponding tract or booklet. FAITH's
gospel presentation consisted of three major parts. The first part,
"Preparation," contained introductory aspects that assess one's interests and religious involvement. These introductory aspects included
discussing the other person's family, hobbies, and/or other interests.
The trainee shared testimonies about his Sunday school class and his
own conversion experience with the other person. These aspects led
to the following key question, "In your opinion, what do you understand it takes for a person to go to heaven?"[41] If the respondent gave a
works-based, negative, or unclear answer, then a transition statement
followed. The personal evangelist began the gospel presentation by
saying, "I'd like to share with you how the Bible answers this question, if it is alright. There is a word that can be used to answer this
question: FAITH."[42] This transition statement led into the actual
gospel presentation.

FAITH referred to the second part of its outline as "Presentation."
The FAITH Presentation began with the letters F-A-I-T-H. These five
letters formulated the following acrostic script for presenting the gospel:

---

40   Carson E. Moseley, "F.A.I.T.H.'s Effect on Evangelism" (DMin dissertation, South-
     eastern Baptist Theological Seminary, 2001), 56.
41   *FAITH: Evangelism through the Sunday School* Outline (Nashville: LifeWay, 1998), 1.
42   *FAITH,* 1.

1. *F* stands for Forgiveness.
2. *A* stands for Available. God's forgiveness is available for all, but not automatic.
3. *I* stands for Impossible. It is impossible for God to allow sin into heaven. This is because God is holy and just and man is sinful.
4. *T* stands for Turn. One must turn from their sin to Jesus Christ.
5. *H* stands for Heaven. Heaven means eternal life for here and the hereafter.[43]

Much like CWT's Model Presentation, FAITH assumed that the other person acknowledged the existence of heaven and the need for forgiveness. The FAITH outline offered biblical support that provided even the most uninformed listener with a theological understanding of the gospel. The FAITH outline concluded with a section called Invitation. The personal evangelist invited an unbeliever to accept forgiveness for his sins through the use of a discipleship pamphlet called *A Step of FAITH*. The personal evangelist then asked, "Understanding what we have shared, would you like to receive this forgiveness by trusting Jesus Christ as your personal Lord and Savior?"[44] If the other person responded in the affirmative, the trainee led him in a prayer of commitment. Unlike the How to Have a Full and Meaningful Life and Eternal Life presentations, the FAITH outline omitted teaching people how to grow in their faith at home. Bobby Welch explained, "Rather, the time [following a faith commitment] is used to bring the person to a personal connection with the local church and Sunday school where it is believed that the individual is able to grow correctly and survive spiritually."[45] FAITH's differences from the two preceding personal evangelism training models included its strong connection with Sunday school and its lack of a tract or

43   *FAITH*, 1–2.
44   *FAITH*, 2.
45   Welch, *Evangelism through the Sunday School*, 122.

a booklet that interested unbelievers could read without a personal evangelist present.

As do LES and CWT, the FAITH model possessed both strengths and weaknesses. First, in its discussion of "*I* stands for Impossible," FAITH utilized James 2:13a completely out of its scriptural context and employed an eisegetical interpretation. The FAITH training manual explained, "God is just. 'For judgment is without mercy.'—James 2:13a, NKJV. God's judgment is against sin. Many verses in Scripture call attention to the just nature of God and his judgment against sin. These are a few verses that refer to the fact that God is just and proclaims judgment against sin: Deuteronomy 32:4; Psalm 9:16; Jeremiah 30:11; Matthew 12:36; Romans 3:23; Hebrews 9:27; Revelation 16:7."[46] As a whole, James 2:13 teaches more about mercy than it does about judgment or God's just nature.

Second, while the FAITH model communicated the gospel effectively to those who possessed a nominal understanding of Christianity, a number of its features inhibited its communication of the gospel to the unchurched. Some of these features included assumptions that the person with whom the gospel is shared: 1) believed in and cared about going to heaven; 2) understood and showed interest in understanding faith as much as a personal evangelist understood and was interested in sharing faith through an acrostic of the word, itself; and 3) was convinced that he needs forgiveness before he was told in the third letter of the acrostic, "Impossible," that he is both sinful and in need of forgiveness. Last, FAITH also shared a weakness that Kelley observed about CWT—the sixteen-week period of the personal evangelism training model exhausted trainees.

In spite of these weaknesses, FAITH also possessed a number of strengths. In his assessment of FAITH, Moseley offered the following strengths of the training model: 1) FAITH combined evangelistic and ministry efforts with simplicity and effectiveness; and 2) the continual enlistment of FAITH team participants each semester by previously certified trainees expanded the size and life of FAITH in

---

46   Welch and Williams, *A Journey in FAITH*, 114.

a church setting.[47] One other strength of FAITH included LifeWay's publication of new training modules for previously certified trainees. These training modules kept the FAITH model fresh. In addition, they ensured a continuation of evangelism training and practice in churches that utilized FAITH.

THE NET

As early as 1998, Bob Reccord led NAMB to design "new training and equipping tools for Southern Baptists to intentionally share the good news of Jesus Christ."[48] NAMB considered a rebuild of CWT; however, perceived changes brought about by postmodern cultural thinking led them to devise a new personal evangelism training model. The Net: Evangelism for the 21st Century emerged as its inaugural evangelism training model of the twenty-first century.[49] Over a period of eight weeks, The Net taught personal evangelists to utilize a guided, rather than a "canned," presentation of the gospel message. Introduced in 2000, NAMB described The Net as "a personal witness development training and deployment process that is designed to be church-driven for effectively equipping believers to share the gospel in a post-modern culture."[50] It implemented The Net's delivery method through national, regional, and local training conferences in coordination with the state conventions and local associations.

The Net resulted from a collaborative partnership between the national NET Task Force, appointed by NAMB, and then-Southeastern Seminary evangelism professors Alvin Reid and Danny Forshee. Together, the national NET Task Force designed The Net to be highly customizable and adaptable for optimal functionality in churches and other ministries. It utilized one's personal testimony in order to

---

47 Moseley, "F.A.I.T.H.'s Effect on Evangelism," 58.

48 "North American Mission Board Report" (1998), 218.

49 Some of these strategies include Heart Call, God's Special Plan for Children, Lighthouses of Prayer, Family to Family, Praying Your Friends to Christ, Prayer Journey, The Ministry Evangelism Toolkit, and Celebrate Jesus 2000. All references to The Net: Evangelism for the 21st Century will be indicated as The Net, unless otherwise noted.

50 "North American Mission Board Report" (2000), 222.

present the gospel message in a postmodern context. Not only did The Net model address how to present the gospel in a postmodern context, but the design and layout of its printed materials appeared much more contemporary and culturally relevant than training models of the past.

The Net took its name from two sources. First, it referred to a first-century fishing analogy for evangelism. In his evaluation of The Net's effectiveness, M. Lindsey Powell explained, "The Net training program is built around the image of fishermen casting their nets into the sea in order to catch fish. The Net teaches those who wish to become 'fishers of men' how to cast their gospel nets into the sea of lost souls in order to draw men to Jesus."[51] This analogy of fishing for souls with a wide net embodied the heart of The Net approach.

Second, The Net's name derived from a concept first taught in "Here's Hope: Share Jesus Now," an evangelistic strategy implemented by the Home Mission Board in the early 1990s. This concept, known as the Spider Principle, illustrated how the Holy Spirit used the witness of numerous believers over time to lead an unbeliever to Christ.[52] The principle diagrammed the connected pattern that resulted from multiple believers evangelizing an unbeliever over time. The Net's *Mentor Handbook* began with a similar illustration. This illustration, called "The Strands of the Net," used different names and situations to tell the story of how the "gifts, abilities, and commitment of different believers [witnessing] create[d] a net from their lives . . . [an] expanding net to reach with world with the gospel."[53] The apparent similarities between the "strands of the web" and the "strands of the net" offered a description of the way The Net functions.

The program's tract, *Your Story . . . How Will It Turn Out*, articulated The Net's formal presentation of the gospel. Reid explained that it "begins by asking the question, 'Your story: How will it turn

---

51 M. Lindsey Powell, "Evaluating the Effectiveness of *The Net* Evangelism Strategy" (DMin dissertation, Southeastern Baptist Theological Seminary, 2004), 51.

52 To view the illustration in detail, see *Adult Roman Road Witness Training Teacher's Guide* (Atlanta: Home Mission Board, 1993).

53 *The Net: Mentor Handbook* (Alpharetta: North American Mission Board, 2000), 6.

out?' It then takes a person through a process of examining his or her life story, and intersecting it with the gospel message."[54] After asking the introductory question, the tract presented four statements with Scripture and an explanation of each statement. These four statements included:

1. God is interested in your life story.
2. We attempt to write our own story.
3. Jesus Christ can change your life story.
4. How Jesus can be the author of your life story.[55]

The testimonial outline, or "Model Story/Testimony" used the headings "The Way," "The Truth," and "The Life," to enable the personal evangelist to share his testimony of faith. "The Way" treated the doctrine of sin. The personal evangelist included an account of his own life before he committed to follow Christ. Next, "The Truth" conveyed the doctrines of God and Christ, making an allowance for the witness to communicate his own salvation experience. Finally, "The Life" explained the benefits of committing one's life to Christ. The witness concluded his presentation by sharing the differences that had occurred since he made his decision to follow Christ, including his views of life significance, meaning, and purpose.

One weakness of this evangelism model involved its promotion. During this same time, both NAMB and LifeWay promoted FAITH, overshadowing the market strategy of The Net. Additionally, the six Southern Baptist seminaries utilized the FAITH training as a part of their evangelism classes; while only one of the seminaries, Southeastern, supplemented FAITH with The Net training in its classes.

Concerning The Net's strengths, its eight-week training period appealed to trainees over the previous evangelism training models, which were much longer. Second, The Net's ease of obtaining access

---

54   Alvin Reid, *Radically Unchurched* (Grand Rapids: Kregel, 2002), 138.
55   *Your Story . . . How Will It Turn Out*, NKJV (Alpharetta, GA: North American Mission Board, 2000), 4, 6, 8, 10.

and use proved helpful to churches seeking to implement an inexpensive and intuitive evangelism strategy.[56] FAITH required a church's pastor to be certified in order to purchase the training material, as did the previously discussed evangelism training models. By not requiring formal instructor training before training, The Net increased its availability to churches.

CONCLUSION

When assessed as a whole, some interesting observations emerge. First, a noticeable difference surfaces in a comparison of LES, CWT, FAITH, and The Net. The former three evangelism training models made assumptions about persons with whom a personal evangelist shares the gospel. The introduction of their gospel presentations revealed these presuppositions, specifically that the other person: 1) believed in and/ or longed for the reality of heaven and 2) believed he stood in need of God's forgiveness. However, The Net took into account the postmodern and/or secular mindset of individuals in its gospel presentation opening. Any assumption about the other person on the part of the witness could prevent him from presenting the gospel in such a way that the other person could clearly understand and comprehend it.

Second, the methods, or delivery systems, of LES, CWT, and FAITH differed from the one utilized by The Net. LES, CWT, and FAITH present the gospel propositionally, or deductively, whereas The Net presented the gospel inductively. Despite the differences in these methods, all four evangelism training models articulated a consistent understanding and proclamation of the gospel.

Finally, all four of the evangelism training models examined in this study utilized a conversion-driven philosophy and approach to evangelism. Such a philosophy and approach to evangelism assumes "a theological agenda framed by the questions, 'What do people need to know in order to be converted?' and 'What do believers need to

---

56 Powell, "Evaluating the Effectiveness of *The Net*," 39.

understand in order to engage in evangelism?'"[57] From the mid-to-late twentieth century until the twenty-first century, Southern Baptists devoted the training materials of LES, CWT, FAITH, and The Net to answer both of these questions. Each of the model presentations answered the first question by its summation of the gospel in outline form. It answered the second question in the weekly training content found in both its trainer and trainee manuals.

Although Southern Baptist baptisms either increased or stabilized in the mid-to-late twentieth century as a result of their conversion-driven philosophical approach to evangelism, it unintentionally affected discipleship in a negative way. Chuck Kelley warned Southern Baptists, "When conversion is presented with such emphasis, other aspects of spirituality may appear less important. The presence of this attitude can result unintentionally in a de-emphasis on the process of sanctification, i.e. maturing in Christian life and thought."[58] Although follow-up content in *How to Have a Full and Meaningful Life*, *Eternal Life*, and *Your Story . . . How Will It Turn Out*, as well as FAITH's follow-up approach of enrolling new converts in Sunday school attempted to remedy this unintentional result, the annual membership of the Southern Baptist Convention, as well as the number of its churches' reported number of baptisms, has continued to plateau and decline into the beginning of the twenty-first century.

---

57   Powell, "Evaluating the Effectiveness of *The Net*," 162.
58   Powell, "Evaluating the Effectiveness of *The Net*," 163.

CHAPTER 22

TWENTY-FIRST-CENTURY DEVELOPMENTS IN EVANGELISM

Paul Akin

The previous chapters have faithfully surveyed the influential leaders and various movements of evangelism in North America over the past three centuries. This chapter will build upon that foundation and direct the focus to the twenty-first century. As Christians move further into the twenty-first century, they must cling to the unchanging nature of the gospel and the Great Commission. For the last two thousand years, God's people have been going into the world, preaching and proclaiming the gospel, and must continue to do so until Christ returns. The message and assignment to be salt and light in the world is unchanging. However, the context and the spiritual environment in which local churches across North America find themselves in today is rapidly changing.

The focus of this chapter will be on twenty-first-century considerations for evangelism in North America. First, this chapter will examine the rapidly changing moral landscape and the impact that is having on churches across North America. Second, this chapter will acknowledge the "new normal" for Christians and churches in twenty-first-century North America. Third, the chapter will close with a timely challenge for Christians and churches in North America as it relates to the primacy and urgency of evangelism in the twenty-first century.

A SOBERING REALIZATION

As Christians in North America strive to be ministers of reconciliation (2 Cor. 5:18) and live as salt and light in the world (Matt. 5:13–16) in the twenty-first century, they would do well to reflect on and learn from the life of the late Lesslie Newbigin. Newbigin (1909–1998) was a British missionary to India for almost forty years. After almost four decades of missionary service in India, Newbigin returned to Britain in 1974 with the eyes of a missionary and soon discovered a sobering reality: churches across Britain had almost entirely succumbed to the modern scientific worldview sweeping across Europe in that day. Most of the people in the churches in Britain had lost confidence in the gospel and were satisfied with relegating their Christian faith to the private realm of life.

In the decades while Newbigin was away in India, Europe had become a predominantly pagan society that was increasingly shaped by its own idolatry. One author in commenting on this reality in Britain at the time, argues that Europe had, "reconfigured the gospel and the church, and the church—tragically—instead of resisting had simply capitulated."[1] Newbigin later commented on this sobering reality when he wrote:

> During the years when I was sitting in discussion with the Hindu friends, Britain was still nominally a Christian country. . . . Preaching the gospel was calling people back to their spiritual roots. There was little distinction between evangelism and revival. *Today the situation is different.* Our large cities have substantial communities of Hindus, Sikhs, Buddhists, and Muslims. Their native neighbors soon discover that they are, in many cases, much more godly, more devout, and more pious than the average native Christian. What, then, is the meaning of evangelism in this kind of society?[2]

---

1   Michael Goheen, *The Church and Its Vocation: Lesslie Newbigin's Missionary Ecclesiology* (Grand Rapids: Baker, 2018), 2.
2   Lesslie Newbigin, *The Gospel in a Pluralist Society* (Grand Rapids: Eerdmans, 1989), 3–4.

Newbigin, looking at his context with the eyes of a missionary, recognized a subtle but striking change in the nature and position of the church in the world. In fact, Newbigin's words and description of the nature of Christian witness in the late twentieth century ring true for many living in North America in 2020. Like Newbigin, Christians in North America today must ask: What, then, is the meaning and nature of evangelism in this kind of society?

A RAPIDLY CHANGING CONTEXT

Today, in 2020, much of the church in North America finds itself in a precarious position as it relates to the rapidly changing moral landscape. Over the last several decades there has been a significant decline in the moral makeup of communities across North America. David Platt in his book *Counter Culture*, adds, "Followers of Christ need to face the reality that contemporary American culture is increasingly anti-Christian."[3] The staggering number of broken homes; the emergence and public agenda of the LGBTQ movement; unfettered access to pornography, drugs, and other addictive indulgences; the aggression and opposition to religious liberty and expression; and a host of other issues highlight the moral collapse currently taking place across North America.

However, Christians and churches are not always keenly aware of the severity of the changes taking place around them. Newbigin's perspective was enhanced because he lived on another continent for almost four decades before returning to Britain, and as a result the contrast was stark and immediately recognizable. Most Christians in North America lack that level of perspective, and as a result tend to recognize changes and trends long after they have already taken root. R. Albert Mohler Jr., writing on the danger of living in a context of moral decline, contends, "Aristotle once described our challenge as the problem of a fish in water. Knowing nothing but life in the water,

---

3   David Platt, *Counter Culture: Following Christ in a An Anti-Christian Age* (Carol Stream, IL: Tyndale, 2017), xii.

the fish never even realizes it is wet. This describes the situation of many Christians in America—they do not even know they are wet."[4] Mohler goes on to add, "We are swimming in one of the most complex and challenging cultural contexts ever experienced by the Christian church. Every day brings a confrontation with cultural message, controversies, and products. . . . How are Christians to remain faithful as we live in this culture?"[5]

Undoubtedly, Christians across North America find themselves in a rapidly changing context. Nevertheless, Christians in every age and every generation remember that Jesus gave His church a mandate, a commission to be witnesses of the gospel regardless of the cultural milieu of the day. It is imperative for Christians and churches in the twenty-first century to recognize and understand the signs of the times. Each image-bearer that hears the gospel of Jesus Christ hears it in a given cultural context. Thus, Christians and churches must labor to understand the culture, engage the culture, and persuasively share the gospel in the midst of this rapidly changing culture. This was true for Christians and churches in the first century and remains true for Christians and churches in the twenty-first century. In fact, there is much about the nature of evangelism and Christian witness in the first century that has implications for Christian and churches in North America today.

THE NEW NORMAL

In light of the cultural and moral shifts taking place in North America, Christians need to first and foremost acknowledge and embrace the "new normal." Christianity is no longer at the center of the moral fabric in North America. Christian values and a Christian worldview can no longer be assumed. Public faith in Jesus Christ has aggressively been pushed to the margins of society. North America, which was

---

4   R. Albert Mohler Jr., *Culture Shift: The Battle for the Moral Heart of America* (Colorado Springs: Multnomah, 2011), xv.
5   Mohler, *Culture Shift*, xv.

previously thought of as a bastion of Christianity, is becoming increasingly secular. Descriptors like "Bible belt" and "cultural Christianity" are monikers of the past. Though nations like the United States and Canada were largely founded on Christian truths and principles, the overwhelming majority of people in those countries have embraced a worldview akin to moralistic therapeutic deism[6] or, even more overtly, some form of secular humanism.[7] Thus, cultural Christianity is fading away across North America at a rapid rate.

The reality is that due the rapidly changing moral landscape and the increasing pressure on religious liberty, Christians are becoming increasingly alien and "strange" in North America. In other words, while there is not a one-to-one correlation between the context and setting that Christians found themselves in during the first century and the context in which North American Christians find themselves in today, there are enough similarities to be instructive. Christians in North America today are in many ways living life at the margins of society, much like Christians in the first century. Yet, the call of Jesus was for his disciples to be salt and light in the world around them. The tendency of many Christians and churches is to shrink back in the face of a rapidly shifting cultural context. While one can understand this temptation, the gospel of Jesus Christ provides a contrary motivation and model for engagement with the world.

Therefore, the alien resident motif,[8] which is present throughout Christian Scripture, can be a helpful identifier, motivator, and model for Christians today as they labor to be salt and light for the gospel across North America. The notion of Christians living as alien residents in the

---

6   Christian Smith and Melina Lundquist Denton, *Soul Searching: The Religious and Spiritual Lives of American Teenagers* (Oxford: Oxford University Press, 2005).

7   Mohler, *Culture Shift*, 57–58.

8   The term "alien resident" is a modification of the term "resident alien." While the two terms appear to be very similar, this author believes it is important to differentiate by emphasizing that in many ways Christians are at home here on earth. Christians are born from above (John 3), which makes them "alien," but they are residents on earth and will be in the restoration of all things (Acts 3:21). Therefore, the preferred description in this dissertation is alien residents. Christians are alien in that they are new creatures in Christ (2 Cor. 5:17), but they are also residents here on the earth and will be after the cosmos is renewed and restored.

world is not something "new under the sun." Rather, this is a theme that has characterized the people of God since their inception with the calling of Abram, and reached its zenith in the first three centuries of the church's existence[9] Russell Moore argues that the call of the Christian life is one of alienation: "Our call is to an engaged alienation, a Christianity that preserves the distinctiveness of our gospel while not retreating from our callings as neighbors, and friends, and citizens."[10]

The alien resident identity strikes a critical balance concerning how followers of Christ can be both at home in the world and also at odds with the world. In commenting on the alien resident nature of Christian witness in the early church, Michael Goheen, an astute Canadian who is intimately familiar with Christianity in North America, writes,

> The exemplary moral lives of ordinary Christians stood out against the rampant immorality of Rome. . . . In the cultural context of the Roman Empire, their "contrary values" led to a "contrary image of community" that was attractive. . . . In the early church, we see something of a community that understood its identity as a people called to bear witness to the kingdom of God in the midst of and for the sake of the world. The early Christians lived in the story of the Bible and thus lived in contrast to the pagan culture surrounding them. Their alternative communal life was on the margins of mainstream society yet was attractive to many and publicly challenged the reigning idolatry of the empire.[11]

---

9   Michael W. Goheen, *A Light to the Nations: The Missional Church and the Biblical Story* (Grand Rapids: Baker, 2011), 6–9. "The members of the church of the first three centuries AD, living in the midst of the pagan and often hostile Roman Empire, defined themselves as resident aliens (*pároikoi*). . . . These early Christians understood themselves to be different from others in their culture, and lived together as an alternative community nourished by an alternative story—the story of the Bible—that was impressed on catechumens in the process of catechism."

10 Russell Moore, *Onward: Engaging the Culture without Losing the Gospel* (Nashville: B&H, 2015), 8.

11 Goheen, *A Light to the Nations*, 8–9.

Therefore, the starting point for North American Christians and churches in the twenty-first century is to recognize and acknowledge the new normal and embrace a different posture in relation to their evangelistic endeavors. The new normal in North America requires that Christians embody a missionary consciousness in regard to their cultural engagement. Missionary consciousness, or a missionary encounter with the culture, implies a keen awareness, critical distance, and prophetic posture in the culture. Goheen states,

> We don't have a deep sense of the religious and idolatrous roots of our cultural story. We need what may be called missionary consciousness. The illustration of the experience of a cross-cultural missionary is helpful. When a missionary goes to a culture where the controlling faith assumptions are rooted in a religion hostile to the Christian faith, she is very careful to analyze that culture with a view to understanding its controlling assumptions and foundational religious beliefs. . . . With this missionary consciousness her antennas are up, sensitive to deep rooted idolatry that shapes her host culture. The missionary consciousness has been blunted in western culture. And it is hard to see because we do not have critical distance from our culture.[12]

The church, as the community of alien residents who have been born again in Christ, must embrace a prophetic role in critiquing the culture and must see the culture through the eyes of a missionary.

Newbigin, in commenting on the prophetic and critical role of the church, argues, "We must always, it seems to me, in every situation, be wrestling with both sides of this reality: that the Church is for the world against the world. The Church is against the world for the world."[13] Os Guinness and David Wells add, "We want to live in the

---

12 Michael W. Goheen, "The Surrender and Recovery of the Unbearable Tension," *JE&CB* 11, no. 1 (2007): 12–13.

13 Lesslie Newbigin, *A Word in Season: Perspectives on Christian World Missions* (Grand Rapids: Eerdmans, 1994), 54.

world in a stance of both Yes and No, affirmation and antithesis, or of being 'against the world/for the world.' This tension is crucial to the faithfulness of the church, and to her integrity and effectiveness in the world."[14] Striking this delicate balance of being both in the world but not of the world is the timeless challenge of the Christian life. Newbigin refers to this struggle as the "unbearable tension." Yet, one must remember, regardless of how unbearable the tension may be, Christians are called to a life of faithfulness that demands engagement and not retreat, critique and not accommodation.

A TIMELY CHALLENGE

From an evangelistic perspective, how should the church carry out its evangelistic mandate in the context of this new normal in North America in the days ahead? In essence, Christians and churches have three options in relation to this question. First, Christians and churches can choose to withdraw from the culture altogether, in a sort of Benedictine attempt to preserve the purity of the Christian faith.[15] Second, Christians and churches in North America could choose to accommodate to the culture and make critical concessions and begin the never-ending process of capitulation. Third, Christians and churches can choose to engage in a missionary encounter with the culture, refusing to isolate or accommodate and zealously striving to bring the biblical story to bear on the governing idolatries of the day. The third approach seems to be the most faithful and the most biblical, and the option best suited for bold evangelistic witness in the century ahead.

In a time of manifold competing cultural narratives, the church must be ready to present and proclaim a convictional and compelling

---

14   Os Guinness and David Wells, "Global Gospel, Global Era: Christian Discipleship and Mission in the Age of Globalization," Lausanne Movement, July 13, 2010, https://www.lausanne.org/content/global-gospel-global-era-christian-discipleship-and-mission-in-the-age-of-globalization.

15   Rod Dreher, *The Benedict Option: A Strategy for Christians in a Post-Christian Nation* (New York: Sentinel, 2017). Though one may disagree with the overall conclusion, there is much to appreciate and learn from Dreher in this book.

alternative story based on the narrative of the Bible. The distinctive and alien resident nature of the early church was nurtured and encouraged by the story of the Bible. The Scriptures had an immense shaping influence on the makeup, nature, and life of the church. The Bible, as the Word of God, is a record and tool of God's redeeming work in the world. As a record, The Bible narrates the story of God's mission and purpose of bringing salvation to the world through the mission of Israel, Jesus, and the church. However, the Bible also is a tool utilized to shape and form the people of God more into the likeness of Christ. Thus, the people of God today must read and understand the alternative story of the world presented in the Bible while simultaneously allowing their lives to be shaped and formed by the same biblical story.

In essence, the witness of the church must be both individual and ecclesial, personal and corporate. From both a communal and individual perspective the church, as the people of God, shaped by the Word of God, is called to witness to the life of the kingdom of God in the midst of the world. As Christians, shaped by the Word and fashioned by an alternative story (the story of God's redemption through Jesus Christ), the verbal declaration and visible demonstrations of the gospel stand in stark contrast to the prevailing ideals and values of the culture. Christians, as new creations in Christ, boldly embody and share the hope, joy, and confidence that they have in the gospel. That all contrasts with the rise of depression, anxiety, fear, and stress that permeates North America today. The contrary values held and personified by Christians and churches eventually leads to a contrary notion of community, a contrary and contrast people that are alien and strange, but also surprisingly attractive. This was true of Christians and churches in the first century and must be true of Christians and churches in the twenty-first century as well. As Christians boldly share and proclaim the gospel to their families, neighbors, and coworkers, they provide hope in a hopeless world, joy in a bleak world, and love in a harsh world. The contrasting nature and identity of Christians in this changing context might be increasingly alien and strange, but also salient and appealing.

Christians across North America have an opportunity to join in Israel's story as a light to the nations. Their Christ-centered identity and Word-shaped lives enable them to function as an attractive contrasting community in the midst of the world. Therefore, when Christians and churches embody the alien resident identity in the midst of the culture, they are joining in the story of Israel and playing a part in God's redemptive purpose in the world. That reality gives confidence, inspires boldness, and empowers Christians to be courageous witnesses as they join in the legacy of the people of God throughout history.

In all of this, North American Christians must actively engage and pursue their families, neighbors, coworkers, and those they encounter with the life-changing message of the gospel. Faith comes by hearing and hearing by the Word of God. The legacy of faithful evangelism that has persisted in North America over the last three centuries has always involved bold verbal proclamation of the gospel of Jesus Christ. Now is not the time to be silent. Christians have been increasingly pushed to the margins, and the temptation in this current cultural climate is to step back and be silent. However, a silent witness is no witness at all. Those who have been changed by the gospel cannot help but speak and share the gospel. Being a witness for Christ requires the courage to speak and to engage lost people with the life-changing message of the gospel. Moore argues,

> Jesus will build his church with or without us. But if we are going to be faithful to him, we must share his mission. This means we don't just talk about lost people; we talk to them. And we don't talk to them as enlightened life-coaches promising and improved future, but as crucified sinners offering a new birth.[16]

The cultural context and climate may have changed in recent decades, but God's means for the salvation of sinners remains unchanged.

---

16   Moore, *Onward*, 215.

Christians must, without hesitation or a sense of timidity, share the good news of the gospel of Jesus Christ. Regardless of the age or cultural milieu, the gospel alone is the only source of hope, joy, and peace in this fallen world. Christians and churches must individually and corporately testify to the beauty and simplicity of the gospel in the midst of the world for the sake of the world.

CONCLUSION

The world is changing, but God's mission to redeem and reconcile those created in his image is unchanging. Therefore, Christians and churches across North America in the twenty-first century find themselves in an oddly familiar place with Christians of the past. The gospel is always an offense in every generation. The gospel is a stumbling block in every culture and context. This is increasingly true today in North America. Nevertheless, the church, the people of God, are called to be salt and light in the midst of the world until Jesus returns. Being salt and light requires both individual and corporate proclamation of the gospel of Jesus Christ in word and deed. As a result, and in light of the changing moral landscape in North America, Christians and churches must be intentional to be even more evangelistic in the days ahead.